PLAYED IN BRITAIN

BRITAIN

MODERN THEATRE IN 100 PLAYS

Also from Methuen Drama:

DECADES OF MODERN BRITISH PLAYWRITING
Series Editors: Richard Boon and Philip Roberts

MODERN BRITISH PLAYWRITING: THE 1950s
by David Pattie
Includes detailed studies of works by T.S. Eliot, Terence Rattigan,
John Osborne and Arnold Wesker

MODERN BRITISH PLAYWRITING: THE 1960s
by Steve Nicholson
Includes detailed studies of works by John Arden, Edward Bond,
Harold Pinter and Alan Ayckbourn

MODERN BRITISH PLAYWRITING: THE 1980s
by Jane Milling
Includes detailed studies of works by Howard Barker, Jim Cartwright,
Sarah Daniels and Timberlake Wertenbaker

MODERN BRITISH PLAYWRITING: THE 1970s
by Chris Megson
Includes detailed studies of works by Caryl Churchill, David Edgar,
Howard Brenton and David Hare

MODERN BRITISH PLAYWRITING: THE 1990s
by Aleks Sierz
Includes detailed studies of works by Philip Ridley, Sarah Kane,
Anthony Neilson and Mark Ravenhill

MODERN BRITISH PLAYWRITING: 2000–2009
edited by Dan Rebellato
Includes detailed studies of works by David Greig, Simon Stephens,
debbie tucker green, Tim Crouch and Roy Williams

Also from V&A Enterprise

PLAYED IN BRITAIN: MODERN THEATRE IN 100 PLAYS, 1945–2010
Available as a tablet App.
Please check the relevant tablet App. store for availability and current pricing.

Introduced by celebrated writer, actor and director Simon Callow, it features
additional video commentary from lead *Guardian* critic Michael Billlington, besides
expanded content, including: additional photographs, first night *Guardian* and
Telegraph reviews, cast lists for original productions, sample extracts for approx.
sixty plays (thanks to Bloomsbury Publishing), and approximately forty short audio
interviews with theatre practitioners.

KATE DORNEY & FRANCES GRAY

PLAYED IN BRITAIN

MODERN THEATRE IN 100 PLAYS

Methuen Drama in association with
V&A Publishing, London

BLOOMSBURY

LONDON · NEW DELHI · NEW YORK · SYDNEY

Contents

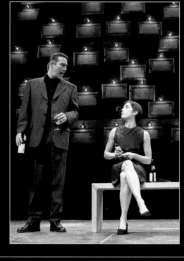

1980–89
PAGE 106

1990–99
PAGE 144

2000–10
PAGE 186

Acknowledgements

We'd like to acknowledge the help and support of our colleagues at the V&A Museum including the Theatre & Performance department, Photographic Studio and V&A Enterprise Ltd. Also, thank you to Jackie Bolton, David Caamano, Aleks Sierz, Linda Schofield, Peter Thomson and Andrew Wyllie.

The authors and publisher gratefully acknowledge the contribution of the following photographers and rights holders in granting permission to reproduce their work:

Simon Annand: *War Horse*, p. 208.

Angus McBean (MS Thr 581). © Harvard Theatre Collection, Houghton Library, Harvard University: *Lady's Not for Burning*, p. 18, *The Cocktail Party*, p. 20, *A Streetcar Named Desire*, p. 22, *Relative Values*, p. 26, *The Mousetrap*, p. 28, *The Deep Blue Sea*, p. 30, *The Pink Room*, p. 32, *The Chalk Garden*, p. 38, *Moon on a Rainbow Shawl*, p. 48.

Douglas McBride: *Europe*, p. 158.

Nobby Clark © Nobby Clark/ArenaPAL: *Amadeus*, p. 104.

Joe Cocks Studio Collection © Shakespeare Birthplace Trust: *Destiny*, p. 94.

John Cowan: *The Hostage*, p. 50.

Robert Day: *Behtzi*, p. 200, *Pornography*, p. 210.

Zoe Dominic: *Saved*, p. 64.

Sophie Grenier: *Far Side of the Moon*, p. 190.

Manuel Harlan: *Black Watch*, pp. 186, 204.

John Haynes © John Haynes/Lebrecht Music & Arts: *The Permanent Way*, p. 196, *Angels in America*, p. 152.

Charles Hewitt © Getty Images: *A View From the Bridge*, p. 42.

Sean Hudson © Communicado Theatre Company, through the good offices of the National Library of Scotland, *Mary Queen of Scots Got Her Head Chopped Off*, p. 138.

Barry Jones © National Library of Scotland: *The Cheviot, the Stag and the Black, Black Oil*, p. 82.

Ivan Kyncl: *Blasted*, p. 160.

Roger Mayne: *The Sport of My Mad Mother*, p. 44.

Steve Morgan: *Bouncers*, p. 118.

Alistair Muir: *The Girlfriend Experience*, p. 212.

Morris Newcombe: *Marat/Sade*, p. 60.

Johan Persson © Johan Persson/ArenaPAL, *England People Very Nice*, p. 214, *Posh*, p. 220.

Courtesy of Theatre Royal Stratford East Archives Collection: *Uranium 235*, p. 14.

© Scarborough Theatre Trust (The Stephen Joseph Theatre) and supplied by Alan Ayckbourn's official website www.alanayckbourn.net: *The Revengers' Comedies*, p. 142.

David Sim: *A Taste of Honey*, p. 46.

© Victoria and Albert Museum, London: *The Deep Blue Sea*, p. 11. *Men Should Weep*, p. 16, *The Pink Room*, p. 32, *Waiting for Godot*, p. 34, *Marat/Sade*, p. 37, *Look Back in Anger*, p. 40, *Happy Days*, p. 52, *Chips With Everything*, p. 54, *Oh What a Lovely War*, p. 55, *The Homecoming*, p. 62, *Rosencrantz and Guildenstern are Dead*, p. 66, *Forty Years On*, p. 68, *What the Butler Saw*, pp. 70, 72, *How the Other Half Loves*, p. 74, *Butley*, p. 76, *The Changing Room*, p. 78, *The Island of the Mighty*, p. 80, *The Rocky Horror Show*, p. 84, *The Island*, p. 86, *Comedians*, p. 88, *No Man's Land*, p. 90, *East*, p. 92, *Abigail's Party*, p. 96, *Bent*, p. 100, *Sus*, p. 102, *The Mysteries*, pp. 107, 126, *The Arbor*, p. 108, *Translations*, p. 110, *The Romans in Britain*, p. 112, *Good*, p. 114, *Top Girls*, p. 116, *Masterpieces*, p. 120, *Glengarry Glen Ross*, p. 122, *Loving Women*, p. 124, *Pravda*, p. 128, *The Castle*, p. 130, *Shirley Valentine*, p. 132, *Road*, p. 134, *Serious Money*, p. 136, *Our Country's Good*, p. 140, *East is East*, pp. 144, 164, *The Fastest Clock in the Universe*, p. 146, *Arcadia*, p. 148, *Beautiful Thing*, p. 150, *My Night With Reg*, p. 154, *Pentecost*, p. 156, *Shopping and Fucking*, p. 162, *Art*, p. 166, *Attempts on Her Life*, p. 168, *The Censor*, p. 170, *Closer*, p. 172, *The Weir*, p. 174, *The Lonesome West*, p. 176, *Yard Gal*, p. 178, *Copenhagen*, p. 180, *The Colour of Justice*, p. 182, *Mnemonic*, p. 184, *Blue/Orange*, p. 188, *Elmina's Kitchen*, p. 192, *Fall Out*, p. 194, *The History Boys*, p. 198, *Nights at the Circus*, p. 202, *Generations*, p. 206, *Jerusalem*, p. 216, *Enron*, p. 218.

John Vickers © University of Bristol/ArenaPAL, *An Inspector Calls*, p. 12, *Saint's Day*, p. 24.

Reg Wilson © Royal Shakespeare Company, *Afore Night Come*, p. 56.

Rolf Fischer: *As Time Goes By*, p. 98.
While every attempt was made to obtain photographer details, none were found.

Foreword by Richard Griffiths

My delight, on first seeing this wonderful collection of one hundred plays presented between 1945 and 2012, was not entirely unmixed by the realisation that ninenty-eight of them premiered in my lifetime. I had no idea I was quite that old. Hardly depressing at all. Still, it was these and other plays that changed my life and rescued me from ... who knows what ... one dreads to think. So, "Thank you, Theatre," would be nice. Come to think of it, without plays, what would our society, our whole world, be like? It would be an awful lot meaner and impoverished for sure.

And yet, plays, all plays, like butterflies, moths and summer morning mists, are classical examples of the ephemeral. Mysteriously, however briefly, we experience their fleeting insubstantial presences; their memory. Their quality, their charms, linger and may dwell in our minds and hearts, long and long.

This volume will be an important resource to scholars and lovers of theatre everywhere. To them, to even the most casual browsers-through, I would ask, however, to bear in mind that plays are never written to be read. They exist only to be listened to in living performance.

No matter what the narrative thrust or authorial purpose of any play; no matter how consciously it probes, reflects, debates or describes events, current concerns or controversies, plays are all and only about us, we human beings. They speak to our condition, our behaviours, our scope, be it micro or macro. I know this may seem rhetorical, fanciful, and overblown. Trust me. It is not.

There cannot be one great play, let alone the one hundred in this book, without there also being many thousands of others that are rotten, crapulous and very sadly, badly written.

"Why are we doing this play? It's rubbish!" I wailed at David Scase, late director of Manchester Library Theatre. And he replied, "We were sent 3000 new scripts in the past year. This, I swear, is the best of the whole pathetic bunch. Now, can we, please, get on!"

Let this collection be a guide to the theatre-goer. Some, possibly several, will not be to your taste. You, the audience member, are allowed, encouraged to be judge, jury and the executioner. Whatever your response, these plays all had a baptism of critical fire and are sure to be worthy of your attention. They earned it!

A word of caution. The plays that meet critical and popular success, do so as much because of the skills and talents of the cast and the production team, over and above the playwright's Art. Recall any classroom play-reading and that truth will reveal itself. When I was fourteen, I went to see my first play, a schools' matinee of a touring production of *Macbeth*. Before I got on the bus home, I vowed never to go into a theatre again. It was that bad.

Three years later, inwardly weeping, I was dragged to see a Nottingham Playhouse production of Albee's *Who's Afraid of Virginia Woolf?* It was electrifying. Next morning, my parents discovered to their heart-breaking dismay, that I *was* going to be an Actor.

To conclude, the plays in this collection are not exclusive. Many other marvellous plays, for want of space, could not be included, but the hundred herein have their place in the canon. The one thing that these and all other plays hold in common is that, when their closing lines are spoken, as Prospero foretold us, they will vanish into air – into thin air.

Enjoy!

Richard Griffiths

Richard Griffiths, OBE
September 2012

Introduction

Just conceivably, some people will have seen the first production of every play in this book. Many more will have lived through the profound social, political and artistic changes that the plays reflect. Others may turn to this book in order to find out something about what made an earlier generation excited or angry or amused. We think it's as good a starting point as any.

What we aim to present is the rich and varied history of theatre in Britain since 1945, told through 100 plays performed on British stages. It draws on the V&A's vast collection of theatre programmes, designs and photographs to create a uniquely visual account of the post-war stage. It brings together well-known plays and lesser-known works to explore how they have shaped the theatre we see today.

There are many theatre histories covering this time span by actors, directors, writers, and critics; each gives their unique take on the period and organise it in a variety of ways. For us, the play's the thing. When we see a play, we're not watching the work of one person (the writer) we're watching the sum total of collaboration between performers, designers, the director and the audience. All of these have a tendency to diversify and change during their lifetime; it is impossible, or at least unwise, to define them. But a published playtext remains more or less the same; this allows us to talk about the text and its various stagings through time as products of a set of social and economic factors. Each time a play is revived, it's received differently, interpreted differently and sometimes staged very differently and the patterns that emerge, of which plays get revived and or studied and which don't, tell us a lot about how theatre and society have changed.

We don't experience life as 'history', as distinct slabs of time made up of significant episodes, but as events which acquire a firmer outline with the benefit of hindsight. The same is true of plays: many of those discussed here were declared ground-breaking on their first production and now look decidedly tame; others acquire new resonance every time they're revived; still others – like Rodney Ackland's *The Pink Room* – have suddenly found their 'moment', decades after their first production.

Some of the reasons can be found in the two major shifts in theatre practice charted here: the end of censorship, and the institution of state subsidy. Subsidy provided writers, directors, producers and designers with the time and opportunity to experiment. In the words of director George Devine, it gave 'the right to fail'. This is as true of *War Horse* and *Les Misérables* (first produced by the Royal Shakespeare Company) as it is of box office disasters like *Saint's Day*. Subsidy also enabled the building of new theatres and the establishment of new companies such as the Royal Shakespeare Company and National Theatre, and the creation of a range of non-building based companies that produced a wide variety of work, much of it a long way from the text-based plays we focus on in this book. The lifting of censorship created an atmosphere in which this creativity could stop looking over its shoulder at a Lord Chamberlain whose function seemed to be counting swear words and dogging the footsteps of companies given, like Joan Littlewood's, to free improvisation.

THE PLAYS

Yes, you will have a long list of plays you would have substituted for ours. And yes, we have left out many that could be described as important, brilliant or significant. What we have done is to select plays that created a stir: provoking public outcry, breaking new ground; plays that marked the beginning, end or highpoint of a career (a very small number of playwrights appear more than once, reflecting their longevity and status), and most of all, plays that engaged with the contemporary world. We have chosen plays that illustrate and respond to a number of themes that animate post-war society: censorship and controversy; race and immigration; gender and sexuality; money and politics.

An important way in which we deliberately limited our choice was to include only plays that we could illustrate from the V&A's theatre collections. Above all this book is a celebration of our collections and the vision of our founder, Gabrielle Enthoven. More than a century ago she began a campaign to establish a department in a national museum devoted to the performing arts that would collect 'playbills, prints, pictures and relics' of performance for the benefit of theatre scholars and practitioners. In a letter to the *Observer* published in 1911 she asserted her ambition:

I want the section to be the place where the producer, actor, author and critic will naturally go for information, both on what is being done in this and other countries at present, and what has been done before.

She realised her ambition in 1924 when the V&A agreed to accept her collection of playbills, prints and other memorabilia. We have been collecting ever since, amassing hundreds of thousands of programmes, playbills and reviews and millions of photographs.

The collection also limited our scope in another important way: it only documents theatre performed in Britain. When international performers and shows come to Britain, we collect material about them, but we don't routinely collect world drama. For this reason the book focuses on plays performed in Britain. Many of them were written here. But not all. We've tried to acknowledge influences from other cultures, especially, perhaps, the USA; sometimes a play reflects pride in a British theatre with the vision to give a home to a play unwelcome in its own theatre, like Arthur Miller's *A View From the Bridge*.

THE PICTURES

The book draws on the extraordinarily rich resources of the Theatre & Performance Department at the V&A which has been collecting programmes, reviews, designs and photographs documenting the history and practice of theatre in Britain for nearly a century. In 2010 the department acquired the archive of prolific theatre photographer Douglas H. Jeffery. One of the first photographers to attend rehearsals as well as photocalls, Jeffery, who began his career in the 1950s and continued to work well into the 2000s captured many of the most iconic productions in post-war theatre. The richness of this collection, combined with other photographic archives held by the department (Houston Rogers, Anthony Crickmay and Graham Brandon) gives us an unparalleled visual record of performance from the 1930s to the present. Production stills enshrine performances in public memory offering a distillation of the event and the performers who created it. Here we are able to combine the iconic images (the first *Waiting for Godot* and *Look Back in Anger*) with rare glimpses of plays and productions often discussed but never seen.

Enthoven's goal – of a collection whose worth lies in demonstrating the relevance of the past to the present and future – is one that we still pursue today. Many of the plays included here have been revived while the book was being written. *Butley*, *Marat/Sade*, *Men Should Weep*, *Moon on a Rainbow Shawl* and *Rosencrantz and Guildenstern Are Dead* have all reappeared on stage, some standing the test of time better than others. We hope this book will spark further revivals and reconsiderations.

HOW TO USE THE BOOK

The book is divided into chronological sections. Each section begins with a contextual overview of the period before going onto the plays. Each play is the subject of an essay divided into three parts: the snapshot gives a brief overview of the plot and themes; impact examines the play's initial reception in Britain; afterlife examines the legacy of the play and its life beyond the first production in Britain (e.g. revivals, other plays it inspired). Below the essay three other works by the playwright are listed to give a sense of their career, while see also suggests other plays that consider the same themes, or use the same techniques. Some of the plays suggested are discussed in the book, others reach far beyond its chronological and geographical scope. Each essay is illustrated by a range of photographs showing early performances and revivals. This visual history reveals changes in set and costume design and in some cases, the progression of actors' careers across the decades.

1945–55

Britain emerged from the Second World War triumphant but exhausted. The theatre that had entertained wartime audiences was a rich mixed bag of the serious and silly, the high-powered and the fluffy. Ivor Novello's musical comedy *The Dancing Years* opened in the West End in 1939, toured the country when the Blitz forced it out of London, returning in 1942 to play until 1944. Noël Coward's ghostly comedy *Blithe Spirit* opened in 1941 and was still going in 1946, playing alongside musical revues and a string of long-forgotten farces. Theatrical titans Laurence Olivier and Ralph Richardson were acting in and directing classical plays with the Old Vic Company at the New Theatre (now the Noël Coward). When the war ended, the froth continued but alongside it sat new work by writers struggling to process the horrors of war. Conscientious objectors Christopher Fry and John Whiting (who later joined the artillery), RAF man Terence Rattigan and French Resistance operative Samuel Beckett produced work that evoked a ravaged post-war world beset with uncertainty. Others, like J.B. Priestley and Ena Lamont Stewart were invigorated by the promise of the Welfare State and envisaged a brighter future in which everyone pulled together for the greater good.

The war literally and metaphorically changed the landscape of British theatre. Bomb damage closed venues across the country, but state-funded touring theatre organised by the Council for the Encouragement of Music and the Arts (CEMA) during the war had shown directors and performers that with enough determination, theatre could be performed anywhere (prisoner-of-war camps, tents, village halls, churches). After the war, CEMA became the Arts Council and the principle of state funding for the arts was established beginning a shift in British theatre from a commercially driven system to a state-subsidised one. The National Theatre was still an aspiration rather than reality, despite official committees and pledges of cash from London County Council, but change was on its way. Up to this point, theatre was either commercial, or subsidised by local dignitaries. Even the de facto national theatre, the Old Vic, had to turn a profit to survive, while the Shakespeare Memorial Theatre in Stratford, predecessor to the Royal Shakespeare Company, was owned and paid for by local brewers Flowers. The most influential management company of the time was H.M. Tennent run by Hugh 'Binkie' Beaumont, a man with deep pockets and an eye for a box-office success, described by critic Kenneth Tynan as having been 'righter, on a higher level, than anyone else in the theatre of his time'. When the war ended in 1945, Tennent was responsible for twelve productions in eight of the thirty-six West End theatres. They had staged fifty-nine plays during the six years of war and would go on to stage many of the most influential plays of the next decade.

Britain attempted to put the war behind it with the Festival of Britain in 1951, a nationwide effort to celebrate the best of British culture, design and industry. Classics aside, much of the most interesting and challenging work was coming from Europe and the US. The Old Vic Company had toured Germany and France in the aftermath of war and seen different styles of acting and producing. When the Comédie-Française came to the Edinburgh Festival in 1954, audiences were astounded by the physicality of the acting. French actor, director and trainer Michel Saint-Denis had returned to London after the war and was working with directors George Devine and Glen Byam Shaw to explore a wider repertoire and teach new ways of acting. Eugène Ionesco's absurdist European drama also exerted a strong influence on Samuel Beckett, Ionesco and Jean Anouilh. Verse drama had another revival with elder statesman T.S. Eliot returning to the stage with *The Cocktail Party* and newcomer Christopher Fry quickly coming to dominate the West End with his quirky, quasi-religious plays and adaptations of French drama.

The influence of American culture and ideals grew steadily in this period. The GIs who swing so confidently through Rodney Ackland's *The Pink Room* were followed by musicals like *Oklahoma!* and *Guys and Dolls* and plays from Tennessee Williams and Arthur Miller. In spite of the Lord Chamberlain's powers of theatre censorship that controlled the way politics and sex could be presented on stage, sex was no longer the preserve of drawing-room comedy or domestic tragedy. The desire at the heart of Tennessee Williams' *Streetcar* is also explored in *The Pink Room* and Rattigan's *The Deep Blue Sea*.

▶ Freddie (Linus Roache) and Hester (Penelope Wilton), *The Deep Blue Sea*, Almeida Theatre, 1993. © *Victoria and Albert Museum, London*

An Inspector Calls

WRITTEN BY
J.B. Priestley (1894–1984)

DIRECTED BY
Basil Dean

DESIGNED BY
Kathleen Ankers (set);
costumes from Old Vic Workshops
and Morris Angels

- First performed at the Kamerny Theatre, Moscow in 1945 (directed by Alexander Tairov, designed by E. Kovalenko).
- First performed in Britain at the New (now Noël Coward) Theatre, London on 1 October 1946.

① Ian McNeil's set for National Theatre production, 1992. © *Victoria and Albert Museum, London*

② Inspector Goole (Ralph Richardson) confronts Gerald Croft (Harry Andrews), New Theatre London, 1946. *Photo by John Vickers,* © *University of Bristol/ArenaPAL*

SNAPSHOT

This three-act fable, set in 1912, begins like a thriller. The enigmatic Inspector Goole disrupts Sheila Birling's engagement party to call her family to account for the suicide of a young woman. All of them prove to have been complicit in her fate. Mr Birling sacked her for union activity. Sheila's fiancé Gerald seduced her. Sheila in a fit of peevishness got her dismissed from her next job in a dress shop. Mrs Birling spitefully refused her charity when she was pregnant (by, it emerges, Sheila's brother Eric, who promptly offered her money stolen from his father). Having reduced their complacency to tatters, the inspector leaves. As the young people ponder their culpability and their parents claw back their smugness, the phone rings: an inspector is on his way to investigate the death of a young woman. Suddenly the play jumps into another dimension – an exploration of time and consciousness, like Priestley's earlier *Time and the Conways*. Who is Inspector Goole? An other-worldly avenger? Or the spirit of a more egalitarian future forged in the 'fire and blood and anguish' of two world wars?

IMPACT

Goole's conviction that 'we are all responsible for each other' was shared by Priestley. A committed socialist, his plays, novels and trenchant wartime broadcasts helped to win the 1945 election for Labour. This was one of the first plays to give a voice to the Britain of the Welfare State. *An Inspector Calls* premiered in Moscow in 1945 – Priestley, one of the few British writers to be invited to the Soviet Union, sent the script as soon as it was finished, rather than wait for a British theatre to become vacant. The production was less stolidly realistic than Basil Dean's Old Vic version the following year, which a disappointed Priestley considered 'merely concerned with a bit of excitement in one night in 1912 ... not an attempt to dramatise the history of the last thirty years or so'. Reviews were mixed, although there was praise for Ralph Richardson's phlegmatic but eerie inspector and for the haunting regret of Alec Guinness as Gerald.

AFTERLIFE

The play was filmed with Alastair Sim as a witty and comical inspector in 1954. By the mid-1950s, the play's relatively conventional format made it unfashionable, although it remained a repertory staple and a favourite for study in schools. The BBC produced a television version in 1982, with Bernard Hepton as Goole. Then, in 1992, Stephen Daldry radically re-imagined the play for the National Theatre in a boldly expressionistic style; the set, designed by Ian MacNeil, was a crazily tilting house marooned in a post-apocalyptic landscape. As in the Moscow production, Goole's clothes placed him in the world of the 1940s to mark him as a messenger from a different world. Hailed as 'the production of the 90s' this revival won an unprecedented nineteen awards, including an Olivier (1993), a Tony and an Outer Critics' Circle Award (1994). It transferred to the Aldwych, then to the Garrick; a restaged version at Wyndham's in 2009 was still touring in 2012. As the *Telegraph* remarked in 2009, 'This Inspector has triumphed over time'.

OTHER WORKS BY
J.B. Priestley
Time and the Conways (1937)
Johnson over Jordan (1939)
The Linden Tree (1947)

SEE ALSO
Waste (1907)
by Harley Granville-Barker
That Face (2007)
by Polly Stenham

Uranium 235

WRITTEN BY
Ewan MacColl (1915–89)

DIRECTED BY
Joan Littlewood

DESIGNED BY
*John Bury and Ruth Brandes
(costumes)*

- First performed in 1946 as part of a Theatre Workshop tour.

① Lola the Smasher (Jean Newlove). *Courtesy of Theatre Royal Stratford East Archives Collection*

② The Scientists. *Courtesy of Theatre Royal Stratford East Archives Collection*

③ The Atom Ballet. *Courtesy of Theatre Royal Stratford East Archives Collection*

SNAPSHOT

Uranium 235 is an extraordinary combination of dance, song and debate on the topic of nuclear science. Written in the wake of the bombing of Hiroshima in 1945, it explains nuclear fission in terms a layperson can grasp. There is a ballet of sub-atomic particles and a gangster movie sketch with Energy threatening, 'how would you like to be a hydrogen proton and live in solitary confinement, eh?' Outlining the growth of atomic science, the play repeatedly asks 'what is the relationship between knowledge and power?' Ultimately, this question is for the audience to decide. Sinister figures of power, a puppet-master and Death, are shown deciding the fate of the world. At the end of the play, the puppet-master and a scientist fight over Energy, who points out that he can work for either peace or war. 'There are two roads. It is for you to choose and me to follow.'

IMPACT

This was a watershed production for Theatre Workshop. When the war disrupted the former Theatre Union, company members — Ewan MacColl, Joan Littlewood, Howard Goorney, Gerry Raffles and Rosalie Williams undertook to study the major theatrical traditions of Europe and regrouped in 1945 (renamed Theatre Workshop) to create popular political theatre. They toured the country in impossible conditions – snow once fell on the stage – and found engaged and lively audiences in non-theatrical venues such as Butlin's Holiday Camp in Filey where *Uranium 235* was well received. The play was Theatre Workshop's fourth production and attracted Sam Wanamaker and Michael Redgrave, who eventually brought it to London for a season at the Embassy Theatre in 1952. This involved enormous energy and considerable faith in the style of the play. London audiences had more preconceptions than novice spectators in the provinces. They were used to sitting in the dark watching an imitation of life, not direct challenges from the actors and dancing atoms. 'There is a message in this play all right, but it is the sort of message which is more commonly conveyed in a slogan or a pamphlet', complained the *Manchester Guardian*. However, the talent of the company was clear. Its dancing was more ambitious than that of some ballet companies (thanks to Rudolf von Laban's assistant Jean

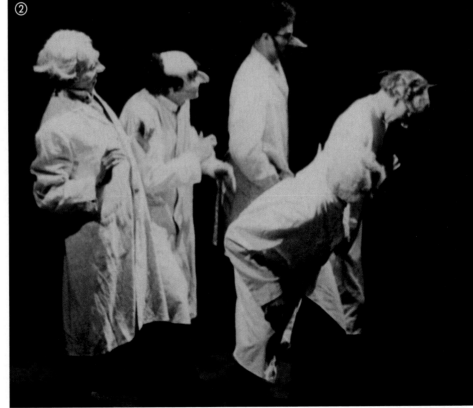

Newlove's input); it included performers of the calibre of Harry H. Corbett and Avis Bunnage; and it was confidently using the style of Bertolt Brecht years before the UK visit of the Berliner Ensemble electrified the imagination of British theatre practitioners. By the following year, the company was established in its permanent home, the Theatre Royal Stratford East. Here, Theatre Workshop developed a reputation as one of the most innovative and important British companies, attributable in large measure to the power of *Uranium 235*.

AFTERLIFE

The production transferred from the Embassy Theatre to the Comedy Theatre on 18 June 1952 but by August the company was back on the road. *Uranium 235* has been revived by a number of student companies. The vibrant mix of music, dance, debate and instruction makes it a challenging masterclass in performance techniques from a variety of traditions. As science itself moves on, audiences need less education in the basics of nuclear energy, but Howard Brenton's *The Genius* and Michael Frayn's *Copenhagen* (see p. 180) owe a debt to this pioneering play.

③

OTHER WORKS BY
Ewan MacColl
Johnny Noble (1945)
Operation Olive Branch (1947)
The Other Animals (1948)

SEE ALSO
Pax (1984)
by Deborah Levy
Copenhagen (1998)
by Michael Frayn

Men Should Weep

WRITTEN BY
Ena Lamont Stewart (1912–2006)

DIRECTED BY
Robert Mitchell

DESIGNED BY
Bet Low

• First performed at the Athenaeum Theatre, Glasgow, 30 January 1947.

① Company in the revival at Theatre Royal Stratford East, 1983. © *Victoria and Albert Museum, London*

② Maggie (Elizabeth MacLennan) and Bertie (Stewart MacFarlane), 7:84 revival at Theatre Royal Stratford East, 1983. © *Victoria and Albert Museum, London*

SNAPSHOT

A powerfully realistic play in Glaswegian dialect by Scotland's first major woman playwright, *Men Should Weep* conveys the hardship of the Glasgow East End tenements in the 1930s. In a tiny flat, Maggie Morrison struggles to keep the family – husband John, mother-in-law and brood of children – on John's occasional scrappy wages. Her childcare routine consists of shouting, slapping and putting sugar on the babies' dummies, while struggling to deal with corrosive rows between her eldest son and his wife, and with her daughter Jenny who is 'living in sin'. As Maggie's sister Lily arrives with a rare treat, a tin of baked beans, Maggie declares her happiness in spite of her circumstances, and at the play's end looks to move to a better house with a yard while waiting for the real prize, a new council house.

IMPACT

Maggie's experience was shared by audiences who had lived through the Depression. 'Hundreds o us, Maggie, beggin' for the chance tae earn enough for food and a roof ower our heids'. Working in a local library and a children's hospital made Lamont Stewart well aware of the deprivation faced by families like the Morrisons: she said that she wrote in a spirit of 'red-hot revolt'. She also understood the support that families like these gained from their neighbours; in the next generation of playwrights, only Arnold Wesker would match her vibrant image of a close-knit (if sometimes censorious) community. As Maggie tells John: 'It's only rich folks can keep theirselves tae theirselves. Folks like us hev tae depend on their neighbours when they're needin help'. The play was written for Unity Theatre, founded in Glasgow in 1940 to focus on working-class issues for a working-class audience. Unity and Lamont Stewart were optimistic that the inadequate housing, ill health and lack of education they showed would be transformed by the new Welfare State.

AFTERLIFE

The play transferred from Glasgow to Edinburgh and then to the Embassy Theatre in London. It attracted little attention. After the collapse of Glasgow Unity, the city's other major theatre, the Citizens, refused to produce Lamont Stewart's work. In 1974, she revised the play to give the women a stronger voice. This version, directed by Giles Havergal, was presented by 7:84 Theatre Company at the Citizen's Theatre in 1982 as part of a 'Clydebuilt' season of Scottish popular socialist plays. This season had a powerful influence on a new generation of Scottish playwrights, including Liz Lochhead. This production also played at the Theatre Royal Stratford East in 1983. In the National Theatre's millennium poll, *Men Should Weep* was voted one of the top 100 plays of the last century. In 2010, it was revived by Josie Rourke at the National Theatre in London; Sharon Small's Maggie was praised by the *Daily Telegraph* as 'full of warmth, resilience, and sudden moments of lacerating despair'. In 2011, it was produced by the National Theatre of Scotland, with songs by the veteran folk singer Arthur Johnstone adding their own social comment.

OTHER WORKS BY
Ena Lamont Stewart
Starched Aprons (1945)
Poor Man's Riches (1947)

SEE ALSO
Juno and the Paycock (1924)
by Sean O'Casey
Chicken Soup with Barley (1958)
by Arnold Wesker

①

The Lady's Not for Burning

WRITTEN BY
Christopher Fry (1907–2005)

DIRECTED BY
Jack Hawkins

No designer credited at the Arts Theatre Club

- First performed at the Arts Theatre Club, London, 10 March 1948.

① Richard (Richard Burton) and Alizoun (Claire Bloom), Globe Theatre, 1949. *Photo by Angus McBean (MS Thr 581).* © *Harvard Theatre Collection, Houghton Library, Harvard University*

② Thomas Mendip (John Gielgud), Chaplain (Eliot Makeham), Jennet Jourdemayne (Pamela Brown), Richard (Richard Burton), Humphrey Devize (Richard Leech), and Hebble Tyson (Harcourt Williams), Globe Theatre, 1949. *Photo by Angus McBean (MS Thr 581).* © *Harvard Theatre Collection, Houghton Library, Harvard University*

③ Jennet Jourdemayne (Pamela Brown), Richard (Richard Burton) and Thomas Mendip (John Gielgud), Globe Theatre, 1949. *Photo by Angus McBean (MS Thr 581).* © *Harvard Theatre Collection, Houghton Library, Harvard University*

SNAPSHOT

The play is a romantic comedy in extravagant verse, set in 'more or less or exactly' 1400, as the Middle Ages are slipping into the Renaissance. Burnt-out soldier Thomas Mendip arrives at the Mayor's house in a small English market town, claiming to have murdered two locals in order to get himself hanged. A crowd of hysterical witch-hunters are there already, to burn Jennet Jourdemayne, the daughter of an alchemist. Jennet wants to live as much as Thomas wants to die. The play becomes a battle of wits between them; of course, they fall in love, and the local Justice of the Peace successfully encourages them to escape.

IMPACT

The figure of the embittered soldier was to appear in many plays of the next two decades, although rarely in such a colourful and optimistic play. It combines an analysis of superstition versus reason, love versus despair, with the light comedy and colourful spectacle for which post-war audiences hungered. The language is decidedly twentieth century, with digs at contemporary bureaucracy. Thomas shouts through the Mayor's window 'I have come to be hanged, do you hear?' only to be asked, 'Have you filled in the necessary forms?' The play was a success for Alec Clunes (playing Thomas) at the Arts Theatre during its short run and tour. It was then secured by John Gielgud and Binkie Beaumont for the West End, with Gielgud as Thomas and the young Richard Burton and Claire Bloom in minor roles that made them stars overnight.

AFTERLIFE

The production sealed Fry's reputation as a master of the comedy of morals. After running for months in the West End, it went to Broadway and received the New York Drama Critics' Circle award for Best Foreign Play of 1950–51. It brought Fry commercial success; shortly afterwards he had three productions on in London (*Venus Observ'd*, *Ring Round the Moon* and *Boy with a Cart*). However, his star was eclipsed by the new realism nurtured by the Royal Court and Theatre Workshop and he turned to television and film.

There have been at least two TV adaptations: an American production with Richard Chamberlain and Eileen Atkins in 1974; and a British one in 1987 with Kenneth Branagh and Cherie Lunghi. The new century has seen several revivals. In 2002, Samuel West made his debut as director with the play at the Minerva Theatre, Chichester. A full production at the Finborough Theatre, London, in 2007 as part of a season of verse-drama was praised by Michael Billington in the *Guardian* for 'exuberant charity'. In 2011, a new company, Parenthesis, staged it off-Broadway.

①

OTHER WORKS BY
Christopher Fry
The Boy with a Cart (1938)
Venus Observ'd (1950)
The Dark is Light Enough (1954)

SEE ALSO
This Way to the Tomb (1945)
by Ronald Duncan
A Man for All Seasons (1960)
by Robert Bolt

The Cocktail Party

WRITTEN BY
T.S. Eliot (1888–1965)

DIRECTED BY
E. Martin Browne

DESIGNED BY
Anthony Holland

- First performed at the Edinburgh Festival 1949.

① An Unidentified Guest (Alec Guinness) and Julia (Nan Munro) in the revival directed by Alec Guinness Wyndham's Theatre 1968. *Photo by Angus McBean (MS Thr 581). © Harvard Theatre Collection, Houghton Library, Harvard University*

② An Unidentified Guest (Alec Guinness) in the revival directed by Alec Guinness Wyndham's Theatre 1968. *Photo by Angus McBean (MS Thr 581). © Harvard Theatre Collection, Houghton Library, Harvard University*

SNAPSHOT

On the surface this is a mildly risqué drawing-room comedy – except that everyone is speaking blank verse. It is Lavinia's party, but her husband Edward finds it hard to explain why she is not there. The elegantly clad guests prattle on. Sociably, they include an uninvited stranger in the conversation, but his refusal to be drawn becomes a running gag. Then everyone is gone but the stranger and Edward confesses that Lavinia has left him – to receive not sympathy but an analysis of his existential poverty. The couple are eventually brought together to make the best of their mediocre marriage by the mysterious guest – a psychiatrist, Henry Harcourt-Reilly. He and the other apparently dizzy partygoers, whose clumsy attempts to separate Edward from his mistress Celia bring a touch of farce to the proceedings, are really 'Guardians'; they preside over the fates of Edward, Lavinia and Celia, whose search for fulfilment leads her to a martyr's death as a missionary. Harcourt-Reilly maintains that she made a meaningful choice and fulfilled her destiny, 'And if that is not a happy death, what death is happy?'

IMPACT

Eliot had dominated English poetry since the 1920s and was awarded the Nobel Prize for *Four Quartets* in 1948. He wanted to penetrate the commercial theatre because, as he said in 1933, 'Every poet would like … to convey the pleasures of poetry … to larger groups of people collectively; and the theatre is the best place in which to do it'. Aided by the serene charisma of Alec Guinness as Harcourt-Reilly at Edinburgh

and then on Broadway, and the star status of Rex Harrison in London, the play ran for almost a year on both sides of the Atlantic. Audiences queued for hours.

The play tapped into Europe's current fascination with Greek mythology (Jean Anouilh's *Antigone* was staged in occupied Paris in 1944, and Jean Cocteau's film *Orpheus* appeared in 1950), although most of the audience probably missed Eliot's use of the myth of Alcestis, who was restored to her husband from the grave by Heracles just as Lavinia is restored to Edward by Harcourt-Reilly. Not all the critics were entirely comfortable with Celia's story. 'Bosh, sprinkled with mystic cologne,' snorted George Jean Nathan. Today, the racist attitude expressed by some characters towards the 'natives' for whom Celia dies is perhaps its least attractive feature. However, in a globalised world, where the death of a young aid worker can make headline news, the play still has the power to disturb.

AFTERLIFE

The play won a Tony Award on Broadway in 1950. Guinness reprised the role of Harcourt-Reilly, for which he had great affection, in his own production at Chichester in 1968. The production moved to Wyndham's the same year and the Theatre Royal Haymarket in 1969. Philip Franks revived the play at the Edinburgh Festival in 1997 to reviews that expressed surprise at its rich vein of comedy. A well-reviewed off-Broadway revival by the Actors Company in 2010 suggests that Eliot can still find the poetically receptive audience he wanted.

OTHER WORKS BY
T.S. Eliot
Murder in the Cathedral (1935)
The Family Reunion (1939)
The Confidential Clerk (1953)

SEE ALSO
Point of Departure (1941)
by Jean Anouilh
Huis Clos (1945)
by Jean Paul Sartre

②

A Streetcar Named Desire

WRITTEN BY
Tennessee Williams (1911–83)

DIRECTED BY
Laurence Olivier

DESIGNED BY
*Jo Mielziner (set and lighting) and
Beatrice Dawson (costumes)*

- First performed at the Ethel Barrymore Theater, New York, 3 December 1947, directed by Elia Kazan, designed by Jo Mielziner (set and lighting) and Lucinda Ballard (costumes).

- First performed in Britain at the Aldwych Theatre, London, 12 October 1949.

SNAPSHOT

The play is a tragedy with modern themes, exploring loneliness, desire and madness. Faded Southern belle Blanche DuBois visits her sister Stella, married to the strong, ambitious and sensual Stanley, in their cramped New Orleans apartment. Seizing her chance for a respectable future, Blanche deploys all her talent for creating 'a little – temporary magic' to captivate Stanley's friend, Mitch. She tells him about her beautiful young husband who shot himself after she found him with a male lover. Irked by Blanche's airs and graces, Stanley uncovers her promiscuous past and scares Mitch away. With Stella in hospital after the birth of their child, Stanley confronts Blanche, carrying her to his bed saying, 'We've had this date with each other from the beginning!' Stella cannot bear the idea that this was a rape – she tells her neighbour, 'I couldn't believe her story and go on living with Stanley'. However, Blanche's fragile sanity crumbles and Stella has her committed to a mental hospital. As the courteous doctor gently leads Blanche away, she confides, 'I have always depended on the kindness of strangers'.

IMPACT

The future of English-speaking theatre at this period seemed to lie with America. Nothing in the UK matched Williams' mix of stark realism and poetic treatment of common speech – Blanche has to 'take a street-car named Desire, then transfer to one called Cemeteries and ride six blocks and get off at – Elysian Fields', reflecting her own metaphorical journey. Williams's use of effects was equally adventurous: the blues soundtrack, alternately plaintive and joyous, expresses not only the life of New Orleans but also Blanche's state of mind. The play was a Broadway success and his raw power as Stanley made Marlon Brando a star. However, to bring to the UK a play about mental illness, rape and homosexuality was a risk for 'stage royals' Laurence Olivier and Vivien Leigh. Even before the opening, questions were asked in Parliament. West End producing giants H.M. Tennent had declared the expensive production exempt from Entertainment Tax as the play was 'partly educational'. One MP sniffed, 'The play is only educational to those who are ignorant of the facts of life'. Olivier's production owed much to Elia Kazan's original, but Leigh's performance, acknowledged as her greatest, was highly individual, all the more poignant for recalling her youthful Scarlett in *Gone with the Wind*. With straggling hair and thick make-up, her disturbed and ageing Blanche embodied the waning of the South itself in the face of dynamic immigrants like Stanley.

AFTERLIFE

The Broadway production won the Pulitzer Prize, the New York Drama Critics' Circle Award and the Donaldson Award. Leigh reprised her role alongside Brando in the 1951 film, which won four Oscars. There have been many revivals. The 1992 production at the Ethel Barrymore Theater (original Broadway venue), starring Alec Baldwin and Jessica Lange, was filmed for television. More recently, Rob Ashford revived the play to great acclaim at the Donmar Warehouse with Rachel Weisz and Elliot Cowan in the lead roles. The play has entered the popular imagination: an episode of The Simpsons shows the long-suffering Marge as Blanche in *Streetcar: the Musical* with the cheery closing number, 'You can always depend on the kindness of strangers'.

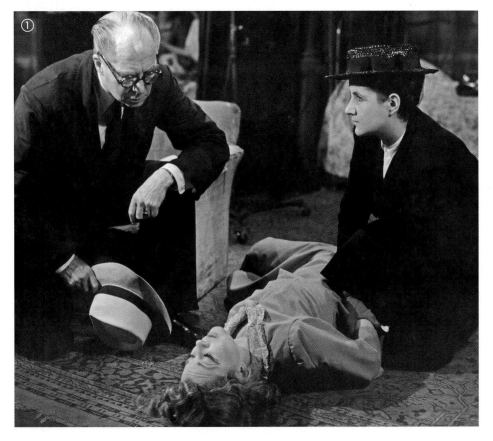

① Doctor (Sidney Monckton), Nurse (Mona Lilian) and Blanche (Vivien Leigh), Aldwych Theatre, 1949. *Photo by Angus McBean (MS Thr 581). © Harvard Theatre Collection, Houghton Library, Harvard University*

② Stella (Renee Asherson) and Stanley (Bonar Colleano), Aldwych Theatre, 1949. *Photo by Angus McBean (MS Thr 581). © Harvard Theatre Collection, Houghton Library, Harvard University*

OTHER WORKS BY
Tennessee Williams
The Glass Menagerie (1948)
Cat on A Hot Tin Roof (1955)
Suddenly Last Summer (1958)

SEE ALSO
The Deep Blue Sea (1952)
by Terence Rattigan
Forever Yours, Marie-Lou (1971)
by Michel Tremblay

Saint's Day

WRITTEN BY
John Whiting (1917–63)

DIRECTED BY
Stephen Murray

DESIGNED BY
Fanny Taylor

- First performed at the Arts Theatre Club, London, 5 September 1951.

SNAPSHOT

A savage parody of genteel pre-war country-house drama, with apocalyptic overtones, *Saint's Day* won First Prize at the 1951 Festival of Britain play competition. The central figure, Paul Southman, is an octogenarian poet living in squalor with his granddaughter Stella and her painter husband Charles in a great house near a village where they are cordially loathed (they never pay bills). Three army deserters are at large, signalling their presence with trumpet calls. When the urbane poet-critic Robert Procathren comes to visit, Southman hopes they will combine forces with the deserters against the villagers. Procathren accidentally shoots Stella before joining the soldiers in a frenzy of destruction; as the play ends, they are preparing to hang Southman and Charles.

IMPACT

Reviews ranged from accusations of 'badness that must be called indescribable' to questioning the author's sanity. The hostility sprang from a lack of fit with the optimism that the Festival was designed to generate: *Saint's Day* must be one of the least festive plays ever written. However, it was also the first clear sign that post-war theatre would make new demands on its audience. It crystallises the anxieties of the period with extraordinary vividness. Wartime propaganda posters depicted an idealised English landscape ('what we are fighting for') – green fields, quaint villages, old churches. Here the trees are dead, the villagers are terrorised and the church is burned down by the rootless and disoriented soldiers. The cruelly bleak ending derived from a personal experience during Whiting's National Service, but the haunting image that it presents is a resonant one: Charles trying to complete the figure of Stella in a vast painting while her body lies on the floor, giving up as the soldiers come to take him away. The audience are left with many questions: if the class system is over, what next? If the war is over but the Cold War is not, what does it mean to be a soldier – or a civilian? If people hate your work, what is the responsibility of the artist? Some theatre figures were drawn to the radical modernity of the play. The forty-year-old Michael Hordern, playing Southman with his trademark tetchy intelligence, was passionately committed to his part. John Gielgud, Peggy Ashcroft and Peter Brook wrote supportive letters to the press. Peter Hall, still an undergraduate, directed his own version at Cambridge.

AFTERLIFE

In 1965, the Stage Sixty Company revived the play at Stratford East and subsequently at the St Martin's Theatre, again with Michael Hordern playing Southman. Mervyn Jones commented in *Tribune*, 'it makes many of the modern plays I have seen seem puny and superficial'. Despite this, it is rarely revived, although Sam Walters directed a production at the Orange Tree, Richmond, London, in 2002 with Ed Stoppard as Charles. Whiting once wrote that playwriting was about 'creation of a world'. The enigmatic, original and bleak world that he put on stage makes sense to an audience familiar with *Serjeant Musgrave's Dance* or *Blasted*.

1945–55

① Paul Southman (Michael Hordern). *Photo by John Vickers, © University of Bristol/ArenaPAL*

② Stella Heberden (Valerie White) and Charles Heberden (Robert Urquhart). *Photo by John Vickers, © University of Bristol/ArenaPAL*

③ Robert Procathren (Ben Warwick) and soldiers, Orange Tree revival, 2002. *© Victoria and Albert Museum, London*

OTHER WORKS BY
John Whiting
A Penny for a Song (1951)
Marching Song (1954)
The Devils (1964)

SEE ALSO
A Sleep of Prisoners (1951)
by Christopher Fry
Serjeant Musgrave's Dance (1959)
by John Arden

Relative Values

WRITTEN BY
Noël Coward (1899–1973)

DIRECTED BY
Noël Coward

DESIGNED BY
Michael Relph

- First performed at the Savoy
Theatre, London, 28 November
1951.

① Nigel (Ralph Michael), Felicity (Gladys Cooper), Don Lucas (Hugh McDermott) and Miranda (Judy Campbell). *Photo by Angus McBean (MS Thr 581). © Harvard Theatre Collection, Houghton Library, Harvard University*

② Admiral Sir John Hayling (Charles Cullum), Lady Cynthia Hayling (Dorothy Batley), Peter (Simon Lack), Felicity (Gladys Cooper), Moxie (Angela Baddeley), Crestwell (Richard Leech). *Photo by Angus McBean (MS Thr 581). © Harvard Theatre Collection, Houghton Library, Harvard University*

③ Moxie (Angela Baddeley) and Felicity (Gladys Cooper). *Photo by Angus McBean (MS Thr 581). © Harvard Theatre Collection, Houghton Library, Harvard University*

SNAPSHOT

'A coincidence in the best tradition of English high comedy,' is how Crestwell, the butler, sums up the situation in *Relative Values*. The Countess of Marshwood is unhappy that her son has decided to marry a movie star, Miranda Frayle. The Countess's maid, Moxie, is even more unhappy: Miranda is her sister, who walked out on her family years ago. To save face all round, the Marshwoods present Moxie as a friend, not a servant. Ill at ease in the country manor, Miranda harps on about the background of 'poverty and squalor' she has invented for herself (complete with alcoholic sister). The Marshwoods egg her on until Moxie erupts in fury. Meanwhile, Miranda's previous boyfriend and co-star, Don, arrives and, with some judicious manipulation on the part of the Countess, wins her back. Crestwell proposes a toast to 'the final inglorious disintegration of the most unlikely dream that ever troubled the foolish heart of man – Social Equality!'

IMPACT

Coward had been a major force in the theatre since the 1920s, but his more recent work had been less successful. *Relative Values* seemed like a triumphant return to the West End and won excellent reviews, except from what Coward called 'the dear little *Daily Mirror*'. However, several critics expressed discomfort at the snobbish premise. Although to Coward's delight Winston Churchill had ousted the Labour Government only a month before, the war had changed Britain. The playwright whose witty subversion of sexual conventions once put him ahead of his times now seemed wilfully behind them. Coward had peevishly resigned from the Festival of Britain Committee and this contribution to the festivities suggested that his opinion of his country was the same as Crestwell's. Increasingly, he found himself at odds with the emerging theatre talents of the decade and reinvented himself as a cabaret performer. By the mid 1960s, however, what he called 'Dad's renaissance' was under way and his work was re-evaluated. Some of the highest praise came from John Osborne and John Whiting.

AFTERLIFE

While Coward's best comedies of the pre-war years, such as *Private Lives* and *Hay Fever*, are frequently revived, *Relative Values* is not. However, at the Chichester production in 1993 some found themselves surprised at its vitality. *Independent* critic Paul Taylor noted, 'I had, to be frank, fully expected to loathe this rare revival'. But the class politics no longer seemed so clear cut. For instance, while there is real affection between the two women, the Countess reflects that she knows almost nothing about Moxie's life. Susan Hampshire was praised for the way that she stressed such 'chips in the charm' of the Countess, while Alison Fiske's down-to-earth Moxie was never the butt of the joke when in disguise. The real figure of fun was her sister, played by Sarah Brightman as a blatant gold-digger trying to master the arcane social codes of the aristocracy. The production moved to its original 1951 venue, the Savoy, with its poster depicting not the stars of the show but Coward himself. An adapted version of the play was filmed by Eric Styles in 2000, with Julie Andrews as the Countess and Stephen Fry, the definitive Jeeves of the 1990s, as Crestwell. This made the American characters – who had not gone down well with US producers – more sympathetic and cut Coward's comedy of eccentricity free of its more reactionary aspects.

①

OTHER WORKS BY
Noël Coward
The Vortex (1924)
Private Lives (1930)
Blithe Spirit (1941)

SEE ALSO
The Young Idea (1921)
by Noël Coward
Hay Fever (1925)
by Noël Coward

The Mousetrap

SNAPSHOT

A murder mystery in the classic setting of a snowbound country house, the play begins with a scream in the dark and a melody that will echo throughout, *Three Blind Mice*. As the lights go up, we hear a voice on the radio reporting a murder and are swiftly introduced to an array of stereotypical suspects – Giles and Mollie Ralston, newly-weds running Monkswell Manor as a boarding house, and their guests: moustachioed Mr Paravicini, phlegmatic Major Metcalf, curmudgeonly Mrs Boyle, highly strung Christopher Wren, and mannish Miss Casewell. Mollie takes a phone call announcing that a Sergeant Trotter is on his way (on skis). Trotter declares a link between the murder – the victim was a farmer's wife convicted of neglecting three foster children, one of whom died – and Monkswell Manor. Initially everyone denies involvement, but Mrs Boyle finally admits she was the magistrate who sent the children to the farm. Her murder brings down the curtain on Act One. In the second act, Sergeant Trotter demolishes everybody's alibis; he also reveals further links between the characters and the abused children. The murderer is exposed in a remarkably short time, tranquilised and taken away. At the curtain call, one of the cast asks the audience not to reveal the solution of the mystery.

IMPACT

A record-breaking London run has made the play a phenomenon and a tourist staple. By November 2012, it will have been playing continuously for sixty years, moving to the St Martin's Theatre for the last thirty-eight years. Some of the cast have set their own records – David Raven played the Major 4,575 times – while others, like Richard Attenborough, the original Trotter, have moved on. It is often forgotten, however, that this was the first truly popular work to raise the subject of institutionalised child abuse in a society where agents of the state still had Mrs Boyle's power to remove children from 'inadequate' parents and send them away. Unmistakably of its period, it reflects a Britain destabilised by war. Many of the characters have lost their families, like Mollie and Giles, or feel rootless, like the sexually ambivalent Christopher; as Trotter points out, 'there aren't any backgrounds nowadays' and people know very little about one another. The 'pale pink' views of the sympathetic Miss Casewell, however, suggest that the new, cradle-to-grave services of the Welfare State will make England a more caring place. Like *An Inspector Calls* (see p. 12), which it strongly resembles in plot and structure, the play takes seriously the question of social responsibility.

WRITTEN BY
Agatha Christie (1890–1976)

DIRECTED BY
Peter Cotes

DESIGNED BY
Roger Furse

First performed at the Ambassadors Theatre, London, 25 November 1952.

AFTERLIFE

This is the longest-running production in the world and has spawned many parodies, including Tom Stoppard's spoof, *The Real Inspector Hound*, in which every convention of the country house murder is ruthlessly satirised. In 1997, Sir Stephen Waley-Cohen, manager of the St Martin's Theatre and owner of the original venue, the Ambassadors, initiated The Mousetrap Foundation, a charity that introduces young people to the theatre.

① Sergeant Trotter makes his entrance on skis. *Photo by Angus McBean (MS Thr 581).* © *Harvard Theatre Collection, Houghton Library, Harvard University*

② Giles Ralston (John Paul), Detective Sergeant Trotter (Richard Attenborough) and Mollie Ralston (Shelia Sim). *Photo by Angus McBean (MS Thr 581).* © *Harvard Theatre Collection, Houghton Library, Harvard University*

③ Christopher Wren (Allan McClellan), Detective Sergeant Trotter (Richard Attenborough) and Major Metcalf (Aubrey Dexter). *Photo by Angus McBean (MS Thr 581).* © *Harvard Theatre Collection, Houghton Library, Harvard University*

1945–55

OTHER WORKS BY
Agatha Christie
Ten Little Indians (1943)
Appointment with Death (1945)
Murder on the Nile (1945)

SEE ALSO
Busman's Honeymoon (1936)
by Dorothy L. Sayers and
Muriel St Clare Byrne
The Real Inspector Hound (1968)
by Tom Stoppard

The Deep Blue Sea

WRITTEN BY
Terence Rattigan (1911–77)

DIRECTED BY
Frith Banbury

DESIGNED BY
Tanya Moiseiwitsch

- First performed at the Duchess Theatre, London, 6 March 1952.

OTHER WORKS BY
Terence Rattigan
After the Dance (1939)
The Browning Version (1948)
Separate Tables (1954)

SEE ALSO
The Pink Room/Absolute Hell (1952)
by Rodney Ackland
Plenty (1978)
by David Hare

SNAPSHOT

This meditation on sexual passion opens with Hester Collyer failing to gas herself in her seedy bedsit. She has left her husband, a respected judge, for a passionate affair with ex-fighter pilot Freddie Page. Page, decorated in the war for his bravery, is scared by the force of Hester's passion and leaves her to become a test pilot in South America. Hester's only comfort is the calm friendship of fellow tenant Mr Miller, who has his own undisclosed sorrows. He encourages her to reject her melodramatic attitude and accept life for what it is: 'to live without hope can mean to live without despair'. The play ends on a hopeful note, with Hester turning on the gas fire and lighting the flame.

IMPACT

Rattigan wrote the play after the suicide of his lover and there has long been speculation that there is a gay version of the play somewhere that Rattigan suppressed. His friends have always dismissed the notion and no script has ever been found. At this point the most successful playwright in the West End, Rattigan claimed to write for a typical audience member – 'Aunt Edna' – a middle-aged, middle-class woman who should be respected but not patronised, challenged, but not scandalised. Edna would appreciate, and even share, Rattigan's enduring preoccupation with surface reserve as a mask for emotional turmoil. As Hester confesses to her husband: 'I was brought up to think that in a case of this kind it's more proper for it to be the man who does the loving'. The other tenants in the house reflect the changing make-up of post-war Britain: the young married Welchs work in the same office; Miller is an Austrian refugee who has been struck off the medical register; and Freddie, at a loss in peacetime, tends to end his attempts to forge a new career in the pub. Though she affects an old-fashioned middle-class froideur and flippancy to conceal her true emotions from her landlady, Hester's own refusal to return to her comfortable marriage and resume her old life suggests that she too is coming to terms with a changing world. Critic Kenneth Tynan noted that the role of Hester was the first serious and lengthy part for a woman since Shaw's *Saint Joan* more than twenty-five years previously. Peggy Ashcroft, the first Hester, commented, 'I feel as if I'm walking around naked'. Despite, or because of, its controversial subject matter, the play ran for over 500 performances; it launched the career of Kenneth More, who played Freddie, and confirmed Ashcroft as one of the major actresses of her generation.

AFTERLIFE

The play made the already successful Rattigan even wealthier and cemented Frith Banbury's reputation as a director, providing the means for them to produce Rodney Ackland's *The Pink Room* (see p. 32), an even franker portrait of post-war London. Though Rattigan – who had once had a record four West End successes running simultaneously – lost his dominance as a new generation of playwrights emerged, *The Deep Blue Sea* is now considered a classic and is frequently revived. The play has been twice filmed, by Anatole Litvak in 1955 with Vivien Leigh, and by Terence Davies in 2011 with Rachel Weisz.

① Mr Miller (Peter Illing), Hester (Peggy Ashcroft) and Sir Wiliam Collyer (Ronald Culver). *Photo by Angus McBean (MS Thr 581).* © *Harvard Theatre Collection, Houghton Library, Harvard University*

② Freddie (Kenneth More) and Hester (Peggy Ashcroft). *Photo by Angus McBean (MS Thr 581).* © *Harvard Theatre Collection, Houghton Library, Harvard University*

The Pink Room (or The Escapists)

WRITTEN BY
Rodney Ackland (1908–91)

DIRECTED BY
Frith Banbury

DESIGNED BY
Reece Pemberton

- First performed at the Lyric Theatre, Hammersmith, London, 18 June 1952.

OTHER WORKS BY
Rodney Ackland
Improper People (1929)
Strange Orchestra (1931)
The Dark River (1942)

SEE ALSO
The Iceman Cometh (1946)
by Eugene O'Neill
The Deep Blue Sea (1952)
by Terence Rattigan

SNAPSHOT

An exploration of the seedy underbelly of London immediately after the war, the play is the story of a private members' club ('La Vie en Rose') literally and metaphorically confronted by a clear-eyed progressive future – in the form of the Labour Party Committee Rooms opposite. In the club, the Bohemian flotsam and jetsam keep reality at bay by drinking, flirting and fantasising about fame and fortune. Manageress Christine is a self-pitying and lonely alcoholic. Members include Hugh Marriner, a writer claiming to be blocked after a damning review, Siegfried Shrager, a refugee and suspected black marketeer and his glamorous companion, Elizabeth. The play is dominated by Christine's attempts to seduce an American serviceman, Butch. Act One ends as Hugh confronts the reviewer and Elizabeth refuses to hear about the fate of a friend liberated from a German camp. By the end of the play, Labour is on the verge of election victory and the club is deserted except for Christine drinking herself into a stupor as the place crumbles around her.

IMPACT

Its realism made *The Pink Room* a commercial risk: H.M. Tennent staged it as 'educational' to avoid Entertainment Tax and Terence Rattigan, who liked the play, financed it to offload some of his own earnings and avoid a high tax bracket. Although the rootless Bohemians would recognise the world of

The Deep Blue Sea, and their frustrated rants would be echoed by Jimmy Porter in *Look Back in Anger* (see p. 40) just four years later, the play did not draw the public in the same way. Reviews were poor: the most influential of its detractors, the critic Harold Hobson, lambasted its 'moral evil' while damning what he saw as a lack of bite: 'Its aim, presumably, is to lash with scorpions ... what in effect it does is to tickle with a feather duster'.

AFTERLIFE

Ackland's career in theatre came to a premature halt. However, in 1988, Sam Walters revived the play at the Orange Tree in Richmond and Ackland, empowered by the absence of the censor, retitled his play *Absolute Hell* and made extensive revisions. The language became more explicit, and hence more natural, and he was able to expose the energies of desire and repression driving the characters. Hugh Marriner has an ex-soldier boyfriend rather than a nagging wife. GI Butch declares that: 'Any form of sex'al innercourse comes natchral to me bar one, I never done it an' I don't intend to – an' that's pay for it'. By altering the sexual dynamics, Ackland was able to paint a far more compelling picture of the club as a refuge for outcasts, and was also able to write a powerful scene between Hugh and boyfriend Nigel about sexuality. After this revival, interest in the play, now seen as a compassionate study of its period, increased. Anthony Page directed it for the BBC in 1991 with Judi Dench as Christine Foskett and Bill Nighy as Hugh; the success of this production led to a performance (again directed by Page) at the National Theatre in 1995 with Dench reprising the role of Christine.

① Christine Foskett (Polly Hemmingway) and Hugh Marriner (David Rintoul) in *Absolute Hell*, the revised version of *The Pink Room*, Orange Tree Theatre Richmond, 1988. © *Victoria and Albert Museum, London*

② Douglas Eden (Terence Brook), Lettice Willis (Betty Marsden) and Michael Crowley (Thomas Heathcote). *Photo by Angus McBean (MS Thr 581).* © *Harvard Theatre Collection, Houghton Library, Harvard University*

Waiting for Godot

WRITTEN BY
Samuel Beckett (1906–86)

DIRECTED BY
Peter Hall

DESIGNED BY
Peter Snow

- First performed in French as *En Attendant Godot* in the Théâtre de Babylone, Paris, 15 January 1953, directed by Roger Blin, designed by Sergio Gerstein.
- First performance in English at the Arts Theatre Club, London, 3 August 1955.

SNAPSHOT

Famously described as 'a play in which nothing happens, twice', *Waiting for Godot* was unique at the time: a powerful injection of European anti-realism. By 'a country road. A tree. Evening' two men, Estragon and Vladimir, wait for the mysterious Godot. They may have asked him for something, they may be awaiting orders. During the apparently endless wait, they pass the time by swapping ritualised insults – and hats – reminiscing, pondering the meaning of life and contemplating suicide. They encounter Pozzo, a bumptious landowner, and his slave, Lucky, trained to 'think' on demand. Lucky recites a monologue, a mix of complex philosophical positions, which so horrifies Vladimir and Estragon that they attack him. Just before the end of Act One, a Boy arrives with a message from Mr Godot, who 'won't come this evening, but surely tomorrow'. In Act Two, the men wait again; Pozzo and Lucky pass by, although Pozzo is now blind and Lucky is dumb. The Boy arrives and denies having seen them before. Asked if he has a message for Godot, Vladimir hesitates, then says: 'tell him that you saw me'. The play ends as it began:

Vladimir: Well, shall we go?
Estragon: Yes, let's go.
[*They do not move*].

IMPACT

British audiences were used to 'lifelike' plots, where actions had consequences and time passing involved change. Not only did *Waiting for Godot* fail to provide such a plot, it also mixed serious debate with trouser-dropping slapstick in the style of Charlie Chaplin; worse, it seemed to be poking fun at the audience's discomfort and boredom, with the characters commenting on the action – 'this is awful' – like music-hall comedians. It was seen as a hoax, an exercise in existential nihilism, an account of Beckett's experiences in the French Resistance and a religious meditation. Beckett – as was his habit – refused to explain the play.

AFTERLIFE

In 1960, Martin Esslin, Head of Radio Drama at the BBC, identified Beckett as one of a group of 'absurd' dramatists. An Austrian Jewish refugee, Esslin saw the connection between the humour of Beckett and that of Eugène Ionesco and the extent of suffering in wartime Europe that had challenged the moral certainties of the West. The label stuck. The influence of Beckett as Absurdist can be seen clearly through many plays of the next two decades, including Tom Stoppard's *Rosencrantz and Guildenstern are Dead* (see p. 66) and Harold Pinter's *The Dumb Waiter*. However, other interpretations of *Godot* inspired very different kinds of production. For the prisoners in San Quentin jail, where actors from the San Francisco Actors Workshop performed it in 1957, using the gallows as a stage, *Godot* meant 'the outside'. In eastern Europe, for example Poland in 1956 and Slovakia in 1969, the play was about hope and longing for regime change. It has been seen in the West End twice – in 1991 with Rik Mayall and Ade Edmondson, a partnership best known for their anarchic TV sitcom *Bottom*, and in 2009, with Patrick Stewart and Ian McKellen employing the comic traditions of their native north of England in Sean Mathias' production at the Theatre Royal Haymarket, where it broke the box-office record. Beckett won the Nobel Prize in 1969.

① Vladimir (Paul Daneman), A Boy (Michael Walker) and Estragon (Peter Woodthorpe), West End transfer, Criterion Theatre, 1955. © *Victoria and Albert Museum, London*

② Estragon (Peter Woodthorpe) and Vladimir (Paul Daneman), West End transfer, Criterion Theatre, 1955. © *Victoria and Albert Museum, London*

③ Estragon (Alan Dobie), Lucky (Richard Dormer) and Vladimir (James Laurenson). Theatre Royal Bath, 2005. © *Victoria and Albert Museum, London*

OTHER WORKS BY
Samuel Beckett
Endgame (1957)
Play (1963)
Not I (1972)

SEE ALSO
Rosencrantz and Guildenstern Are Dead (1966)
by Tom Stoppard
Boesman and Lena (1969)
by Athol Fugard

1956–68

At a symposium about the state of British theatre held at the Royal Court in November 1956, Arthur Miller declared 'that the British theatre is hermetically sealed against the way the society moves'. Even as he made this pronouncement, theatre was changing, and by 1968, it had changed radically. The National Theatre and the Royal Shakespeare Company had been established and produced bold new work alongside fresh revivals of classic plays. The Lord Chamberlain's powers of censorship had been abolished as a result of writers, directors and producers challenging what could be shown on stage and *Saved*, one of the plays examined here, was instrumental in bringing this about. But before any of this happened, in May 1956 an angry young man burst on to the stage of the Royal Court and started a phenomenon. Jimmy Porter, the protagonist in John Osborne's *Look Back in Anger*, was a rebel without a cause, and his youth and anger captured the imagination of critics and audiences across the country. The play opened the same year as Miller's *A View from the Bridge* and Bertolt Brecht's Berliner Ensemble's *Mother Courage* and is conventional in comparison (and indeed in comparison to many other plays at the Royal Court and elsewhere), but this did nothing to diminish its impact.

Porter was decidedly conservative next to the youths in Ann Jellicoe's *The Sport of My Mad Mother* or Geof and Jo in Shelagh Delaney's *A Taste of Honey*. He even had conservative taste in music, preferring jazz to the new rock and roll that would become the soundtrack of a generation. Music features in many of the plays discussed here: the improvised jazz interludes of *A Taste of Honey*; the popular songs of the Edwardian era revisited in *Oh What a Lovely War* showed the Brechtian influence on Theatre Workshop, now settled in an old-fashioned Victorian theatre in Stratford, East London. Determined to engage their local audience, they performed classical plays alongside new ones and encouraged a new generation of musical theatre writers who created work about the surrounding area and contemporary issues. Although designed for locals, a number of these productions transferred to the West End, taking their best actors with them which ultimately led to the dismantling of the company.

It wasn't only young writers who captured the zeitgeist. Photos of *The Chalk Garden* may give the impression that the play was a superbly clad country house comedy but in fact, it dealt with crime, punishment, child abuse and teenage sexuality. Elsewhere in the West End, Brian Rix's straight sex farces were enjoying an uninterrupted run of success at the Whitehall Theatre, complemented in the 1960s by Joe Orton's heavily coded homosexual ones elsewhere in the West End. The RSC set up camp at the Aldwych Theatre, premiering new works by Harold Pinter and David Rudkin to be viewed alongside Peter Daubeny's World Theatre Seasons. The seasons gave audiences the chance to see companies from places like Japan, Czechoslovakia, Israel, Poland, as well as France and Italy, and helped form new theatrical styles. Far from being hermetically sealed against the way society moved, theatre had become a key way of debating where it would move next.

▶ Charlotte Corday (Anastasia Hille) and de Sade (David Calder), *The Persecution and Assassination of Marat as Performed by the Inmates of the Asylum of Charenton Under the Direction of the Marquis de Sade*, National Theatre, 1997.
© Victoria and Albert Museum, London

The Chalk Garden

WRITTEN BY
Enid Bagnold (1889–1981)

DIRECTED BY
John Gielgud

DESIGNED BY
Reece Pemberton

- First performed at the Ethel Barrymore Theater, Broadway, 26 October 1955, designed by Cecil Beaton.
- First performed in the UK at the Theatre Royal Haymarket, London, 11 April 1956.

SNAPSHOT

The Chalk Garden is an artificial black comedy set in the home of eccentric Mrs St Maugham. She is interviewing governesses for her untruthful pyromaniac teenage granddaughter Laurel. The only candidate not intimidated, Miss Madrigal, joins them and their manservant Maitland, who wearily copes, while the unseen butler, Pinkbell, tyrannises from his sickbed. The play follows two struggles. One is the relationship between Laurel and her family. She claims she saw her father's suicide and was sexually assaulted prior to her mother's much-resented remarriage. Madrigal gently unpicks these lies and Laurel returns to her mother. The other struggle is Madrigal's – she has just finished a sentence for murder (although she may be innocent). The judge who condemned her comes to lunch. In a tense, funny scene, Madrigal's identity is gradually revealed as the judge indulges Laurel's passion for true crime stories and Madrigal gets tipsy on wine and terror. At the end, Mrs St Maugham asks, 'Did you do it?' But she is able to endure Madrigal's refusal to tell, because she will have her company, and they will restore the dying garden by planting things appropriate to a chalky soil, just as Laurel has been 'replanted' in her true home.

IMPACT

The West End production ran for 658 performances; its more celebrated contemporary, *Look Back in Anger* (see p. 40), had 280 (152 in the first run and West End transfer, 128 in the 1957 revival). It was a triumph for Edith Evans as Mrs St Maugham, applying the aristocratic vocal swoops of her famous Lady Bracknell to everything from her false teeth to Laurel's alleged rape ('by some extraordinary carelessness she was violated in Hyde Park'), and also for Peggy Ashcroft, whose Madrigal hinted at a groundswell of passion beneath an orderly exterior. The starry cast, the set – including that symbol of everything old-fashioned in the theatre, French windows – and the box-office success concealed the play's real originality. Bagnold challenged male dominance in the West End and focused on relationships between women. She dealt with sensitive subjects – teenage sexuality, abuse, capital punishment – and showed the breakdown of the family and the class system, embodied in the repressive Pinkbell, whose death is a kind of mental liberation for everyone, including the judge. This radicalism may account for the timidity with which managements on both sides of the Atlantic approached the play. Bagnold paid tribute to the tenacity of Irene Selznick, the New York producer. Best known for her 1935 novel *National Velvet*, filmed with a young Elizabeth Taylor in 1944, Bagnold never found it easy to get her work staged and did not write another play until 1960.

AFTERLIFE

Following a six-month run on Broadway, Bagnold was awarded a medal by the American Academy of Arts and Letters. The play was filmed in 1964 and Edith Evans won the National Board of Review USA Award for Best Supporting Actress. It has had many revivals. A production by Michael Grandage at the Donmar warehouse in 2008 encapsulated 1950s England on the brink of change. It received excellent reviews – notably for Margaret Tyzack as Mrs St Maugham, described by Michael Billington as an 'arthritic ogre … trapped inside a self-created persona'.

1956–68

① Laurel (Karal Gardner), Madrigal (Valerie White), Judge (Allan Jeays), Maitland (David Evans), and Mrs St Maugham (Fay Compton) in the Theatre Royal Haymarket tour of *The Chalk Garden*, 1956. *Photo by Angus McBean (MS Thr 581).* © *Harvard Theatre Collection, Houghton Library, Harvard University*

② Mrs St Maugham (Fay Compton) and Laurel (Karal Gardner) in the Theatre Royal Haymarket tour of *The Chalk Garden*, 1956. *Photo by Angus McBean (MS Thr 581).* © *Harvard Theatre Collection, Houghton Library, Harvard University*

③ Mrs St Maugham (Margaret Tyzack), Laurel (Felicity Jones) and Madrigal (Penelope Wilton), Donmar Warehouse, 2008. *Photo by Angus McBean (MS Thr 581).* © *Harvard Theatre Collection, Houghton Library, Harvard University*

OTHER WORKS BY
Enid Bagnold
The Last Joke (1960)
The Chinese Prime Minister (1964)
Call Me Jacky (restaged as *A Matter of Gravity*) (1967)

SEE ALSO
Bill of Divorcement (1921)
by Clemence Dane
The Children's Hour (1934)
by Lillian Hellman

Look Back in Anger

WRITTEN BY
John Osborne (1929–94)

DIRECTED BY
Tony Richardson

DESIGNED BY
Alan Tagg

- First performed at the Royal Court Theatre, London, 8 May 1956.

① Jimmy (Richard Coyle) and Alison (Mary Stockley) in *Look Back in Anger*, Theatre Royal Bath, 2006. © *Victoria and Albert Museum, London*

② Jimmy (Kenneth Haigh) and Alison (Mary Ure) in *Look Back in Anger*. © *Victoria and Albert Museum, London*

③ Alison (Mary Ure), Cliff (Alan Bates), Helena (Helena Hughes) and Jimmy (Kenneth Haigh). © *Victoria and Albert Museum, London*

SNAPSHOT

'The best young play of its decade,' wrote Kenneth Tynan, declaring, 'I doubt if I could love anyone who did not wish to see *Look Back in Anger*'. 'A formal, rather old-fashioned play,' said Osborne himself later. Both descriptions are true. Though not formally different from the work of Noël Coward or Terence Rattigan, the play had a new kind of protagonist. Jimmy Porter has a self-appointed mission to puncture moribund social norms and express his own passionate vitality. The opening image became iconic – Jimmy and his friend Cliff deep in the Sunday papers, as Alison, wearing Jimmy's shirt, does the ironing in their dingy bedsit. Jimmy relentlessly hectors Alison, the main target for his resentment of all who accept the status quo; when he finally storms out, she tells Cliff she is pregnant. A temporary truce is shattered when Alison's friend Helena arrives and becomes the focus of Jimmy's malice. Alison leaves with her father, Colonel Redfern. Helena and Jimmy have a furious row culminating in an (inevitable) embrace. Act Three opens with Helena at the ironing board, but despite, or because of, the fact that her tougher personality is a match for Jimmy, when Alison returns after losing the baby, the marriage is mended and the play ends with their sentimental game of 'bears and squirrels'.

IMPACT

Reviews overall were moderately favourable, if not as exuberant as Tynan's. The play was on the brink of closure until a televised excerpt brought Jimmy's tirades to a wider audience. It struck a chord with a generation repelled by the smug imperialism of 1950s Britain. The resulting box-office success saved the fortunes of the English Stage Company, which under George Devine set out to be a 'Writers' Theatre' and offer a platform to new talent, making the Royal Court a powerhouse of British theatre for more than fifty years. The production made a star of Kenneth Haigh (whose ferocious Jimmy was actually slapped by a spectator). Language coined to discuss *Look Back in Anger* became a cultural shorthand; everybody understood the term 'kitchen-sink drama' (though Jimmy and Alison's flat doesn't have a sink), and the phrase 'angry young man', used by Royal Court press officer George Fearon to describe Jimmy, summed up a generation of literary heroes from Kingsley Amis's *Lucky Jim* to Colin Wilson's *Outsider*. Although other productions – such as *Waiting for Godot* (see p. 34) or the visiting Berliner Ensemble's staging of Bertolt Brecht's *The Caucasian Chalk Circle* – arguably had greater long-term influence, *Look Back in Anger* unquestionably symbolised the new theatrical mood.

AFTERLIFE

The play toured nationally and internationally – at one point to Russia. It was filmed by Tony Richardson in 1959 with Richard Burton as Jimmy, and again by Judi Dench in 1989 for TV with Kenneth Branagh. It has been frequently revived; the most notable Jimmy of recent years was Michael Sheen at the Royal Exchange, Manchester, described in *The Times* as 'a Midlands Hamlet: funny, desperate, passionate, lacerating'. Osborne's last play, *Déjà Vu*, staged at the Comedy Theatre in 1992, presented Jimmy in middle age and, like his author, now politically right wing but as vitriolic as ever.

①

1956–68

OTHER WORKS BY
John Osborne
The Entertainer (1957)
Luther (1961)
A Patriot for Me (1966)

SEE ALSO
Private Lives (1930)
by Noël Coward
Who's Afraid of Virginia Woolf (1962)
by Edward Albee

A View from the Bridge

WRITTEN BY
Arthur Miller (1915–2005)

DIRECTED BY
Peter Brook

DESIGNED BY
Peter Brook

- First performed at the Comedy Theatre, London, 11 October 1956.

OTHER WORKS BY
Arthur Miller
Death of a Salesman (1949)
The Crucible (1953)
Broken Glass (1994)

SEE ALSO
Point of Departure (1941)
by Jean Anouilh
Men Should Weep (1947)
by Ena Lamont Stewart

SNAPSHOT

The language of *A View from the Bridge* is that of working-class Italian Americans; the structure is that of Greek tragedy. Longshoreman Eddie Carbone takes in two illegal immigrants, Rodolpho and Marco, cousins of his wife Beatrice. Rodolpho, young, charming and popular, courts Eddie's orphan niece, Catherine. Sick with a jealousy he cannot understand, Eddie betrays the brothers to the Immigration Bureau, an unforgivable crime in the eyes of the local community. The night before Rodolpho and Catherine's wedding, he and Marco are arrested. Swearing revenge, Marco confronts Eddie, who produces a knife. In the scuffle, it is Eddie who is stabbed. He dies calling for Beatrice. Eddie's lawyer, Alfieri, who has acted as a chorus-figure and explained to the audience the honour code shaping Eddie's world, comes forward to mourn Eddie's folly but also to assert that 'something perversely pure calls to me from his memory'.

IMPACT

The play has a complex history. Miller and director Elia Kazan worked on a film, *The Hook*, about corruption at the docks (the theme of Kazan's 1954 film, *On the Waterfront*). Hollywood was in the grip of the House Un-American Activities Committee and demanded changes to the 'unpatriotic' script that Miller refused to make. He then wrote a one-act verse play, based on a true story similar to Eddie's. It had a poor reception (and was reported on by an FBI informant). With the help of Peter Brook, Miller revised this version as a two-act prose tragedy. It was the first Miller play to premiere in London, where Miller's wife Marilyn Monroe was working with Laurence Olivier. However, it struck more censorship problems. This time the issue was not politics, but a scene where Eddie humiliates Rodolpho by kissing him on the lips. Realising the box-office value of the controversy, the producers refused to cut anything and staged the play as part of a 'banned' season (including Tennessee Williams' *Cat on a Hot Tin Roof*) at the New Watergate Club, created at the Comedy Theatre by a cabal of West End producers specifically to evade the censor. Reviews were mixed; some used the word 'masterpiece', while *The Times* complained that Miller 'elevate[d] these ordinary men and women to the rank of heroes and heroines of high tragedy'. Most agreed that, as Eddie, Anthony Quayle gave the performance of his life.

AFTERLIFE

The passion of Miller's play was a shot in the arm to the newly emerging generation of British playwrights; Miller's interest in *Look Back in Anger* (see p. 40) also stimulated the cautious Olivier to work with John Osborne on *The Entertainer*. Now seen as one of Miller's finest works, *A View From the Bridge* is frequently revived. It was filmed by Sidney Lumet in 1962. In 1987, Alan Ayckbourn staged it at the National Theatre with Michael Gambon as Eddie – a noted performer in Ayckbourn's own comedies. Widely praised for its powerful evocation of a whole community, it won Gambon an Olivier for Best Actor. Lyric Opera Chicago premiered an operatic setting of Miller's text with music by William Bolcom in 1999.

① Beatrice (Elizabeth Bell), Catherine (Suzan Sylvester) and Eddie (Michael Gambon), National Theatre, 1987.
© *Victoria and Albert Museum, London*

② Beatrice (Megs Jenkins), Catherine (Mary Ure), Marco (Ian Bannen) and Eddie (Anthony Quayle). *Photo by Charles Hewitt,* © *Getty Images*

The Sport of My Mad Mother

WRITTEN BY
Ann Jellicoe (1927–)

DIRECTED BY
George Devine and Ann Jellicoe

DESIGNED BY
Jocelyn Herbert

- First performed at the Royal Court Theatre, London, 25 February 1958.

① Fak (Phillip Locke), Patsy (Sheila Ballantine), Caldaro/Dean (Jerry Stovin) and Dodo (Avril Elgar). © *Roger Mayne, Photographer*

② Greta (Wendy Craig), Caldaro/Dean (Jerry Stovin) and Cone (Paul Bailey). © *Roger Mayne, Photographer*

③ Fak (Phillip Locke), Cone (Paul Bailey), Greta (Wendy Craig), Patsy (Sheila Ballantine), Caldaro/Dean (Jerry Stovin) and Dodo (Avril Elgar). © *Roger Mayne, Photographer*

SNAPSHOT

The Sport of My Mad Mother is free-flowing ritual jazz, unlike anything else on the stage of its time. A gang of East End teenagers, Fak, Patty and Cone, is under the sway of a mysterious figure called Greta. A musician, Steve, accompanies the action with a variety of improvised instruments, occasionally talking to the audience. The teenagers entertain themselves with a mix of creative play and petty violence towards outsiders. Cone eventually attacks Greta before realising she is pregnant. In a scene combining slapstick with piercing cries of pain, Greta bears a child, crying 'Birth! Birth! That's the thing!' Steve decides the child is his. He dismisses the audience, saying, 'I'm blowing this place up; bring your own axes'.

IMPACT

The play won third prize in the 1956 *Observer* competition for new playwrights, but the production at the Royal Court ran for only fourteen performances. Many reviews seemed to miss the point – *The Times* oddly remarking that Jellicoe 'appears to see life in a series of newspaper clichés'. It was, however, unmistakably a pioneering work. Jellicoe was not only the first woman in a predominantly male generation of playwrights, but also radically anti-naturalistic in style. Despite exuberantly presenting recognisable teenagers in the language of the streets (Jellicoe met her husband, Roger Mayne, when he photographed the play as part of an exploration of teenage culture), it tapped into powerful myths of female sexuality and violence. It also played joyful games with language; the act of perming a girl's hair became a surreal rite with the instructions on the packet chanted in chorus. Jellicoe, an experienced actress, director and tutor at the Central School of Speech and Drama, was a key figure in the Royal Court Writers' Group. This was a forcing house for many of the new generation of playwrights, allowing them to explore improvisation, masks and performance styles from a variety of cultures. It not only opened up new dramaturgical possibilities but also, as Jellicoe said, proved the Court's commitment to the idea that 'theatre could only be really changed by writers'.

AFTERLIFE

Sport did more to break down barriers between stage and audience than any other play of its time. It is revived all over the world in a variety of languages. Its influence can be seen in plays as diverse as Jez Butterworth's *Jerusalem* (see p. 216) and Sarah Kane's *4.48 Psychosis*. Jellicoe had a commercial success with *The Knack* in 1962; filmed by Richard Lester, it won the 1965 Palme d'Or at Cannes. In 1978, Jellicoe set up the Colway Theatre Trust to explore the concept of Community Plays and continued to develop large-scale works involving the public.

OTHER WORKS BY
Ann Jellicoe
The Knack (1961)
The Rising Generation (1967)
The Western Women (1983)
with Fay Weldon and John Fowles

SEE ALSO
Yard Gal (1998)
by Rebecca Prichard
Jerusalem (2009)
by Jez Butterworth

①

A Taste of Honey

WRITTEN BY
Shelagh Delaney (1938–2011)

DIRECTED BY
Joan Littlewood

DESIGNED BY
John Bury

• First performed at the Theatre Royal Stratford East, London, 27 May 1958.

OTHER WORKS BY
Shelagh Delaney
The Lion in Love (1960)
The House that Jack Built (1978)

SEE ALSO
The Arbor (1980)
by Andrea Dunbar
When I Was a Girl I Used to Scream and Shout (1984)
by Sharman MacDonald

SNAPSHOT

A Taste of Honey is a nineteen-year-old's account of working-class northern life as she saw it. All the characters experience fleeting moments of 'honey' in lives limited by poverty. Schoolgirl Jo moves with her flighty mother Helen to a grim flat in Salford. Helen has an on-off relationship with a youngish car salesman, Peter. When he finds it difficult to live with an adolescent girl, Helen leaves with him. Jo is consoled by a black sailor; she likes to imagine that he is a prince. In the second act, Jo is pregnant and the sailor hasn't returned. She is looked after by a gay art student, Geof. Far more maternal than Jo, he looks forward to the baby. Helen, dumped by Peter, moves back and bullies Geof into leaving; as Jo's labour pains begin, Helen swans off for a drink.

IMPACT

Delaney wrote the play in two weeks after Terence Rattigan's *Variations on a Theme* failed to impress her. Having seen Theatre Workshop in Manchester, she sent the script to Joan Littlewood, one of the few directors willing to tackle interracial relationships, homosexuality and single motherhood without sensationalism. Littlewood, as was her habit, made changes. Helen and Jo gained some comic asides. Avis Bunnage, a seasoned Workshop performer, excelled at these and Frances Cuka had done some revue work before joining the company. A jazz trio played incidental music, underlining the dreamlike atmosphere in which events flow from decisions taken off stage. Perhaps less successfully, entrances and exits were marked with dances. Overall, the aim was to preserve the youthful quality of the play. Negative reviews harped on Delaney's age and class. 'If there is anything worse than an Angry Young Man it's an Angry Young Woman,' announced the *Daily Mail*; others claimed to be shocked by the play's 'vulgarity'. Murray Melvin recalls that when playing Geof he expected extreme hostility from the audience. However, they were almost invariably warmly responsive. Jo's powerlessness, poverty and tolerance reflected the experience of many whose wartime childhoods had meant austerity but a less limited view of the world.

AFTERLIFE

The play transferred to the West End in 1959 and ran for over a year, during which Delaney received the Charles Henry Foyle award for best new play and an Arts Council bursary. On Broadway, Joan Plowright played Jo, winning a Tony for her performance, and Angela Lansbury played Helen. Tony Richardson directed the film, released in 1961, starring Rita Tushingham and Dora Bryan, with Murray Melvin reprising his stage role as Geof. It won four BAFTA awards, including one for Delaney's screenplay, and helped to launch the New Wave in British cinema. *A Taste of Honey* is one of the most frequently revived plays by a female playwright; there were numerous productions to celebrate the play's fiftieth anniversary in 2008; the Royal Exchange, Manchester focused on the play's roots in the north, with *Coronation Street* star Sally Lindsay as Helen. Delaney wrote a number of screenplays and works for radio, but the theatre failed to nurture her. A year before Delaney died, Jeanette Winterson noted, 'She had all the talent and we let her go'.

① Jo (Kaye Wragg) and Geof (Ashley Artus), Watford Palace, 2000. © *Victoria and Albert Museum, London*

② Geof (Murray Melvin) and Jo (Frances Cuka), Wyndhams Theatre, 1959. © *David Sim, Photographer*

Moon on a Rainbow Shawl

WRITTEN BY
Errol John (1924–88)

DIRECTED BY
Frith Banbury

DESIGNED BY
Loudon Sainthill

- Original version performed on BBC radio as 'Small Island Moon', 27 May 1958.
- First staged at Manchester Opera House, 27 October 1958.

SNAPSHOT

This is a vibrantly naturalistic study of poverty in Trinidad just after the Second World War. The characters live in Old Mack's ramshackle yard, but dream of better things. Bus driver Ephraim wants to go to Liverpool. Sophia next door wants education for her daughter Esther, who has won a scholarship, but doesn't trust her husband Charlie to provide. When the takings are stolen from Old Mack's café, Rosa confides to Ephraim that she has unwittingly betrayed Charlie to the police. Furious, Ephraim leaves, even though Rosa is pregnant; Sophia attempts in vain to persuade him to stay. When someone else is accused of the theft, Charlie owns up. A heartbroken Esther runs away. Sophia assures Rosa she will help with the baby but, as Old Mack's voice summons Rosa, it's clear where the money will come from. Just before the curtain falls, Esther returns – a small note of hope.

IMPACT

Errol John had his own company in Port of Spain, but found few opportunities as an actor when he moved to London in the 1950s. Although there was a black and Asian population of 180,000, this was only the second West Indian play to be staged in Britain. It won the *Observer* competition for new playwrights in 1957 and an unexpected postponement at the Royal Court freed a slot for it in 1958 – just ten years after HMS *Windrush* docked at Tilbury carrying 493 West Indians intending, like Ephraim, to start a new life in the UK. The play was well – if sometimes patronisingly – received. 'The coloured cast were excellent,' announced *Theatre World*. The complexity of its sexual politics was largely ignored, as was Charlie's account of the prejudice that destroyed his career as a cricketer (based on the experience of John's father) – perhaps the theatre's best-ever speech about the politics of sport. The only member of the original cast to find success in the UK was Jacqui Chan, a charming Esther, who became a familiar face on British television.

AFTERLIFE

The play was televised by ITV in 1960. John wrote only one further play, *The Exiles*, for BBC TV in 1969. However, in 2003, a group of black practitioners met to create a new company, Eclipse, and chose *Moon* as their first production. On tour, Victor Romero Evans was praised for his balanced performance, showing both the cruelty of Ephraim and his understanding of the youthful hope of Esther; Dystin Johnson also received good reviews for the mix of maternal love and judgemental narrowness in her Sophia. The play was a major factor in establishing the Eclipse company. In 2008, the Cayman National Cultural Foundation organised a conference on Caribbean Theatre, centred on *Moon* as a pioneering classic. It continues to be revived, most recently by the National Theatre in 2012.

① Charlie (John Boule), American Soldier (Leonard Davis), Prince (Leo Carera), Sophia (Vinnette Carroll) and Mavis (Barbara Assoon). *Photo by Angus McBean (MS Thr 581).* © *Harvard Theatre Collection, Houghton Library, Harvard University*

② Sophia (Vinnette Carroll), Old Mack (Lionel Ngakane) and Rosa (Soraya Rafat). *Photo by Angus McBean (MS Thr 581).* © *Harvard Theatre Collection, Houghton Library, Harvard University*

③ Mavis (Ellen Thomas), Almeida, 1988. © *Victoria and Albert Museum, London*

1956–68

OTHER WORKS BY
Errol John
The Exiles (1960)

SEE ALSO
Redemption Song (1984)
by Edgar White
Elmina's Kitchen (2003)
by Kwame Kwei-Armah

The Hostage

WRITTEN BY
Brendan Behan (1923–64)

DIRECTED BY
Joan Littlewood

DESIGNED BY
Sean Kenny

- First performed at the Damer Theatre, Dublin, in Irish (An Giall), 16 June 1958.
- Translated into English and first performed in the UK at the Theatre Royal Stratford East, London, 14 October 1958.

SNAPSHOT

The Hostage mixes farce and political cabaret with a naturalistically treated love story. In Belfast, an eighteen-year-old boy waits in jail to be hanged for killing a policeman; the IRA takes a hostage, a young English soldier called Leslie, threatening to kill him if the sentence is carried out. They hide Leslie in the last place they think anyone will look – a Dublin brothel owned by an ancient rebel and run by his one-legged sidekick. The whores – male and female – assure Leslie the threats are only a bluff and he begins a tentative romance with a Catholic waif, Teresa. However, he is betrayed by one of the brothel tenants, the sanctimonious Mulleady ('I'm a secret policeman and I don't care who knows it'), and is shot in a botched raid. Leslie rises in a green spotlight to lead the cast in a chorus of 'The bells of hell go ting-a-ling-a-ling'.

IMPACT

Behan translated the play – based on a true story – from his naturalistic one-act play in Gaelic, *An Giall*, which was full of references to Irish history incomprehensible to an English audience. There was a widespread assumption that in handing his text over to Joan Littlewood, Behan lost control of it. But he concurred with her that 'music hall is the thing to aim at'. The relationship between actors and audience is full of asides and theatrical in-jokes. 'Brendan Behan, he's too anti-British,' complains Leslie; an IRA man retorts, 'Too anti-Irish, you mean', and threatens Behan for 'making fun of the Movement'. The music-hall conventions allow the actors to speak directly and forcibly to the audience about Behan's real targets: capital punishment (still in force), colonialism (in Kenya and Cyprus as well as Ireland), and sexual and racial intolerance. Those at the bottom of the pecking order noisily celebrate themselves: the black client of transvestite whore Rio Rita marches about with a sign reading 'Keep Ireland Black'. However, Leslie's ordinary decency always counterpoints the laughter and reminds the audience of their own vulnerability in an unjust society. The surreal vitality of *The Hostage* prompted Kenneth Tynan to remark that Behan, like Oscar Wilde or Sean O'Casey before him, was fulfilling the perennial mission of Irish playwrights to 'kick the English drama from the past into the present'.

AFTERLIFE

The Hostage transferred to Wyndham's Theatre on 11 June 1959, then to the Cort Theater, Broadway on 20 September 1960. It was filmed for German television as *Die Geisel* in 1977. Behan, an epic drinker celebrated in songs by bands as diverse as Thin Lizzy and the Pogues, died in 1964 aged only forty-one; he produced an autobiography, *Borstal Boy*, and some travel writing, but *The Hostage* was his last play. Along with *The Quare Fellow*, it has secured his reputation as a dramatist and has been extensively revived. In 1994, it was staged at the Barbican with John Woodvine. A revival in Dublin marked the fortieth anniversary of Behan's death. In 2009, Alice Coghlan's site-specific version for Wonderland Productions transformed the birthplace of Padraic Pearse, leader of the Easter Rising, into Behan's brothel. *An Giall* has also been revived more than fifty times.

① Colette (Yootha Joyce), Meg (Eileen Kennally), Teresa (Celia Salkeld), Pat (Howard Goorney) and Leslie (Alfred Lynch), Wyndhams Theatre transfer, 1959. © *John Cowan, Photographer*

①

② Pat (Howard Goorney), Colette (Yootha Joyce), Old Ropeen (Leila Greenwood), Meg (Eileen Kennally), Leslie (Alfred Lynch) and IRA Volunteer (Clive Barker), Wyndham's Theatre transfer, 1959. © *John Cowan, Photographer*

③ Pat (Dermot Crowley) and Monsewer (John Woodvine), Barbican, 1994. © *Victoria and Albert Museum, London*

②

③

OTHER WORKS BY
Brendan Behan
The Quare Fellow (1954)
An Giall (1958)
Richard's Cork Leg (1972) completed
posthumously by Alan Simpson

SEE ALSO
The Shadow of a Gunman (1923)
by Sean O'Casey
The Freedom of the City (1973)
by Brian Friel

Happy Days

WRITTEN BY
Samuel Beckett (1906–89)

DIRECTED BY
George Devine

DESIGNED BY
Jocelyn Herbert

- First performed at the Cherry Lane Theater, New York, 17 September 1961, directed by Alan Schneider).

- First performed in the UK at the Royal Court Theatre, London, 1 November 1962.

SNAPSHOT

Beckett was challenged by his friend Maureen Cusack to 'write a happy play'. *Happy Days* shows a life even more deprived of movement and energy than *Waiting for Godot* (see p. 34), but it is nevertheless a comedy, with occasional moments of cheeky, seaside postcard humour. In changeless blazing light, in a scorched and barren landscape, Winnie stands buried in a mound of earth up to her waist. Her husband Willie moves in and out of a hole at the back of the set and makes the occasional remark. The next day, Winnie is buried up to her neck. Willie says just one word, and at the end is crawling towards his revolver. However, Winnie sings.

IMPACT

George Devine originally cast Joan Plowright as Winnie. When she withdrew, Brenda Bruce was a last-minute replacement and Beckett guided her through the role. Bruce was mainly known for comedy and gave full rein to Winnie's bawdy humour and the dogged resilience that makes the most of small events – brushing her teeth, watching an ant, memories of courtship. Beckett's style no longer surprised the critics, though there seemed to be a determination to take nothing at face value. 'The message seems slight and faintly debilitating,' said the *Guardian*.

Beckett clearly anticipated this sort of response. Winnie recalls a man called Shower – or maybe Cooker – gaping at her and demanding, 'What's it meant to mean?' Some lines were treated as purely poetic – for example, Winnie's query, 'Do you think the earth is losing its atmosphere?' (The same applied to David Rudkin's image of the crop-duster in *Afore Night Come* (see p. 56).)

AFTERLIFE

Peggy Ashcroft, who once described the role of Winnie as the female equivalent of Hamlet, played it for a year in Peter Hall's Old Vic production, which transferred in 1976 to the National to celebrate Beckett's seventieth birthday. This version had a darker edge: Willie's struggle to reach the gun hinted more strongly that he intended to commit suicide and Ashcroft was most memorable for the mounting terror she showed at the possibility, her song stripped of any sense of hope. Billie Whitelaw, an actress much admired by Beckett, worked with him for six weeks on a production for the Royal Court in 1979. She described rehearsals as like 'working with a painter, a sculptor, a conductor' in terms of the precision with which he directed; her song at the end was based on Beckett's own performance of it (although more tuneful). He praised the 'profound frivolity' of her characterisation, younger and more sexual than some earlier Winnies, and the near-madness with which she seized the props that she used to structure her day. The play has had many revivals and was filmed in 2000. Most recently it has been performed by Pauline McLynn, who appeared in the surreal Irish sitcom *Father Ted* and compared Winnie to her character Mrs Doyle – both, she said, believed that 'I talk, therefore I am'.

① Winnie (Peggy Ashcroft), Old Vic, 1975. © *Victoria and Albert Museum, London*

② Winnie (Natasha Parry), Riverside Studios, 1997. © *Victoria and Albert Museum, London*

③ Winnie (Brenda Bruce). © *Victoria and Albert Museum, London*

OTHER WORKS BY
Samuel Beckett
Waiting for Godot (1953)
Endgame (1957)
Play (1963)

SEE ALSO
Rockaby (1980)
by Samuel Beckett
Shirley Valentine (1986)
by Willy Russell

Chips With Everything

WRITTEN BY
Arnold Wesker (1932–)

DIRECTED BY
John Dexter

DESIGNED BY
Jocelyn Herbert

* First performed at the Royal
  Court Theatre, London,
  27 April 1962.

① Squadron Leader (Robert Hewitt), Wing Commander
(Howard Marion Crawford), Pilot Officer (Corin
Redgrave) and Pip (Gary Bond), Royal Court, 1963.
© *Victoria and Albert Museum, London*

② Richardson (John Noakes) and Seaford (Terence
Taplin), Royal Court, 1963. © *Victoria and Albert Museum,
London*

③ Hill (Alan Dobie), Seaford (Terence Taplin) and
Richardson (John Noakes), Royal Court, 1963. © *Victoria
and Albert Museum, London*

SNAPSHOT

Chips with Everything is a stylistic mix of 'found'
theatre, quoting verbatim from Wesker's own
National Service training, and expressionistic
set pieces. It shows a troupe of mainly working-
class youths gradually adapting to the RAF.
Among them is upper-class Pip, who has refused
officer training. He encourages the others in acts
of rebellion – like stealing coke for their chilly
hut – and in doing so proves himself a leader.
When Smiler, the weakest recruit, is bullied by
a pair of NCOs, the men care for him. Pip urges
the other officers not to charge the men, as he
puts on his own officer's uniform. The play ends
with the recruits giving a perfect display of drill
to the sound of the National Anthem.

IMPACT

This was Wesker's first commercial success:
'The first anti-Establishment play of which the
establishment has cause to be afraid', wrote
Harold Hobson. Wesker correctly assumed that
audiences would enjoy watching displays of
skill, such as the intricate marching rituals or
the equally disciplined coke-stealing sequence.
Most critics also found the anger of the class
politics exhilarating and the performances –
including the debut of a young Ronald Lacey
as a cherubic Smiler – were highly praised.

Bamber Gascoigne in *The Spectator* dissented:
'I hear Mr Wesker is contemplating a play on
the life of Jesus, no doubt another stage in
his autobiography'. This shrewdly isolated a
problem in the play: at times Wesker seems to
idealise the priggish and authoritarian Pip. For
instance, at a party for all ranks, Pip coerces
the recruits into challenging the officers with
their performance of an old rebel song, 'The
Cutty Wren'; it is theatrically chilling, but also
patronising towards the men's own taste, as if
Elvis Presley was somehow intrinsically inferior
to British folk music.

AFTERLIFE

The play transferred to the Vaudeville
Theatre, and then to the Plymouth Theater
on Broadway in 1963. It was made into a BBC
television play in 1975. It was most recently
revived at the National in 1997, with Rupert
Penry-Jones as an aristocratic Pip. While
the director Howard Davies was praised for
a lively sense of period, the play seemed
dated and its language relatively tame, unlike
Wesker's naturalistic and still potent *Roots*.
Later treatments of National Service life, such
as John McGrath's *Events While Guarding the
Bofors Gun* in 1966, were more graphic and
more directly challenging to the censor.

OTHER WORKS BY
Arnold Wesker
*The Wesker Trilogy: Chicken Soup
with Barley; Roots; I'm Talking
About Jerusalem* (1958–1960)
The Kitchen (1959)
Their Very Own and *Golden City*
(1965)

SEE ALSO
*Events While Guarding the
Bofors Gun* (1966)
by John McGrath
Dingo (1967)
by Charles Wood

Afore Night Come

WRITTEN BY
David Rudkin (1936–)

DIRECTED BY
Clifford Williams

DESIGNED BY
John Bury

- First performed at the Arts Theatre Club, London, 7 June 1962.

① Jim (David Warner), Albert (Joe Gibbons), Ginger (Timothy West), Taffy Hughes (Brian Jackson), Jumbo (Freddy Jones), Roche (Gerry Duggan) and Jeff (Henley Thomas). *Photo by Reg Wilson, © Royal Shakespeare Company*

② Johnny Hobnails (Peter McEnery) and Tiny (Henry Woolf). *Photo by Reg Wilson, © Royal Shakespeare Company*

③ The Killing of Roche. Jeff (Henry Thomas), Ginger (Timothy West), Jim (David Warner), Roche (Gerry Duggan) and Albert (Joe Gibbons). *Photo by Reg Wilson, © Royal Shakespeare Company*

SNAPSHOT

Afore Night Come begins as a play about work and ends in ritual violence. A group of rural labourers are harvesting pears in a Midlands orchard, quarrelling uneasily. At first their aggression appears to focus on Larry, a naive student. Two 'regulars', Johnny Hobnails, on release from a mental hospital, and his friend, Tiny, both born-again Christians, are drawn to Larry, Johnny with inarticulate sexual longing. Hostility eventually crystallises around a mysterious poetic Irish hobo, Roche. In the grip of a nameless fear, Tiny and Johnny persuade Larry to leave. The group then surround Roche, slash his body with a cross, cut off his head and bury him 'reverently'. As the boss and the foreman, Spens, appear, Johnny leaves for good. Larry returns and Spens adds his name to the list of pickers for the season. Alone, Larry picks up one of the knives used to stab Roche.

IMPACT

Originally written for students, the play reflects Rudkin's interest in Antonin Artaud. Artaud's book *The Theatre and its Double* outlines a Theatre of Cruelty – cruel in the sense that it used violently physical acting to show the audience truths they do not wish to see. In 1962, Peter Hall made *Afore Night Come* central to a summer of new plays exploring violence, surrealism and ritual, avoiding the censor by billing them as club performances. Audiences were gripped by the mesmerising rhythms that orchestrated the violence. On the first night, a spectator fainted as the head of Roche rolled downstage and was briskly silenced by Harold Pinter. Only weeks after the opening, the aggression towards 'outsiders' shown in the play took on a sharper political significance as one of the UK's first race riots occurred in the Midlands.

AFTERLIFE

The play received an *Evening Standard* award for most promising playwright. The RSC revived it for their Theatre of Cruelty season in 1964 at the Aldwych, which included not only Rudkin's play but also Peter Weiss' *Marat/Sade* (see p. 60). Both works became the focus of an attack by the impresario Emile Littler, one of the company's own governors, who called them 'dirty plays', incompatible with 'having the Queen as our patron'. Critics as different in outlook as Harold Hobson and Kenneth Tynan came to the defence of the plays and the RSC for its commitment to performing modern playwrights alongside Shakespeare. They also upheld the RSC's right to subsidy, which Littler evidently grudged them. The play was extensively revived in Europe and the USA. One revival in Wuppertal in 1969 caused a massive rift between older members of the audience, who reiterated Littler's charge of 'filth', and the passionately engaged spectators of the post-war generation. It was revived at The Other Place, the RSC's small experimental venue in Stratford, in 1974, an effective symbol of the desire of its director, Ron Daniels, to return to the provocative and innovative spirit of the 1960s. The Young Vic staged the play in 2001, a production hailed by Gregory Burke, author of *Black Watch*, as 'the best performance I've ever seen'. Rudkin's carefully evoked landscape, an earth polluted by pesticides that make the workers infertile, acquired a new topicality and power.

①

1956–68

Oh What a Lovely War

WRITTEN BY
Charles Chilton (1917–),
Joan Littlewood (1914–2002)
and Theatre Workshop

DIRECTED BY
Joan Littlewood

DESIGNED BY
John Bury

- First performed at the Theatre Royal Stratford East, London, 19 March 1963.

SNAPSHOT

Oh What a Lovely War is popular theatre, created by the people. It's a collage of songs of the First World War, which looks at the experience of those who had been inspired or enraged by them; it was put together by Joan Littlewood and Theatre Workshop based on a radio programme by Charles Chilton. It shows the progress of the war from the cynical power games that began it, to the experience of troops led by incompetent generals to die in their thousands for tiny amounts of territory – men who called themselves 'lions led by donkeys'. The company was anxious to avoid flooding the stage with khaki uniforms and realistic death scenes; hence, the play is staged as one of the seaside pierrot concert parties popular in the early 1900s. A Master of Ceremonies welcomes the audience to 'the ever-popular war game'; the company performs routines to the hit songs of the day alongside satirical sketches. Everything is played against projected footage of the war in all its grimness and statistics about casualties appear in lights.

IMPACT

In 1961, Joan Littlewood left Theatre Workshop for two years, complaining that the West End had stolen her best work, such as *A Taste of Honey*, from the East End community for which it was created. But in *Oh What a Lovely War* the relevant community was huge: all families in the Britain of the early 1960s were affected in some way by the Great War. The younger generation was sharply aware of the possibility of nuclear conflict, especially after the Cuban missile crisis. Reviews were positive, several critics finding themselves surprised by the mixture of nostalgia and pain generated by the songs. It proved a hard piece to classify: in America, it received a Tony nomination for Best Musical; others preferred to think of it as a documentary; Joan Littlewood liked the term 'entertainment'.

AFTERLIFE

The play transferred to Wyndham's in June 1963, and then to the Broadhurst Theater, Broadway, in 1964. Victor Spinetti, who played the MC and had been a key member of the group that shaped the pierrot style, won a Tony Award for Supporting Actor in a Musical. Richard Attenborough filmed it in 1969, retaining the concert-party style; the film won six BAFTA awards. *Oh What a Lovely War* has decisively coloured the way the First World War has been understood; though a later generation of conservative historians regarded it as unfair on the leadership, shows such as *Blackadder Goes Forth* perpetuate its image of the war as a game for those far from the front line and hell for the working-class troops in the thick of it. The play is constantly revived by both amateur and professional companies, although Littlewood resisted an attempt in 1998 to stage it at the National Theatre; instead, it was played in a circus tent and subsequently toured the country like Theatre Workshop in its pre-Stratford years.

① Chiwetel Ejiofor, National Youth Theatre production, Bloomsbury Theatre, 1994. © *Victoria and Albert Museum, London*

② Pierrots, Wyndhams Theatre transfer, 1963. © *Victoria and Albert Museum, London*

③ Pierrots, National Theatre, 1998. © *Victoria and Albert Museum, London*

SEE ALSO

Journey's End (1928)
by R.C. Sherrif
Dingo (1967)
by Charles Wood

The Persecution and Assassination of Marat as Performed by the Inmates of the Asylum of Charenton Under the Direction of the Marquis de Sade

WRITTEN BY
Peter Weiss (1916–82)

DIRECTED BY
Peter Brook

DESIGNED BY
Sally Jacobs

- First performed at the LAMDA Theatre, London, 12 January 1964.

OTHER WORKS BY
Peter Weiss
The Investigation (1965)
The Insurance (1969)

SEE ALSO
The Fool: Scenes of Bread and Love (1973)
by Edward Bond
The Danton Affair (1986)
by Pam Gems

① The Company. © *Morris Newcombe, Photographer*

② Rossignol (Freya Copeland), Kokol (Dave Fishley) and Marat (Corin Redgrave), National Theatre, 1997.
© *Victoria and Albert Museum, London*

SNAPSHOT

Marat/Sade is, as its title suggests, a multilayered play, one of the first in which the surreal and dreamlike style of the Absurd clashes directly with the cooler political debate of Brechtian theatre. In 1808, mentally-ill patients under the direction of fellow asylum inmate the Marquis de Sade are acting out the 1793 French Revolution. The central conflict is between de Sade, who sees revolutionary violence as conducive 'to the withering of the individual and a slow merging into uniformity', and the radical Marat, who believes people can change if society is changed. This debate is constantly challenged and sometimes overwhelmed as the inmates present a wild physical theatre spectacular, often working against the words: the activist Charlotte Corday is played by a patient with sleeping sickness, egged on to assassinate Marat by an erotomaniac who paws her as he speaks high-minded sentiments. De Sade's production is often interrupted by Coulmier, the Bonapartist director of the asylum, who steps into the whirling anarchy wearing a top hat. Peter Brook's production for the RSC was the product of weeks of public workshops exploring the Theatre of Cruelty. The actors' immersion in Antonin Artaud's work produced extraordinary images: a splashy guillotine sequence with buckets of paint for blood (red or aristocratic blue); Glenda Jackson in her first major role as Corday, whipping de Sade with her hair; and 'lunatics' in a final orgy of destruction suddenly morphing into actors giving the audience a slow handclap.

IMPACT

Inevitably, responses were passionate and polarized. Sexual mores were changing and new attitudes to war and authority emerged, especially among the young, as US involvement in Vietnam began to escalate. For some, the imagination and scope of the production crystallized the energy of the mid-1960s. Bernard Levin described it in the *Daily Mail* as 'one of the half-dozen most amazing achievements … the English Theatre has seen in my lifetime'. David Edgar, who saw it aged sixteen, recalled, 'It suddenly made clear to me what theatre could do'. Others sided with Emile Littler, who had ignited the 'dirty plays' controversy over *Afore Night Come* (see p. 56) and *Marat/Sade*. This broader debate raged in the press for weeks.

AFTERLIFE

The play opened on Broadway at the Martin Beck Theater on 27 December 1965. It won four Tony Awards in 1966 and the New York Drama Critics' Circle Award 1966. Since then there have been many revivals. Their perspectives have often shifted – Weiss rewrote several times, emphasising Marat, not de Sade, as the intellectual centre of the play. Christopher McElroen staged an all-male, all-black 2007 production at the Classical Theater of Harlem in New York. Most recently, the RSC performed it at Stratford as part of its fiftieth birthday celebrations, in a production by Anthony Neilson that brought the action up to date to evoke the Arab Spring: Marat used a laptop; Corday dressed as a terrorist and tortured de Sade with a Taser. The old controversy was partly re-ignited. There were audience walkouts and the *Daily Mail* complained about RSC subsidies, the 'left-wing' ideology and the fact that an actor from *Midsomer Murders* appeared in a rape scene. However, many of those who supported the RSC's right to experiment and praised some of the more interesting innovations, such as giving the key role of the narrating Herald to an actress, Lisa Hammond, nevertheless felt that the updating and the barrage of shock effects had over-simplified the play.

①

②

The Homecoming

WRITTEN BY
Harold Pinter (1930–2008)

DIRECTED BY
Peter Hall

DESIGNED BY
John Bury

- First performed at the Aldwych Theatre, London, 3 June 1965.

SNAPSHOT

The term 'comedy of menace' coined to describe the early work of Pinter fits *The Homecoming* as far as any label can fit this ambiguous play, in which there is no rational, understandable basis for the characters' actions. Teddy, a philosophy professor in the USA, brings his wife Ruth to his old north London home. The rest of his family are there: the patriarch, Max, a retired butcher, and his chauffeur brother Sam, and Teddy's brothers, hopeless boxer Joey and Lenny, a pimp. There is only one violent incident, when Max hits Joey, but ferocious aggression underpins even trivial disputes over a cheese roll or a newspaper: 'I'll chop your spine off', says Max when Lenny interrupts him. Ruth and Lenny have a sexually charged encounter. Later, she and Joey engage in energetic foreplay in front of the whole family, including Teddy. Finally, Ruth agrees to stay in the household and work as a prostitute, and Teddy leaves. As the lights go down, Max, the dying, or possibly dead, Sam, and Joey are all at Ruth's feet. Lenny watches.

IMPACT

This was Pinter's third full-length play; he sent it to Peter Hall, the start of an enduring writer-director relationship, in the wake of the 'dirty plays' controversy. This time there were no complaints about the subject matter. Though baffled by the motivations of the repellent characters, critics felt they understood the style in Hall's production, with its snappy exchanges and uncomfortable 'Pinteresque' pauses orchestrated with as much care as the RSC's recent Shakespeare cycle. Noël Coward wrote to Pinter of his admiration for the 'arrogant, but triumphant, demands' made on the audience.

The play spoke to the changing sexual attitudes of the 1960s. Infidelity on stage still tended to be portrayed as furtive and guilt-ridden or as a basis for farce. *The Homecoming* dispenses with shame. The Oedipal conflicts and economic imperatives that drive the family are made brutally explicit. Vivien Merchant made Ruth a figure of extraordinary power – not just sexually, but intellectually. Ruth is the only character who converses with both the violent and sexist Lenny and the philosopher Teddy in their own kind of language. Both Peter Hall and Pinter identified Teddy as the villain of the play, suggesting that engagement with life, however unpleasant, is better than withdrawal.

AFTERLIFE

The play transferred to the Music Box in New York in 1967 and won four Tony Awards. Merchant again played Ruth, as she did in a 1973 film made by Peter Hall. The role has continued to offer actresses an extraordinary challenge, particularly since feminists have deconstructed the assumption that the male characters take for granted – that women are all whores or mothers. It has become a period piece about a woman unconsciously seeking her own liberation. Keith Allen at the National Theatre in 1997 made Teddy insufferably patronising, a reason for Lindsay Duncan's burning coldness as she begins to discover the possibility of a different life. The play was staged at Stratford-on-Avon as part of the RSC's fiftieth anniversary season. Praising the highly controlled and powerful Ruth of Aislin McGuckin as 'the one realist in a household of dreamers', Michael Billington added, 'It is still the best new play the RSC has discovered in its history'.

① Lenny (Nicholas Woodeson), Ruth (Cherie Lunghi) and Joey (Douglas McFerran), Comedy Theatre, 1991. © *Victoria and Albert Museum, London*

② Teddy (Michael Bryant), Ruth (Vivien Merchant), Joey (Terence Rigby) and Max (Paul Rogers). © *Victoria and Albert Museum, London*

③ Ruth (Lia Williams), Max (Ian Holm) and Teddy (Nick Dunning), Comedy Theatre, 2001. © *Victoria and Albert Museum, London*

OTHER WORKS BY
Harold Pinter
The Caretaker (1960)
No Man's Land (1975)
Ashes to Ashes (1996)

SEE ALSO
Buried Child (1978)
by Sam Shepard
Love and Understanding (1997)
by Joe Penhall

Saved

WRITTEN BY
Edward Bond (1934–)

DIRECTED BY
William Gaskill

DESIGNED BY
John Gunter

- First performed by the English Stage Society at the Royal Court Theatre, London, 3 November 1965.

SNAPSHOT

In thirteen stripped-down scenes, *Saved* charts the emotionally stunted lives of a group of working-class south Londoners. A young woman, Pam, picks up Len for sex. He becomes the family lodger, an optimistic presence in a household marked by grim silences between Pam's parents. Pam ditches Len for Fred, one of a group of young men who hang about together, and has his child. Only Len takes much notice of the baby, whose crying is ignored as the others watch TV and argue. Left with Fred in the park, the baby is tortured and stoned to death by Fred and his mates. When Pam returns, she fails to notice that the baby is dead. Fred is convicted of the crime, but on his release from prison Pam tries to win him back. As the play ends, the family is locked in silence while Len mends a broken chair.

IMPACT

The Lord Chamberlain's Office refused *Saved* a licence. The Royal Court's management risked staging it as a club performance, but was prosecuted for violating club conditions, found guilty and given a conditional discharge. *Saved* was the beginning of the end for theatre censorship, but the debate was prolonged and painful, especially as it coincided with terrible revelations in the press about the murders of three young people by Ian Brady and Myra Hindley, a case that led some to demand more censorship of potentially 'corrupting' literature. Even reviews supporting Bond's right to his subject tended to express shock rather than analysis. However, a number of theatrical luminaries defended the play in the spirit of Sir Laurence Olivier, who remarked in court that it was 'for grown-ups'. Tony Selby, cast as one of the young men along with Dennis Waterman and Ronald Pickup, recalls that director William Gaskill's aim was to express the 'delicacy' of the text: the queasy individual reservations expressed by most of the men in the park before their atavistic communal violence; and the rare moment of tender comedy as Pam's mother flirts with Len, making him mend the stocking she is wearing, a scene forbidden by the censor. This 'delicacy' precludes simplistic motivation, such as poverty – the characters live in a reasonably prosperous society, which nevertheless alienates them from their own humanity. In the absence of any figure who offers direct moral comment, it is for the audience to judge them and their world.

AFTERLIFE

Notable revivals include Peter Stein's 1967 production at the Kammerspiele in Munich (voted best production of the year by Theater Heute) and Danny Boyle's at the Royal Court in 1984. Most recently, in Sean Holmes's production at the Lyric Hammersmith in 2011, it was clear that the minimalist style was familiar to the audience through the work of writers such as Sarah Kane, who have acknowledged their debt to Bond. The audience was able to consider the murder in its context, and reviews responded to the fraying relationship between Lia Saville's Pam and Morgan Watkins' awkward Len as much as to the overt violence.

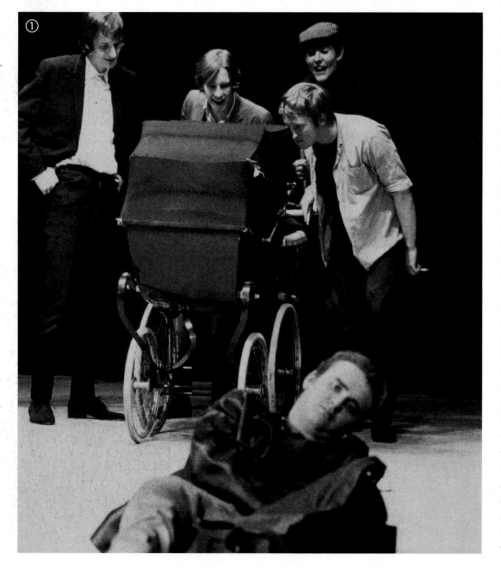

① Pete (Ronald Pickup), Colin (Dennis Waterman), Mike (John Bull), Barry (William Stewart) and Fred (Tony Selby). © *Zoe Dominic, Photographer*

② Baby stoning; Pete (Ronald Pickup), Barry (William Stewart), Colin (Dennis Waterman) and Fred (Tony Selby). © *Zoe Dominic, Photographer*

③ Liz (Alison Frazer) and Pam (Barbara Ferris).
© *Victoria and Albert Museum, London*

OTHER WORKS BY
Edward Bond
Lear (1972)
Bingo: Scenes of Money and Death (1973)
The Fool: Scenes of Bread and Love (1975)

SEE ALSO
No One Was Saved (1970)
by Howard Barker
Blasted (1995)
by Sarah Kane

1956–68

Rosencrantz and Guildenstern Are Dead

WRITTEN BY
Tom Stoppard (1937–)

DIRECTED BY
Derek Goldby

DESIGNED BY
Desmond Heeley

- First performed at the Old Vic (National Theatre), London, 11 April 1967.

SNAPSHOT

In this comic meditation on the nature of theatre and life, Stoppard puts Rosencrantz and Guildenstern, minor characters from Shakespeare's *Hamlet*, centre stage; the main action of *Hamlet* becomes a backdrop. As another minor character, the Player, also promoted to a leading role, explains: 'We do on stage the things that are supposed to happen off. Which is a kind of integrity if you look on every exit as being an entrance somewhere else'. Elizabethan versions of Vladimir and Estragon from *Waiting for Godot*, the pair amuse themselves by playing verbal games, debating probability, existence and death as they toss a coin, which always comes down heads. They are oblivious to the unfolding drama that determines their destiny: they die, without ever knowing why, in obedience to the laws of tragedy explained by the Player (with a bit of help from Oscar Wilde): 'The bad end unhappily, the good unluckily. That is what tragedy means'.

IMPACT

Rosencrantz and Guildenstern Are Dead is probably the most successful student play of all time. Initially staged by Oxford Theatre Group at the Edinburgh Fringe festival, it was spotted by Kenneth Tynan, then dramaturg at the National Theatre, and programmed as the only new play in the National's next season. It was an apt choice for a relatively new institution. The play is partly a dialogue with Peter Hall's 1965 *Hamlet* for the RSC, in which David Warner's prince, a troubled and shabby figure who would look at home in a student protest, was a poster boy for 1960s youth. It offered significant opportunities to the National's younger members: John Stride, a star since his Romeo opposite Judi Dench in 1960, and Edward Petherbridge in his first major role. It explored a number of themes animating theatre and public life in the 1960s, including questions of authority and free will sparked by the Vietnam War, the Cultural Revolution in China and the build-up to the Prague Spring. Excellent reviews – Harold Hobson labelled the play 'the most important event in the British professional theatre of the last nine years' – established Stoppard as a presence in the theatre for the next forty years.

AFTERLIFE

The play transferred to Broadway where it ran for a year and won four Tony Awards. In 1990, Stoppard adapted and directed a film version starring Tim Roth and Gary Oldman, which won the Golden Lion at the Venice Film Festival. Trevor Nunn revived the play in 2011, at the Chichester Festival Theatre and subsequently at the Theatre Royal Haymarket in the West End. Reviews were mainly positive, although some felt the joke had worn thin and the play lacked both the political energy and the human warmth of Stoppard's later work.

① The Players perform in front of Guildenstern (Edward Petherbridge) and Rosencrantz (John Stride). © *Victoria and Albert Museum, London*

② Rosencrantz (John Stride) and Guildenstern (Edward Petherbridge). © *Victoria and Albert Museum, London*

②

1956–68

OTHER WORKS BY
Tom Stoppard
Jumpers (1972)
Every Good Boy Deserves Favour
(1977) with André Previn
Rock 'n' Roll (2006)

SEE ALSO
Waiting for Godot (1955)
by Samuel Beckett
Bingo: Scenes of Money and Death
(1973) by Edward Bond

Forty Years On

①

WRITTEN BY
Alan Bennett (1934–)

DIRECTED BY
Patrick Garland

DESIGNED BY
Julia Trevelyan Oman

- First performed at the Apollo Theatre, London, 31 October 1968.

SNAPSHOT

Forty Years On, a play about a play, has strong affinities with revue, the form Bennett knew best. The boys and staff of a run-down public school, Albion House, celebrate the retirement of the Headmaster with a play about an upper-class couple, Moggie and Hugh, and their old Nurse, sitting out the Second World War in the basement of Claridge's. In a series of freewheeling sketches, the schoolboys show the unfolding events of the twentieth century until they meet the time frame of Hugh and Moggie. As Bennett has said, the play is full of 'terrible' puns and throwaway jokes. At the heart of it, however, is a key moment in Britain's history: the transition from appeasement to defiance of Hitler. In September 1939, Labour leader Arthur Greenwood rose to denounce Neville Chamberlain's feeble response to Hitler's invasion of Poland. From the backbenches came a cry of 'Speak for England, Arthur!' 'Speak for England, Arthur!' is the title of the play within the play, suggesting that *Forty Years On* aims to do just that.

IMPACT

Bennett was one of the Oxbridge graduates who wrote and performed *Beyond the Fringe*, a revue that set the tone of British satire for the 1960s. Its main target was old-style Toryism – snobbish, colonialist and authoritiarian – symbolised by the current Prime Minister, Harold Macmillan. The play similarly parodies an authoritarian culture opposed to 'that bunch of rootless intellectual, alien Jews and international pederasts who call themselves the Labour Party'. The sexual timidity of that culture is also mocked in the school chaplain's near-incomprehensible facts-of-life speech: 'It's not pretty, but it was put there for a purpose. Point taken, Foster?' Albion House, England in miniature, is described as 'A valuable site at the cross-roads of the world' – a society in which race, sexuality and class are all at a cultural watershed. One of the boldest features of Patrick Garland's production was the casting of John Gielgud, who at that time rarely worked in new plays, as the Headmaster; although initially alienated by the satirical tone, Gielgud supported the play through some rocky encounters with shocked audiences on tour and established it as a West End hit. His career took a new direction, as the eccentricity and pathos of his comedy and the gravitas he brought to the final speech made him natural casting in David Storey's *Home* and Harold Pinter's *No Man's Land* (see p. 90).

AFTERLIFE

The play won the inaugural *Evening Standard* Special Award in 1968, although poor reviews in the *New Yorker* prevented a transfer to Broadway. Paul Eddington, the junior master Franklin in the original production, played the Headmaster in a revival at Chichester Festival Theatre in 1984 and the bewildered dignity of his performance was praised by several critics as funnier than that of Gielgud. The play was revived at the Theatre Royal, York, in 2011, the theatre's fifth play by the Yorkshireman Bennett.

① **The pupils.** © *Victoria and Albert Museum, London*

② **Headmaster (John Gielgud).** © *Victoria and Albert Museum, London*

1956–68

OTHER WORKS BY
Alan Bennett
Habeas Corpus (1973)
Talking Heads (1992)
The History Boys (2004)

SEE ALSO
Skyvers (1963)
by Barry Reckord
Slags (1970)
by David Hare

1969–79

The end of theatre censorship in 1968 gave theatre in the 1970s a new freedom, allowing alternative and experimental work to thrive. The anti-authoritarian attitudes that characterised the swinging sixties in Britain could now be articulated on stage: swearing was permissible, and political satire and work exploring race, gender and sexuality and other contemporary issues became a major part of the theatrical scene. Caryl Churchill was one of a growing band that gave women a significant and sustained voice on the stage. Increases in Arts Council funding enabled more touring companies to produce increasingly experimental work. Regional theatres continued to flourish, offering actors, directors and playwrights the chance to learn their craft and hone their ideas. Some, like the Liverpool Everyman, put their creative energy into fostering new and local writing talent, providing opportunities for Alan Bleasdale, Willy Russell, Chris Bond and John McGrath.

Theatre blossomed everywhere in the 1970s: in pubs, found spaces and in the streets, as well as in newly-built theatres. When the National Theatre opened on the South Bank in 1976, it embraced the fringe aesthetic, inviting Ken Campbell (another alumnus of Liverpool Everyman) to stage his ten-hour spectacular *Illuminatus* in the Cottesloe. The Royal Shakespeare Company also established a number of smaller spaces, hiring the Place in London in 1971 and creating a 330-seat auditorium, then opening the 140-seat Other Place in Stratford-upon-Avon in 1974. Regional theatres followed this trend, establishing black-box studio theatres alongside their main auditorium.

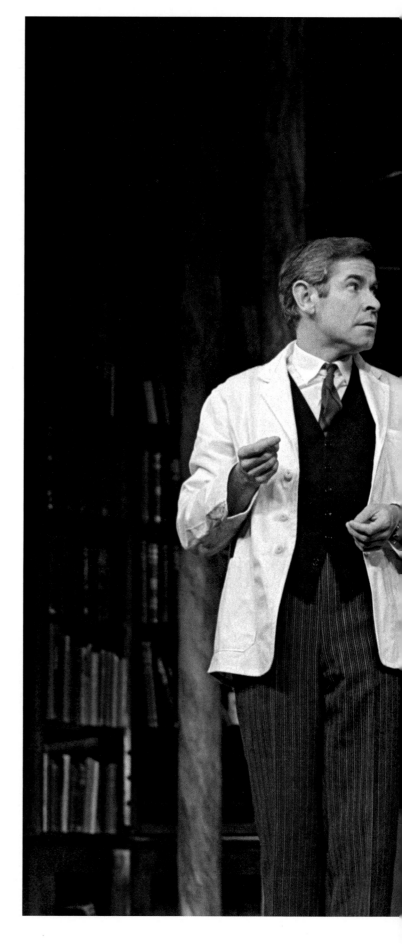

▶ Prentice (Stanley Baxter) and Rance (Ralph Richardson), *What the Butler Saw.* © *Victoria and Albert Museum, London*

What the Butler Saw

WRITTEN BY
Joe Orton (1933–67)

DIRECTED BY
Robert Chetwyn

DESIGNED BY
Hutchinson Scott

- First performed at the Queen's Theatre, London, 5 March 1969.

① Mrs Prentice (Coral Browne) and Nick (Hayward Morse). © *Victoria and Albert Museum, London*

② Mrs Prentice (Betty Marsden) and Sergeant Match (Kevin Lloyd), Royal Court, 1975. © *Victoria and Albert Museum, London*

SNAPSHOT

This fast-moving farce set in a psychiatric clinic puts a new spin on the idea of the lunatics taking over the asylum. Busily seducing Geraldine, a young applicant for the post of secretary, Dr Prentice is interrupted by his wife and bellboy Nick, who is blackmailing her. The Prentice marriage is based on mutual contempt: 'You were born with your legs apart. They'll send you to the grave in a Y-shaped coffin'. Matters are complicated by the arrival of clinic inspector Dr Rance, from 'your immediate superiors in madness'. Rance's madness *is* superior – the only authentic madness in the play; the rest only act madly to bolster their own frantic lies. Geraldine and Nick swap clothes, resulting in a string of mistaken identities and innuendo-laden gags. The play ends with the revelation that Geraldine and Nick are the Prentices' long-lost twins and the recovery of a vital part of a statue of Winston Churchill, which killed Geraldine's adoptive mother in an explosion.

IMPACT

By the time *What the Butler Saw* was produced, Orton was infamous, having been battered to death by his lover Kenneth Halliwell, who then committed suicide. Eagerly anticipated, the play was lavishly mounted by the most powerful managements in the West End, Lewenstein-Delfont and H.M. Tennent, and cast with theatre aristocrats: Ralph Richardson as Rance, and Coral Browne and Stanley Baxter as the Prentices. Baxter's reputation as one of the great pantomime dames gave extra oomph to Mrs Prentice's sneer 'Have you taken up transvestism? I'd no idea our marriage teetered on the edge of fashion'. The play flopped disastrously, its first night audience so hostile that Baxter initially thought the theatre had been invaded by drunks. What disconcerted audiences and critics alike was the way Orton un-domesticated farce. For years, notably at the Whitehall Theatre with Brian Rix, farce offered audiences uncontroversial fun. Orton presented his sexually omnivorous characters without moral baggage; he then plunged them into a chaos that disrupted their sense of self, sanity and sexuality. By the end, they find they have all committed incest, but their reunion is joyful and they decide to 'put on our clothes and face the world'.

AFTERLIFE

It took Lindsay Anderson's revival at the Royal Court in 1975 to establish the play as an icon of modern drama – not simply through Anderson's brilliantly vicious treatment of the social satire, but through a change in public taste. The censor – in whose shadow a nervous Oscar Lewenstein had altered Winston Churchill's penis to a cigar – had gone. Shows such as Richard O'Brien's *The Rocky Horror Show* (see p. 84) were relaxed about sexual ambiguity. The transfer of *What the Butler Saw* to the home of the respectable farce, the Whitehall, indicated how far things had changed. Revivals are rare, but the 2005 production at Hampstead Theatre (and later in the West End) with Joanna Page as Geraldine and Malcolm Sinclair as Rance, took for granted – as Michael Billington approvingly noted – 'Orton's suggestion that gender is provisional and madness ubiquitous'. It also ran for three months at the Vaudeville Theatre in 2012.

①

1969–79

OTHER WORKS BY
Joe Orton
Fred and Madge (written 1959)
Entertaining Mr Sloane (1964)
Loot (1965)

SEE ALSO
Plunder (1928)
by Ben Travers
The Rocky Horror Picture Show
(1973) by Richard O'Brien

How the Other Half Loves

WRITTEN BY
Alan Ayckbourn (1939–)

DIRECTED BY
Alan Ayckbourn

- First performed at the Library Theatre, Scarborough, 31 July 1969.

SNAPSHOT

A comic study of marriage across the social spectrum, *How the Other Half Loves* has an ingenious set combining two living rooms, one full of pretentious reproduction antiques, the other shabbily suburban, allowing the audience to see simultaneously into the lives of two separate couples. Frank and Fiona, in the posh half of the set, have a passionless marriage, while Frank's employee Bob, in the dowdy half, leaves his wife Terry to cope with their baby while he enjoys an affair with Fiona. Both Bob and Fiona make use of a boring married couple, the Featherstones, to provide them with alibis, but when Frank and Terry separately invite the Featherstones to dinner things come unstuck. The dinner parties, although they take place on consecutive evenings, are staged at the same time. Perched on swivel chairs, the helpless Featherstones repeatedly swing from one set of hosts to the other in a nightmare of accusations, tantrums and an angrily hurled bowl of soup.

IMPACT

The West End production of his comedy *Relatively Speaking* in 1967 marked Ayckbourn out as a talented playwright. It also marked out Scarborough as a place to watch. Ayckbourn had long been associated with the Library Theatre (later renamed the Stephen Joseph) and eventually became its artistic director. This small provincial theatre became a unique forcing-house for Ayckbourn's brand of social comedy. The close proximity of the audience to the tiny in-the-round stage gave performances a special tension. Ayckbourn not only directed the first production of *How the Other Half Loves* but also played Frank for part of the run, with Elizabeth Sladen, later known for her work in

the TV series *Doctor Who*, as Fiona. This kind of engagement with such a broad spectrum of theatrical activity gave Ayckbourn confidence in his technical craftsmanship. Meanwhile, the tiny space also encouraged a remarkably honest and intimate characterisation of the female characters; the couples at the end of *How the Other Half Loves* have to be economical with the truth to secure the happy ending. While some of the wives' problems are very much of their period, they also reflect a dilemma that Ayckbourn would explore in many of his future works: that of an intelligent woman stuck with a man who prefers not to move with the times into a more equal and hence more challenging relationship.

AFTERLIFE

Producer Peter Bridge brought *How the Other Half Loves* to the Lyric Theatre. Robin Midgley directed the larger-than-life star Robert Morley as Frank. Morley dominated the production, unbalancing Ayckbourn's carefully constructed ensemble piece. However, it was still praised for the precision of its craftsmanship. 'Mr Ayckbourn goes out of his way to court danger,' noted critic Irving Wardle. It ran for 869 performances before touring Canada and Australia. The Broadway production featured Phil Silvers, a major star since his TV series *Sergeant Bilko*. The play has had several revivals, most recently by Ayckbourn at the Stephen Joseph Theatre in 2009. Ayckbourn has continued to experiment with time and space on stage, introducing a river onto the stage in *Way Upstream* (this flooded the National when the play transferred) and constructing two interlinked plays to run simultaneously in two auditoria in *House and Garden*.

① Bob (Ian McCulloch) and Fiona (Jan Holden), Lyric Theatre, 1970. © *Victoria and Albert Museum, London*

② Terry (Mary Miller) and Frank (Robert Morley), Lyric Theatre, 1970. © *Victoria and Albert Museum, London*

③ Frank (Robert Morley) and Fiona (Jan Holden), Lyric Theatre, 1970. © *Victoria and Albert Museum, London*

OTHER WORKS BY
Alan Ayckbourn
Absurd Person Singular (1972)
Way Upstream (1981)
House and Garden (1999)

SEE ALSO
Noises Off (1982)
by Michael Frayn
Dinner (2002)
by Moira Buffini

Butley

WRITTEN BY
Simon Gray (1936–2008)

DIRECTED BY
Harold Pinter

DESIGNED BY
Eileen Diss

- First performed at the Criterion Theatre, London, 14 July 1971.

OTHER WORKS BY
Simon Gray
Quatermaine's Terms (1981)
The Common Pursuit (1984)
The Late Middle Classes (1999)

SEE ALSO
After Haggerty (1970)
by David Mercer
Educating Rita (1980)
by Willy Russell

SNAPSHOT

Butley is a dark comedy about an embittered English Literature lecturer, Ben Butley. In the course of one dreadful day, his housemate Joey quarrels with him, his estranged wife asks for a divorce so she can marry their mutual friend Tom, his despised colleague Edna finds a publisher for her book, and Joey moves in with a new man. Meanwhile, Butley wriggles out of as many tutorials as possible with cries of 'Too much administration', though the exceptionally determined Miss Heasman manages to read him an essay. Its title sums up his life: 'Hate and redemption in *A Winter's Tale*'. Like Leontes, the protagonist of Shakespeare's play, Butley destroys himself with jealousy and redemption is a long way off.

IMPACT

Harold Pinter, Gray's chosen director, was drawn to the central character 'who hurls himself towards destruction while living, in the fever of his intellectual hell, with a vitality and brilliance known to few of us'. While the play was unspecific about the nature of the relationship between Butley and Joey, it was nonetheless one of the first West End plays since the legalisation of homosexuality in 1967 to contain such a strong homoerotic element. The pain of the situation is clearly, if entertainingly, expressed through a comedy of territory. Like the characters in Pinter's *The Homecoming* (see p. 62), Butley uses physical space to stake his claim on people; sharing an office with the tidy Joey, Butley colonises Joey's half with a mess of books and papers just as he attempts to take over his life. The play was an immediate success. Alan Bates, already a star from John Osborne's *Look Back in Anger* (see p. 40) and Ken Russell's film *Women in Love*, gave the performance of his life. His comic timing and droll campery enhanced the endearing qualities that make Butley hilarious as well as repellent. While the play makes no acknowledgement of the fact that student revolts in Paris in 1968 had led to some radical rethinking about the nature of university education right across Europe, the audience of 1971 might well have been prompted to reflect on an educational system that lets someone like Butley waste himself. Amid all the peevish rant, there are vivid glimpses of the brilliant teacher he once was.

AFTERLIFE

The play won the *Evening Standard* Best Play Award in 1971. It transferred to Broadway where Bates won a Tony, and was made into a film, Pinter's first as director. Butley himself remained a reference point for critics discussing characters like Frank, the drunken Open University lecturer in Willy Russell's *Educating Rita*, and Bill Maitland in John Osborne's *Inadmissible Evidence*. In 2011, Lindsay Posner directed a revival at the Duchess Theatre with Dominic West as Butley. Although the witty *schadenfreude* of the hero was as lively as ever, there was a new emphasis on the tragic aspects of Butley's failure to acknowledge his sexual nature and the lethal self-deception beneath the whimsical quotations from Beatrix Potter.

① Joey (Jeff Rawle), Gardner (John Patrick-Deery) and Butley (John Nettles), Fortune Theatre, 1984. © *Victoria and Albert Museum, London*

② Anne (Colette O'Neill) and Butley (Alan Bates). © *Victoria and Albert Museum, London*

The Changing Room

SNAPSHOT

The Changing Room is famous for three things: nudity – still novel on the British stage, though the American musical *Hair*, in which all the cast stripped off, was running in the West End – northern dialect and a large cast. On a bitterly cold day, a rugby league team are in the changing room, bantering with one another, the coach and hangers-on. The audience sees their rituals, routines, hopes and fears. Twenty-two men, some of them naked, occupy the stage in shifting patterns, until at last the game is finished, the communal bath over and the room abandoned to Harry, the cleaner.

WRITTEN BY
David Storey (1933–)

DIRECTED BY
Lindsay Anderson

DESIGNED BY
Jocelyn Herbert

- First performed at the Royal Court Theatre, London, 9 November 1971.

IMPACT

Storey galvanised audiences and critics by putting the minutiae of work on stage, as Arnold Wesker had in *The Kitchen*. His earlier play, *The Contractor*, staged the erection and dismantling of a marquee every night. *The Changing Room* took this further, keeping the actual work offstage and focusing on its preparation and aftermath – a process Storey likened to an actor's activity backstage. A former rugby league player, Storey knew the world about which he wrote. Lindsay Anderson, always alert to the fine details of stage naturalism, had the whole cast coached by the noted rugby player Bev Risman; at one point in rehearsal, the cast performed the first act, then played a match before returning to perform the second half of the play. Anderson also respected the precision of Storey's stage directions. The simplest actions teach the audience all they need to know about the complexities of a man's social class, relationships or sporting confidence. A player combs his hair, ordering Harry to pass him a coat hanger; another, in a room where casual nudity is the norm, carefully swathes his towel about his waist. For Harold Hobson the play had poetic overtones: 'Behind the ribbing, and the swearing, and the showing off, the piece is permeated by a Wordsworthian spirit'. The poetry lies in the way the everyday lives of the players contrast with the physical discomfort of the game, which nevertheless brings them glory.

AFTERLIFE

The play had a sold-out run at the Royal Court before transferring to the Globe (now Gielgud) Theatre in the West End. In 1973, Michael Rudman directed it on Broadway where it collected a string of awards, including a Tony for John Lithgow. Many of the original UK cast went on to considerable success in film and television, including Warren Clarke, Brian Glover, Mark McManus, Michael Elphick and Alun Armstrong. Glover and McManus were also part of Bill Bryden's company in the Cottesloe auditorium of the National Theatre where they played in Tony Harrison's *The Mysteries* (see p. 126). The large cast means the play is rarely performed professionally, although it was revived by the Royal Court in 1996 as part of its 'classic' season. Paul Taylor of the *Independent* appreciated it as a 'timeless study of male bonding rites and a preservation in art of a fast-vanishing culture'. The minutely detailed exploration of the world of work inspired Richard Bean to write *Toast*, set in the canteen of a Hull bakery threatened with closure.

① **Preparing for the game.** © *Victoria and Albert Museum, London*

② **The team practice.** © *Victoria and Albert Museum, London*

③ **Copley (Geoffrey Hinsliff), Clegg (Matthew Guinness), Luke (Don McKillop), and Crosby (Barry Keegan).** © *Victoria and Albert Museum, London*

②

OTHER WORKS BY
David Storey
In Celebration (1969)
The Contractor (1969)
Home (1970)

SEE ALSO
Up 'n' Under (1984)
by John Godber
Toast (1999)
by Richard Bean

③

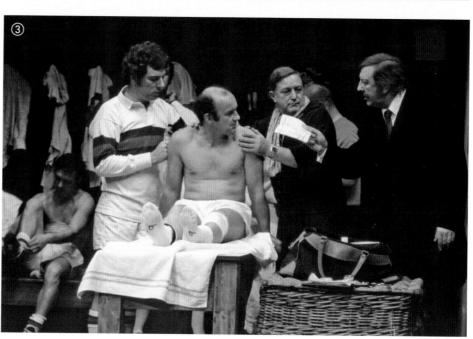

The Island of the Mighty

WRITTEN BY
John Arden (1930–2012) and
Margaretta D'Arcy (1934–)

DIRECTED BY
David Jones

DESIGNED BY
Tazeena Firth and Timothy O'Brien

• First performed at the Criterion
Theatre, London, 14 July 1971.

OTHER WORKS BY
John Arden
Serjeant Musgrave's Dance (1959)
Armstrong's Last Goodnight (1963)
Pearl (1978)

SEE ALSO
The Romans in Britain (1980)
by Howard Brenton
Goddodin (1988)
by Brith Gof and Test Department

SNAPSHOT

A heady mix of Celtic myth and political analysis, this trilogy about King Arthur has a strong focus on characters generally ignored in the story – the workers and the poor. Britain, threatened with Saxon invasion, is weakened by warring factions. One is led by the ageing Arthur, stubbornly adhering to rules laid down by the Romans. Against him are the starving, pagan but politically flexible Picts. The first part shows Arthur's noblemen engaging disastrously with Pict culture. In the next, Arthur's power crumbles in a battle with his wife Gwenhwyvar and his incestuous son Medraut. The final part shows the subversive bard Aneurin struggling to make sense of the waste and injustice.

IMPACT

The first-night audience encountered a picket line. Arden and D'Arcy claimed that the RSC distorted the anti-imperialism of their play and fruitlessly demanded a debate with the audience. Arden announced, 'We will never write for you again'. Some critics concentrated on the writer/director dispute: 'BRAIN STOPS PLAY', blared the *Sun*. Others admired the poetry and spectacle, but found the play incoherent. This perhaps confirmed the writers' point that, in cutting the trilogy into a single play with Arthur as hero (Patrick Allen playing a fallen giant rather than a peevish conformist), the RSC got it wrong. Arden was the most original – and uncommercial – playwright

of the New Wave. His *Serjeant Musgrave's Dance* at the Royal Court in 1959 was the most creative response to Bertold Brecht that England had yet produced. D'Arcy, an Irish writer-performer, created theatre with a wide spectrum of people – actors, political groups, local communities. Arden/D'Arcy joint works invariably sparked controversy – about their audience, performers and subject. British troops entered Northern Ireland in 1969. In January 1972, thirteen civilians were killed by members of the Parachute Regiment during a civil rights demonstration in Derry. Attempts to address the situation directly on stage, such as Portable Theatre's *England's Ireland*, struggled for a hearing. Arden and D'Arcy's oblique analysis of dissidence and a dying imperialist culture evolved during a trip to India; its colourful, populist and epic drama seemed to them a useful model. However, *The Island of the Mighty* was never seen in complete form. The tempestuous preview overwhelmed discussion about politics or style. (A similar fate overtook Howard Brenton's *The Romans in Britain* (see p. 112), also using the Arthurian legend to explore Anglo-Irish relations in 1980.)

AFTERLIFE

One immediate legacy was the creation of the Theatre Writers' Union, the first body to address the rights of playwrights over their work. Arden and D'Arcy never wrote again for the British stage but worked in Ireland, with a mix of professional and political groups, maintaining their commitment to explore British policy in Ireland. They also wrote for BBC Radio. Arden's play *Pearl*, broadcast on BBC Radio 4 in 1978, won a special Giles Cooper Award. The story of two playwrights attempting to shape the English revolution of the 1640s, it is a passionate hymn to theatre as an agent of political change. While both writers find an audience in Ireland, Arden remains undervalued in the UK. As director Dominic Dromgoole observed: 'Arden was and is a giant of modern playwriting. He aimed high and he got there. He deserves a little more respect'.

① Strathclyde (Anthony Pedley). © *Victoria and Albert Museum, London*

② Balin (Roger Rees) and Balan (David Calder). © *Victoria and Albert Museum, London*

②

The Cheviot, The Stag and The Black, Black Oil

WRITTEN BY
John McGrath (1935–2002)

DIRECTED BY
John McGrath

DESIGNED BY
Eileen Hay, Nick Redgrave and Irene Wells

- First performed at the Criterion Theatre, London, 14 July 1971.

SNAPSHOT

The Cheviot, The Stag and The Black, Black Oil examines the abuse of the natural resources of Scotland from 1813 onwards. In sketches and songs, it explores the clearing of the Scottish Highlands to make way for the profitably hardy Cheviot sheep, the Victorian exploitation of Scotland as a blood sport paradise for aristocrats and the big corporations' control over North Sea oil. McGrath designed the play as a ceilidh, for people who might not attend a theatre but would go to a community centre or a dance hall. Many of the company were accomplished musicians. Dolina McLennan was a Gaelic singer. Allan Ross, whose ancestors had suffered from the clearances, was a virtuoso fiddle player. They would sing before the play began, inviting the audience to join in. To round off the evening they became a dance band.

IMPACT

Typically, 7:84 Theatre Company (so called because 7% of the population own 84% of the wealth) launched the play as a work-in-progress. They gave a reading at an Edinburgh conference called 'What kind of Scotland?' on 31 March 1973. The response was applause, advice and fresh input. The first full performance was in Aberdeen, where many in the audience were affected by rocketing prices as the oil companies moved in. As Elizabeth MacLennan, McGrath's wife and one of the 7.84 founders, points out, 'Information on the stage is important' and the play named the companies then profiting from North Sea oil. Delighted to hear their concerns directly addressed, the audience gave 7.84 an excited reception and invited them to return. This was a typical response. There followed more than 100 performances, to 30,000

1969–79

people, across 17,000 miles. The demands on the company – musical talent, debate and comedy – made it a valuable training ground for actors such as Bill Paterson, who gave a vibrant performance in Country and Western style as Texas Jim, an oil profiteer.

AFTERLIFE

Its success prompted BBC1 to present *The Cheviot* as a *Play for Today* in 1974. This involved McGrath in complex negotiations over lines deemed too 'political'. Eventually, it was shown in the context of a documentary about 7.84, as if to underline that the fact that the BBC took no responsibility for the views expressed. Viewing figures were excellent, however. McGrath's defiantly celebratory vision of political theatre and his conviction that theatre should be carried right into the community resonated strongly with the burgeoning fringe theatre companies of the 1970s, and directors as diverse as Richard Eyre and Jude Kelly cite him as a major influence. His episodic and inventive style influenced several generations of Scottish writers, including Greg Burke and Liz Lochhead. McGrath left 7.84 Scotland in 1988 after disagreements with the Scottish Arts Council about the political nature of the company. However, he had decisively proved that a Scottish National Theatre would find an audience. A rehearsed reading of *The Cheviot* was given in June 2011 at the Tron, Glasgow, as part of the National Theatre of Scotland's 'Staging the Nation' series.

③

① Harriet Beecher Stowe (Liz McLellan), 1973. *Photo by Barry Jones,* © *National Library of Scotland*

② The 7:84 company in Bowmore, Islay touring with *Cheviot,* 1973. *Photo by Barry Jones,* © *National Library of Scotland*

③ Queen Victoria (Chris Martin), 1973. *Photo by Barry Jones,* © *National Library of Scotland*

OTHER WORKS BY
John McGrath
Events While Guarding the Bofors Gun (1966)
Blood Red Roses (1980)
Hyperlynx (2001)

SEE ALSO
Armstrong's Last Goodnight (1964) by John Arden
Can't Pay? Won't Pay! (1974) by Dario Fo

The Rocky Horror Show

WRITTEN BY
Richard O'Brien (1942–)

DIRECTED BY
Jim Sharman

DESIGNED BY
*Brian Thomson (set)
and Sue Blane (costumes)*

- First performed at the Royal Court Theatre Upstairs, London 16 June 1973.

SNAPSHOT

The Rocky Horror Show fuses outrageous musical numbers and a Glam Rock aesthetic to create a parody of 1950s Hollywood horror films. Two small-town kids, Brad and Janet, are caught in a storm and take refuge in the castle of Dr Frank N Furter, a transvestite from the planet Transexual with a crew of sinister servants and a failed experiment in creating life, Eddie. He is celebrating his creation of a new creature, the beautiful Rocky Horror. After killing off the vengeful Eddie, Frank introduces the couple to the joys of sex. His servants finally kill him and return to their home planet.

IMPACT

The show was an immediate critical and commercial success. The ironic nods to the B-movie, a joyous anarchy and the catchy songs all fitted perfectly with the freer attitudes to sexuality that characterised the 1970s. Designer Brian Thomson set it in a derelict

cinema, and Sue Blane sourced some of the leather, rubber and bondage gear from sex shops. This meant that its look was not only distinctive, anticipating the punk clothing of Vivienne Westwood, but also cheap to copy. This fitted a play that goes far beyond audience participation; it involves and invades the audience with an intensity similar to Living Theatre's *Paradise Now* or the political plays of 7.84 theatre company. Early in its run, audiences took to dressing as the characters and joining in with the dialogue and songs, as they continue to do. It offers a personal style and a safely enjoyable way to explore and express different kinds of sexuality. Many fans pay multiple visits, especially when a key role changes hands.

AFTERLIFE

After a brief transfer to a small cinema on the King's Road, it took up residence in the King's Road Theatre and ran for seven years plus another year in the West End at the Comedy Theatre, a run of 2,960 performances. It was revived in 1990 in the West End (the first major UK revival was a tour in 1984) and continues to tour. While Tim Curry's original Frank remains a key influence on the overall style, the role has become a kind of accolade granted to popular performers; it has been played by figures as different as Tim McInnerny, best known from the TV series *Blackadder*, Anthony Head, star of *Buffy the Vampire Slayer*, Robin Cousins, the skater, and Jason Donovan. There have been numerous runs and revivals in Europe, America, Australia and Brazil. In 1975, it was made into a film, *The Rocky Horror Picture Show*, with Meatloaf as Eddie, and many of the original cast. This has also drawn costumed and fully participating audiences, notably at midnight showings – it has had more of these than any film in history. In 2005, it was added to the Library of Congress's National Film Preservation Board Film Registry in recognition of its influence on Anglo-American culture. In 2006, it was voted the Royal Court's most popular show in fifty years. The current cast of the stage show, along with Richard O'Brien, organised a mass performance of its best-known dance number, 'The Time Warp', in Trafalgar Square, London, in July 2006.

① Riff Raff (Richard O'Brien), Magenta (Patricia Quinn), Columbia (Little Nell), Rocky (Raynor Boughton) and Frank (Tim Curry). © *Victoria and Albert Museum, London*

② Magenta (Patricia Quinn) and Riff Raff (Richard O'Brien) do the Timewarp. © *Victoria and Albert Museum, London*

③ Janet (Julie Covington), Brad (Christopher Malcolm), Frank (Tim Curry) and Rocky (Rayner Boughton). © *Victoria and Albert Museum, London*

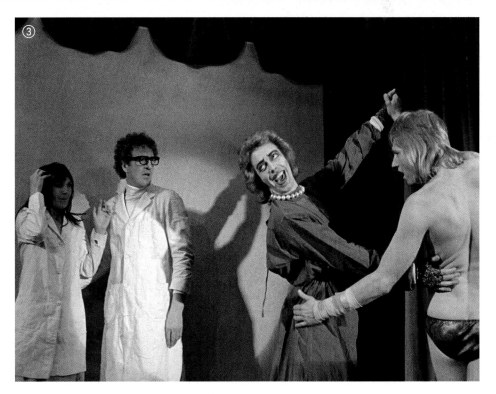

OTHER WORKS BY
Richard O'Brien
Top People (1984)

SEE ALSO
What the Butler Saw (1969)
by Joe Orton
Return to the Forbidden Planet (1983)
by Bob Carlton

The Island

WRITTEN BY
Athol Fugard (1932–),
John Kani (1943–)and
Winston Ntshona (1941–)

DIRECTED BY
Athol Fugard

- First performed at the Space Theatre, Cape Town, 2 July 1973.
- First performed in the UK at the Royal Court Theatre Downstairs, London, 29 December 1973.

① Winston (Winston Ntshona) and John (John Kani), National Theatre, 2000. © *Victoria and Albert Museum, London*

② John (John Kani) washes out Winston's (Winston Ntshona) eye. Royal Court, 1974. © *Victoria and Albert Museum, London*

SNAPSHOT

A unique fusion of devised theatre and classical Greek tragedy, *The Island* brought home the brutality of apartheid to British audiences. It follows two prisoners on Robben Island, where Nelson Mandela and other political activists were imprisoned. Like Mandela, who organised Shakespeare readings in prison, they are staging a play – Sophocles' *Antigone*, the western world's most famous play about the relationship between the individual and state repression. As they struggle to cope with forced labour and the tantalising prospect of release, the prisoners debate the meaning of the text. The play reflects the experiences of the actors, John Kani and Winston Ntshona. Their earlier play, *Sizwe Bansi is Dead*, had been seized and used as evidence in their trial. Hence *The Island* had no printed script but was workshopped in clandestine performances to black audiences. To circumvent the repressive pass laws that restricted black people's movements, Kani and Ntshona had to be described on their pass books as 'chauffeur' and 'gardener' to the white Fugard.

IMPACT

The Island was first performed in the UK as part of a South African season at the Royal Court Theatre alongside two other plays outlining the brutal regime: *Sizwe Bansi is Dead* and Fugard's *Statements After an Arrest under the Immorality Act* (with a young Ben Kingsley). It had a massive impact. Every reviewer was affected by the opening scene, in which the prisoners perform their pointless and humiliating daily labour of digging piles of sand and replacing them; for fifteen minutes the actors worked in silence, allowing the audience to absorb their pain and to see the silent bond that enables them to cope. At one point, Ntshona's eye is hurt; Kani urinates into his hand and tenderly cleans the wound. Director Peter Brook commented, 'It was one of the greatest things I've ever seen in the theatre in terms of its relation between imagination and absolute truth'. The gentle comedy of the later scenes and the real affection between the characters also reflected bonds that stretched beyond the confines of the play, as the names of real activists and details of their lives were woven into the discussion.

AFTERLIFE

The Island toured internationally after London. In 1975, the Broadway production won Kani and Ntshona an unusual distinction, a joint Tony Award for Best Performance in a Play. There was a notable revival in 1999, again starring Kani and Ntshona, which toured to the theatre most associated with Brook, the Bouffes du Nord in Paris, and then to the National Theatre in London in 2000. They also appeared at the Old Vic in 2002. As South Africa changes (its first multiracial democratic election was in 1994), the dignity of these two campaigners, who have given decades of their lives to bear witness to the struggle, continues to be praised by audiences and critics.

OTHER WORKS BY
Athol Fugard
Blood Knot (1961)
Sizwe Bansi is Dead (1972) with
John Kani and Winston Ntshona
Master Harold ... and the Boys (1982)

SEE ALSO
Woza Albert! (1981)
by Percy Mtwa, Mbongeni Ngema
and Barney Simon
Our Country's Good (1989)
by Timberlake Wertenbaker

①

②

Comedians

WRITTEN BY
Trevor Griffiths (1935–)

DIRECTED BY
Richard Eyre

DESIGNED BY
John Gunter

- First performed at the Nottingham Playhouse, 20 February 1975.

① George McBrain (Stephen Rea) takes the stage, Old Vic, 1975. © *Victoria and Albert Museum, London*

② Eddie Waters (Jimmy Jewell) and Gethin (Jonathan Pryce), Old Vic, 1975. © *Victoria and Albert Museum, London*

③ Gethin (Jonathan Pryce) on stage, Old Vic, 1975. © *Victoria and Albert Museum, London*

SNAPSHOT

Despite unusual demands on the audience, *Comedians* is severely naturalistic; a clock on the set shows real time. Six men, taking an evening class in stand-up at a decrepit Manchester college, are about to make their club debut. The chief principle of their tutor, former comic Eddie Waters, is that 'a true joke ... has to liberate the will and the desire, it has to change the situation'. A London agent, Challenor, arrives, looking for 'someone who sees what the people want and knows how to give it them'. In the second act, each student performs. Some retain Eddie's observational style, others incorporate misogynist and racist gags to please Challenor. Eddie's star pupil, Gethin Price, concludes with a surreal, disturbing mix of whiteface mime and class rage, haranguing a couple of expensively dressed dummies before viciously stabbing the female one. The final act, after Challenor employs two students with clichéd but effective routines, is a showdown between Eddie and Gethin. Eddie accuses Gethin of wallowing in hate. Gethin counters that Eddie has lost the political rage that once drove him. He leaves to wait for the revolution he believes is imminent. Eddie welcomes a potential recruit to his next class.

IMPACT

Griffiths's earlier plays were praised for political complexity. *Comedians* was a box-office and critical success, praised for what the *Financial Times* called the play's 'marvellous and original framework'. Vintage comedian Jimmy Jewel was acclaimed for his surefooted timing as Eddie; the savage grace of Nottingham Playhouse regular Jonathan Pryce as Gethin got stellar reviews. Peter Hall chose Richard Eyre as a possible successor at the National on the strength of his production. The comedians' class is a microcosm of 1970s (male) working-class England. The issues raised in their jokes and their personal lives – race, class, poverty, gender relations – were being fought out across the country. National Front membership had just risen to 14,000 and white nationalist marches studded the decade. The toxic jokes in many working men's clubs of the period did nothing to alleviate the situation; Griffiths considered each of the Challenor-style jokes on the Granada TV series *The Comedians* 'a lead pellet aimed at somebody in my country and society'. It was a bold stroke to transform the audience in the second act into members of the club, forcing them to judge and assess their own laughter, or lack of it.

AFTERLIFE

Comedians transferred to the National Theatre at the Old Vic and subsequently to Wyndham's. Mike Nichols directed it on Broadway in 1976, with Milo O'Shea as Eddie. Pryce, the only original cast member, won a Tony Award. In 1987 – with the nature of humour a matter of public debate, and alternative comedy winning substantial audiences – Griffiths reworked the play with female comedians, including Jenny Lecoat and Pauline Daniels, for Kate Rowlands' version at the Liverpool Everyman. Here, the final confrontation was more explicitly feminist than the original, whose focus on the debate between reformist and revolutionary politics left the misogyny of Gethin's routine unexplored. There have been many revivals. Responses to one of the most recent, at the Lyric Hammersmith in 2009, suggest that the confessional monologues encouraged by Eddie have become comedy clichés, but the central conflict still disturbs.

OTHER WORKS BY
Trevor Griffiths
Occupations (1970)
The Party (1973)
The Gulf Between Us (1992)

SEE ALSO
School for Clowns (1975)
by Ken Campbell
Dead Funny (1994)
by Terry Johnson

1969–79

No Man's Land

WRITTEN BY
Harold Pinter (1930–2008)

DIRECTED BY
Peter Hall

DESIGNED BY
John Bury

- First performed at the Old Vic Theatre, London, 16 April 1975.

① Hirst (Harold Pinter) and Foster (Douglas Hodge), Almeida, 1993. © *Victoria and Albert Museum, London*

② Spooner (John Gielgud) and Hirst (Richardson). © *Victoria and Albert Museum, London*

③ Ralph Richardson and John Gielgud take direction from Peter Hall. © *Victoria and Albert Museum, London*

SNAPSHOT

No Man's Land, like Pinter's *The Homecoming* (see p. 62), explores the fight for territory and the fear of loss. Hirst, a 'man of letters', is fossilising in his palatial home in a drunken miasma. Spooner, an unsuccessful poet he met in a pub, ingratiates himself with passive-aggressive tactics, claiming to possess 'strength' that can penetrate literary 'flabbiness'. Spooner betrays no surprise as Hirst, previously monosyllabic, cries out that no man's land 'does not move ... or change ... or grow old ... remains ... forever ... icy ... silent' before leaving on all fours. He emerges in a dressing gown, unsure what day it is, and doesn't recognise Spooner, leaving him to the mercies of the servants, cocky Foster and stolid Briggs. Spooner is locked in, plunged into darkness, served a champagne breakfast and subjected to a long monologue by Briggs about directions to Bolsover Street. A reinvigorated and dapper Hirst appears, hailing Spooner as an old friend. Spooner seizes his chance to initiate a discussion about their social set in the 1930s, which becomes a hilariously savage game of one-upmanship. Hirst claims to have slept with Spooner's wife. Fuelled by whisky, he becomes assertive, while Spooner flounders, begging for a secretarial post. Hirst, Foster and Briggs seem a solid unit, although it is not clear who is in charge. As the curtain falls, all four seem fixed in no man's land.

IMPACT

In the 1975 National Theatre season, Peter Hall hit his stride. The Richardson–Gielgud partnership was a major coup – their second in a modern play that decade (the first being David Storey's *Home* at the Royal Court in 1970). Gielgud as Spooner stole the show in a grubby pinstripe suit, disgusting socks and sandals, a look he modelled on the poet W.H. Auden. In Hall's opinion, the obvious relish with which Gielgud delivered lines like 'Do you often hang about Hampstead Heath?' overshadowed Richardson's magnificently stolid despair: 'I do not think any other actor could fill Hirst with such a sense of loneliness and creativity as Ralph'. Most reviewers admired the play – Frank Marcus praised 'the best double act since Laurel and Hardy' – but were at a loss to explain events on stage. Michael Billington suggested Spooner and Hirst personified Pinter's worst fears: the failed poet he might have been and the wealthy recluse he might become. Richardson pointed out that interpretation is unnecessary, because in real life none of us 'quite know who we are'. He said his nightly task was to 'dream from the moment he came onstage', and that was glad he personally suffered from nightmares because they fuelled his performance.

AFTERLIFE

The production transferred to the West End and then to Broadway. It was recorded for television in 1978. There were no revivals for almost twenty years, a hiatus Pinter ascribed to the reluctance of actors to follow such authoritative performances. In 1993, Pinter revived the play at the Almeida, playing Hirst to Paul Eddington's Spooner. It was subsequently revived at the National Theatre (in 2001) with John Wood as Spooner and Corin Redgrave as Hirst. In 2008, Michael Gambon and David Bradley played Hirst and Spooner alongside David Walliams as Foster and Nick Dunning as Briggs.

①

1969–79

OTHER WORKS BY
Harold Pinter
The Birthday Party (1958)
Betrayal (1978)
Celebration (1999)

SEE ALSO
Home (1970)
by David Storey
Speed-the-Plow (1988)
by David Mamet

East

WRITTEN BY
Steven Berkoff (1937–)

DIRECTED BY
Steven Berkoff

- First performed at the Traverse Theatre, Edinburgh, 26 August 1975.

① Harley Davidson Les (Barry Phillips) and Mike (Steven Berkoff), Greenwich Theatre, 1976. © *Victoria and Albert Museum, London*

② Les (Barry Phillips), Sylv (Anna Nygh) and Mike (Steven Berkoff), Greenwich Theatre, 1976. © *Victoria and Albert Museum, London*

③ Les (Barry Phillips), Greenwich Theatre, 1976. © *Victoria and Albert Museum, London*

SNAPSHOT

East is a fast-moving impressionistic study of London's East End in Berkoff's own youth. The central characters establish the style of the play immediately:

> Les: Donate a snout, Mike?
> Mike: OK I'll bung thee a snout, Les.
> Mike: Now you know our names.

In this stylised Shakespearean-Cockney argot (which leaves the printed text thickly studded with footnotes), Mike (played by Berkoff) and Les fight over a girl, bond while being stitched in A&E, cope with tedious jobs and the nostalgia of Dad for his fascist youth, and search for aggro and sex. There are moments of joy, notably a spectacular sequence where the lads transform themselves into a Harley-Davidson and its rider. Their girl, Sylv, keeps her end up in the sex war, although she is aware men have the power. She speaks for the young with a final 'speech of resolution', concluding 'we will not end our days like this'.

①

IMPACT

Berkoff studied physical theatre in Paris under Jacques Lecoq. He then wrote and starred in several stage adaptations of novels by Kafka, including *Metamorphosis*, the tale of a man transformed into an insect. A number of plays in verse followed, of which *East* was the first. He described it as 'a testament to youth and energy. It is a scream or a shout of pain. It is revolt'. Berkoff wanted to create a theatre full of shock and excitement; his most admired actor was Laurence Olivier, for the sense of danger he could impart. Before the founding of Théâtre de Complicité or Kneehigh theatre company, he conveyed a vibrant physicality. *East* also confronted one of theatre's remaining taboos with 'Mike's cunt speech', a sentimental hymn to one-night stands that harped on the forbidden word to diminish its power (and in Berkoff's performance grew more absurdly graphic every time). Responses were mixed. No one could deny the power and impact of the performance. However, some were ill at ease with the aggressive masculinity and the casting of the mother as a man in drag; others felt that the play did not reflect the real East End, even that of Berkoff's younger days, but was a mix of Cockney clichés going back to the nineteenth century. However, the toxic monologues of Dad, who holds the failure of British fascism in 1938 responsible for the 'Pandora's bleeding box' of the present, were an unnerving testament to the rise of the National Front in that same present.

AFTERLIFE

The play transferred to the National Theatre (Cottesloe) on 18 July 1977. Berkoff restaged it for a twenty-fifth anniversary production at the Churchill Theatre, Bromley. This toured to the Edinburgh Festival. It opened at London's Vaudeville Theatre on 15 September 1999. The run was short. Berkoff subsidised it for some weeks. It won considerable praise even if the play's shock value had diminished – the *Evening Standard* admired its 'faintly camp and even delicate sensibility'. A revival at Leicester Haymarket in 2005 by Paul Kerryson also received praise for the 'high-adrenaline' opportunities it offered the cast. Brian May's first solo album after the death of Freddie Mercury contains the line 'I'm scared of Steven Berkoff'.

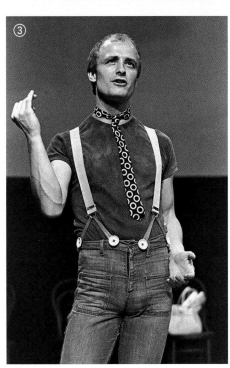

OTHER WORKS BY
Steven Berkoff
Metamorphosis (1969)
Greek (1979)
Brighton Beach Scumbags (1991)

SEE ALSO
Saved (1965)
by Edward Bond
Serving It Up (1996)
by David Eldridge

Destiny

WRITTEN BY
David Edgar (1948–)

DIRECTED BY
Ron Daniels

DESIGNED BY
Di Seymour

- First performed at the Other Place, Stratford-on-Avon, 22 September 1976.

SNAPSHOT

Destiny is a state-of-the-nation play exploring the growth of the Far Right. The action begins in 1947, with the British Army preparing to quit India on Independence Day, an event shown from four perspectives: Colonel Chandler, old-school Tory and a relic of the Raj; Major Rolfe, coldly disapproving of the British government's offer of citizenship to Indians; Corporal Turner, instinctively certain of his own racial superiority; and Khera, the Indian servant. There is an immediate shift to the English Midlands in the 1970s, where Colonel Chandler's death has triggered a by-election. His nephew Peter Crosby, one of the new breed of financial whizz-kids, is the new Conservative candidate. Turner, whose antiques business has been wrecked by a shadowy conglomerate, becomes an active right-winger and is adopted by the Nation Forward Party who carefully groom him as their candidate. A strike against racial discrimination, organised by Khera and uneasily supported by the Labour candidate, becomes the key election issue. Nation Forward exploit it to take a significant number of votes from Labour: although they lose to the Tories, they gain markedly in credibility. Over celebratory sherry with a wealthy Nation Forward supporter – none other than Major Rolfe – Turner discovers that the party is financed by the very conglomerate that ruined him.

IMPACT

The Stratford production could not have been more timely: in July, the National Front gained a substantial share of the vote in a Thurrock by-election. Some reviewers were confused by Edgar's unwillingness to simplify nascent British fascism with scenes full of jackboots and swastikas. Rather, there is a strain of comic amateurism – a key meeting has Union Jacks hung upside down and dodgy microphones; but there is compassion for potential recruits to Nation Forward as they articulate grievances about the decline of British manufacturing, free-marketeering and the huge changes wrought by immigration on the social landscape, only to have them smoothly translated into dangerously potent fascist rhetoric. Most critics, however, felt that, after years of single-issue plays on tiny budgets, political theatre had come of age: 'The panoramic political play that writers of Mr Edgar's generation have been straining after', remarked the *Observer*. Edgar's confident Brechtian techniques, such as short episodic scenes and direct address to the audience, let him draw complex historical links across thirty years. The performances – notably Ian McDiarmid's bitter, perplexed Turner – matched Edgar's clarity. Although the play was geared to the big open stages of the new provincial playhouses, it also suited the intimacy and excitement of the Other Place, the RSC 's tiny tin hut for experimental work.

AFTERLIFE

Destiny transferred to the Aldwych in May 1977, where it was seen by 20,000 people. It opened during the Queen's Silver Jubilee, an event looking back across a similar time period with rather more nostalgia. Edgar won the John Whiting Award and began a fruitful relationship with the RSC, for whom he produced several large-scale works, including *Nicholas Nickelby*. *Destiny* was televised by the BBC in 1978, finding a national audience in the year the National Front was nearing the peak of its popularity.

① Platt (Clyde Pollit), Kershaw (Dennis Clinton), Crosby (Paul Shelley) and Mrs Ward (Judith Harte). *Joe Cocks Studio Collection © Shakespeare Birthplace Trust*

② Major Rolfe (Michael Pennington), Turner (Ian McDiarmid), Khera (Marc Zuber) and Colonel Ward (David Lyon). *Joe Cocks Studio Collection © Shakespeare Birthplace Trust*

③ Cleaver (Bob Peck), Liz (Cherie Lunghi), Maxwell (John Nettles) and Tony (Leonard Preston). *Joe Cocks Studio Collection © Shakespeare Birthplace Trust*

OTHER WORKS BY
David Edgar
Maydays (1983)
*The Life and Times of Nicholas
Nickleby* (1980)
Playing with Fire (2005)

SEE ALSO
England People Very Nice (2009)
by Richard Bean
A Day at the Racists (2010)
by Anders Lustgarten

Abigail's Party

DEVISED AND DIRECTED BY
Mike Leigh (1943–)

DESIGNED BY
Tanya McCallin

• First produced at the Hampstead Theatre, London, 18 April 1977.

OTHER WORKS BY
Mike Leigh
Ecstasy (1979)
Two Thousand Years (2005)
Grief (2011)

SEE ALSO
Absurd Person Singular (1972)
by Alan Ayckbourn
Clybourne Park (2010)
by Bruce Norris

SNAPSHOT

Abigail's Party is a comedy of manners devised over ten weeks by Mike Leigh and the cast. Laurence and Beverley hold a party in a house crammed with spanking new mod cons. He is a workaholic; she preens, flirts and domineers. He likes Beethoven; she likes schmaltzy Mediterranean pop. Their guests are new neighbours Angie and Tony, and anxious divorcee Sue, endlessly fretting about another party, that of her teenage daughter Abigail, across the road. As the evening progresses, Beverley and Tony flirt, everyone drinks too much gin and tempers flare. Laurence has a fatal heart attack to the thunder of his favourite Beethoven track. Beverley wails and accidentally flicks ash over his face while Angie administers CPR. As the play ends, Tony is massaging Angie's aching shoulders after her failed lifesaving efforts, Sue is phoning Abigail and Beverley is sobbing. Laurence, as usual, is ignored.

IMPACT

The play is perhaps the most successful improvised play ever. Leigh's method involves the actors working on the characters for some time before being introduced, then improvising within a structure to create a precise script. The result is confident characterisation with bold comic images – such as Alison Steadman's Beverley, determinedly gyrating to a track she finds 'sexy' and needling Laurence with scarcely-veiled taunts about his potency while he sits head in hands. The play was an instant success, although opinion was – and remains – divided. Some found it elitist, including playwright Dennis Potter, who disliked the 'rancid disdain' for its subjects. Others found sharp truths in the way the characters need expensive tat – Laurence's unread, leather-bound Shakespeare, the kitsch painting Beverley prefers to his beloved Van Gogh – to mask their dying relationships. Bernard Levin's *Sunday Times* review diagnosed the characters as 'torn loose from history, faith, spirit and even language'. Despite the differences in class and income, he could be talking about Edward Bond's *Saved* (see p. 64), or looking forward to the materialism analysed in Caryl Churchill's *Serious Money*. That this sort of analysis can co-exist with the audience's pleasure in Beverley's catchphrases such as 'little top-up?', 'a little cheesy pineapple one?' suggests that Mike Leigh correctly describes the care and affection with which he and the cast approached the characters, 'it's about us, and that's why it works'.

AFTERLIFE

Steadman won the *Evening Standard* Award for Best Actress and only her pregnancy prevented a West End transfer. Instead, the play was shown as a BBC *Play for Today* and has since been seen by millions on DVD. Simon Stephens called it 'TV's *Waiting for Godot*. It affected everything', and it is cited as a major influence by Julia Davis, creator of the TV series *Nighty Night*, and Tony Jordan, producer of *EastEnders*. It was voted one of the plays of the century in the National Theatre poll. A National Theatre platform reading with the original cast in 2000 was so popular it had to be screened for the overflow audience outside, many of whom knew the script word for word. *Abigail's Party* is one of the most regularly revived plays of its time; a West End production at the New Ambassadors and then the Whitehall marked its twenty-fifth anniversary in 2002. The most recent revival was at the Menier Chocolate Factory in London in 2012.

① Beverley (Alison Steadman) and Tony (John Salthouse). © *Victoria and Albert Museum, London*

② Beverley (Alison Steadman). © *Victoria and Albert Museum, London*

As Time Goes By

WRITTEN BY
Drew Griffiths (1947–84) and
Noël Greig (1944–2009)

DIRECTED BY
Noël Greig

DESIGNED BY
Paul Dart

- First performed at the Campaign for Homosexual Equality conference, Nottingham, 26 August 1977.

① Hans (Phillip Timmins) and Lenny (Alan Pope). *While every attempt was made to find the rights holder, none were found*

② Lenny (Alan Pope). © *Rolf Fischer, Berlin. While every attempt was made to obtain photographer details, none were found*

③ Kurt (Drew Griffiths) rips off the Blue Angel. *While every attempt was made to find the rights holder, none were found*

SNAPSHOT

As Time Goes By was the first gay chronicle play, a mix of naturalism and cabaret. The opening section is set in a Victorian male brothel where the young rent boys live on the edge of poverty. One steals the night's takings; when the other is unfairly accused, he retaliates by bringing in the police. Only the brothel-keepers are arrested; the wealthy clients sail off to France. In the second section, set in Berlin, Lenny, half of a drag double act, works with Magnus Hirschfield, a gay Jewish scientist attempting to prove a biological basis for homosexuality. Lenny's drag partner, Kurt, begins a relationship with Hans, a young waiter, gradually becoming politicised. As the Nazis tighten their grip on the city, it becomes clear that the Left has failed to stand up for homosexuals. In the third section, members of the Black Power and women's movements unite with gay men to evict a policeman menacing a drag queen in the Stonewall bar. The Stonewall riot of 1969 begins.

IMPACT

This was a new direction for gay theatre in the UK. Drew Griffiths founded Gay Sweatshop in 1974 with Gerald Chapman. By 1977, it had split into two companies. While the women's company selected a naturalistic and topical play about child custody, Greig and Griffiths wanted

to reclaim their history, portraying gay men 'continually caught up in history yet alienated from it by the violence practised against them'. Their sophisticated treatment of context was something new, giving insight into every character's situation. The class-bound world of the brothel exploits the young rent boys, but even the wealthy clients, who bolt to France and are unwilling to change a society where they are 'rather near the top', undergo the pain of losing their families – 'we're dogs to them now'. In Berlin, the Left scores cheap points by outing prominent gay Nazis: 'One step more and we'll be the root cause of fascism', says Hirschfield's young lover sourly. The audience is both exhilarated by the songs, which gleefully rip off well-known standards, and challenged by their fierce commentary on the action. At the close, a singer begins the romantic classic 'As Time Goes By', but the last phrase hangs in mid-air as a piano picks out the Nazi anthem. It is for the audience to consider what happens next.

AFTERLIFE

The play was so well received that the first Gay Times Festival in 1978 was based on *As Time Goes By*. Because the writers deliberately left the fate of each character to the imagination of the audience, groups could usefully discuss what might have happened next and the political reasons for it. One response went further than discussion. Playwright Martin Sherman, drafted in to help with the American accents in the Stonewall scene, was enormously moved by the scene where Lenny leaves carrying a suitcase with a pink triangle. He wrote *Bent* (see p. 100) for Gay Sweatshop, but the company decided the play deserved a wider audience and passed it to the Royal Court. As Greig and Griffiths's Drag Queen says, 'Our stories continue'. Drew Griffiths was killed in a homophobic attack in 1984. Noel Greig wrote several other major plays for Gay Sweatshop and also become one of the UK's most influential and respected teachers of playwriting.

OTHER WORKS BY
Drew Griffiths and Noël Greig
The Dear Love of Comrades (1979)
by Noël Greig
Poppies (1983) by Noël Greig
Mister X (1975) by Drew Griffiths
and Roger Baker

SEE ALSO
Bent (1979)
by Martin Sherman
Night After Night (1993)
by Neil Bartlett

Bent

WRITTEN BY
Martin Sherman (1938–)

DIRECTED BY
Robert Chetwyn

DESIGNED BY
Alan Tagg

- First performed at the Royal Court Theatre, London, 3 May 1979.

SNAPSHOT

Bent is partly a historical document, highlighting the appalling Nazi treatment of homosexuals, and partly a call to arms for the 1970s' gay rights movement. It is also a love story. One night, Max brings home a Nazi storm trooper to the apartment he shares with his lover, Rudy. It is the notorious Night of the Long Knives and the SS assassinate the storm trooper in the apartment. Terrified, Max and Rudy try to flee Berlin but are captured and sent to Dachau. On the train, Max beats Rudy to death rather than acknowledge him as his partner. He gets himself classified as a Jew, so he can wear a yellow star on his uniform rather than the pink triangle denoting a homosexual, a category even lower than the Jew in concentration camp hierarchy. Max is befriended by Horst, a gay man who tells him the key to survival is to 'never notice, never watch' and never help a fellow prisoner. Max and Horst fall in love and, when Horst is shot, Max reclaims his gay identity by donning Horst's jacket with its pink triangle, before committing suicide by walking into the electric fence.

IMPACT

More than ten years after the decriminalisation of homosexuality, it was unusual to find a play in a major theatre focused solely on gay experience. The Royal Court found some actors reluctant to be associated with the roles. However, there was considerable praise for the production and especially for Ian McKellen in what critic Benedict Nightingale called a 'deepening ... darkening performance' as his Max changed from selfish chancer to martyr. His scene with Tom Bell, as Horst, in which they stand distantly apart but make love with words, was a major factor in the huge success of the play.

AFTERLIFE

Bent transferred to the Criterion Theatre in the West End and McKellen won an Olivier award. The play went to Broadway, with Richard Gere in the role of Max, and Sherman was nominated for a Tony. There have been a large number of revivals, and the play has been seen in over forty-five countries and performed in twenty-one different languages. McKellen reprised his role in a benefit performance for the gay rights organisation Stonewall, in which he had become active, at the Adelphi Theatre in 1989. It was directed by Sean Mathias, who also staged a full production at the National Theatre in 1990. The play made a significant change in public consciousness of gay history. In 1978, a US TV series, *Holocaust*, had reminded a new generation about the persecution of European Jews, but had failed to mention the presence of homosexuals in the concentration camps. In 2006, Daniel Kramer directed a production at the Trafalgar Studios, which won high praise for Chris New, fresh from drama school, as Horst. At the first-night curtain, Martin Sherman announced the death of Tom Bell, the original Horst.

① Max (Ian McKellen) and Horst (Tom Bell). © *Victoria and Albert Museum, London*

② Rudy (Jeff Rawle) and Max (Ian McKellen). © *Victoria and Albert Museum, London*

③ Max (Ian McKellen) and Horst (Tom Bell). © *Victoria and Albert Museum, London*

1969–79

Sus

WRITTEN BY
Barrie Keeffe (1945–)

DIRECTED BY
Ann Mitchell

DESIGNED BY
Inigo Espejel

- First performed at Soho Poly, London, 18 June 1979.

SNAPSHOT

A shocking and naturalistic play based on a true event of the 1960s, the play was a response to growing abuse of the 'sus' law, which allowed the police to stop and search anyone they suspected of intending to commit an offence. Like most victims of this process, the central character, Leon Delroy, is black. Taken in on the night of Margaret Thatcher's election victory in 1979, he has no idea of what crime he is suspected of committing. Only slowly do the two policemen, absorbed in the election results, reveal that his wife is dead. They go on to suggest that Delroy killed her in the course of a botched abortion. Bewildered, Delroy asks for a solicitor, prompting the senior officer, Karn, to say that he has now made things 'formal'. Delroy is made to empty his pockets. The other officer, Wilby, repeatedly beats him. In the small hours, Karn brings news that the post-mortem has exonerated Delroy and they release him. They tell him he was detained on sus in order to avoid any allegations of wrongful arrest or brutality. Karn advises him: 'you're not a unique case'.

IMPACT

Keeffe had been associated with the innovative new-writing theatre, the Soho Poly, for some time and its director, Verity Bargate, was confident enough in the play's power to change the schedules and rush the opening forward to within six weeks of Thatcher's election victory. Ann Mitchell's production struck an immediate nerve. The tiny thirty-five-seat theatre staged three shows a day, sometimes with a standing audience of around 100. The intimacy made the brutality – psychological as much as physical – truly shocking to watch.

① Delroy (Paul Barber) and Karn (Stuart Barren), Royal Court Theatre, 1979. © *Victoria and Albert Museum, London*

② Wilby (Will Knightley), Delroy (Tony Hippolyte) and Karn (Karl Howman), Soho Poly, 1984. © *Victoria and Albert Museum, London*

③ Delroy (Paul Barber) and Karn (Stuart Barren), Royal Court Theatre, 1979. © *Victoria and Albert Museum, London*

AFTERLIFE

The production moved to the Royal Court Theatre. It was also staged in libraries and social clubs on behalf of the 'Stop Sus' campaign before Philip Hedley, newly appointed artistic director of Theatre Royal Stratford East, offered it a season. It was received with great excitement by predominantly black audiences, Stuart Barren's Karn attracting visceral responses. Ten years later, the play was staged at the Greenwich Theatre shortly after the racist murder of teenager Stephen Lawrence in nearby Eltham. For three nights after the show, Stephen's parents and the local police debated the killing, an instant response to a situation whose terrible outcome was explored in depth in Richard Norton Taylor's *The Colour of Justice*. *Sus* has been staged in the US, India, Pakistan, Australia and all over Europe. It was filmed in 2010 and revived at the Young Vic. The sus law was repealed in 1981, but subsequent legislation has meant that Delroy's experience is still recognisable to many. Keeffe comments, 'I'm surprised and rather saddened that a play I wrote thirty-one years ago and thought then was, as one critic described it, a piece of "instant political theatre" ... still does have a painful resonance'.

OTHER WORKS BY
Barrie Keeffe
Gimme Shelter (1977)
A Mad World My Masters (1977)
Frozen Assets (1978)

SEE ALSO
Rat in the Skull (1984)
by Ron Hutchison
Fallout (2003)
by Roy Williams

1969–79

Amadeus

WRITTEN BY
Peter Shaffer (1926–)

DIRECTED BY
Peter Hall

DESIGNED BY
John Bury

MUSIC ARRANGED BY
Harrison Birtwistle

- First performed at the Olivier,
  National Theatre, London,
  2 November 1979.

① Constanze (Felicity Kendal) and Mozart (Simon
Callow). *Photo by Nobby Clark, © Nobby Clark/ArenaPAL*

② Salieri (Paul Scofield). *Photo by Nobby Clark, © Nobby
Clark/ArenaPAL*

③ Salieri (Paul Scofield) and the Venticelli. *Photo by
Nobby Clark, © Nobby Clark/ArenaPAL*

SNAPSHOT

Shaffer's tragicomedy draws on a variety of
historical and fictional sources to present a
theatrically spectacular re-imagining of the
relationship between Antonio Salieri, the most
famous and revered composer of eighteenth-
century Vienna, and Wolfgang Amadeus
Mozart, whose worth only Salieri recognised
at the time. The focus is Salieri, tormented by
envy of a true genius; worse, a genius who is
crude and childish in his private life. The story
unfolds backwards, beginning with Salieri's
memories of his first meeting with Mozart,
before moving on to his decision to block the
younger man's career. After watching Mozart's
Don Giovanni, Salieri realises that the key to
Mozart's destruction lies in his Oedipal terror
of his father, and he proceeds, in disguise, to
haunt him to the grave. The play closes with
Salieri morally bankrupt and forgotten as an
artist. Salieri's challenge to the audience, 'I
present to you – for one performance only –
my last composition, entitled The Death of
Mozart, or Did I Do It?' makes it clear that this
is a play about theatricality and that we may
never get the whole truth.

IMPACT

This was a landmark production designed
to showcase the resources of the National
Theatre. John Bury's set heightened the
theatrical nature of the play – a 'stage of ice
blue plastic' changing colour under the lights.
Upstage was a proscenium arch complete
with gilded cherubs, used for projections and
backdrops of eighteenth-century Vienna.
John Birtwistle's arrangements of Mozart
– and of Salieri's own surprisingly strong
compositions – conveyed the sense that the
music was emerging straight from Salieri's
tormented memory. Paul Scofield was highly
praised for his Salieri, an ingratiating courtier
in public who broods on assassination in
private, his hands involuntarily reaching out
as if to strangle an imaginary Mozart while
he howls his rage at God for denying him an
equal talent. Simon Callow made his name
as Mozart, a naughty child who nevertheless
seemed capable of creating divine sounds. The
play itself divided critics. Many considered it
too long – Shaffer's original five-hour script
was continually trimmed in rehearsal. There
was also a prolonged debate about the limits
of dramatic licence. Director Peter Hall recalls
Prime Minister Margaret Thatcher's refusal to
believe that Mozart could be such a potty-
mouthed lout. She announced that 'it was
inconceivable that a genius who had written
such elegant music would have used such
inelegant language'.

AFTERLIFE

Amadeus won the 1979 *Evening Standard*
Award for Best Play. The production
transferred from the National to Her Majesty's,
London with Frank Finlay as Salieri, before
touring the UK. In 1980, it was produced at
the Broadhurst Theater, New York, starring
Ian McKellen as Salieri, Tim Curry as Mozart
and Jane Seymour as Constanze. The play
was filmed by Milos Forman in 1984 with a
completely new cast. In 1999, the play was
revived at the Old Vic by Peter Hall with
Michael Sheen as Mozart and David Suchet as
Salieri, and the production transferred first to
Los Angeles and then to Broadway.

①

OTHER WORKS BY
Peter Shaffer
Royal Hunt of the Sun (1964)
Equus (1973)
Lettice and Lovage (1987)

SEE ALSO
Bingo: Scenes of Money and Death
(1973) by Edward Bond
The Habit of Art (2009)
by Alan Bennett

1980–89

If the 1970s were about freedom and the exploration of different identities and ways of working, the 1980s were all about money and politics; the haves and the have-nots. With Margaret Thatcher at its head, the Conservative government proceeded to roll up state investment in health, education and the arts and promote an individualistic, capitalist attitude. This was captured beautifully in Howard Brenton and David Hare's *Pravda: a Fleet Street Comedy* in which an avuncular family newspaper business is taken over by a rapacious, morally bankrupt entrepreneur. Caryl Churchill, Alan Ayckbourn and David Mamet all produced plays exploring the new mode of capitalism, while Andrea Dunbar and Jim Cartwright showed its effect on the poor. Other writers turned to history to provide parallels with Britain in the 1980s, notably Brenton's *Romans in Britain* and Brian Friel's *Translations*, which took a long view of the relationship between England and Ireland. Timberlake Wertenbaker used history to prove the importance of theatre at a human level rather than an economic one in *Our Country's Good*, and also highlighted the experience of women in penal colonies. Women's experience was a topic whose urgency increased rather than diminished during the reign of the first woman Prime Minister, with Churchill, Sarah Daniels, Pam Gems, Liz Lochhead and Willy Russell all exploring the issue.

All these plays were produced in state-subsidised theatres increasingly under pressure to find alternative sources of funding. By the end of the decade, the blockbuster musical was dominating subsidised and commercial stages, with the RSC's hit adaptation of *Les Misérables* providing the company and its director, Trevor Nunn, with an alternative source of income. Michael Billington noted that the musical, with its celebration of the individual, was 'Thatcherism in action'.

▶ Noah (J.G. Devlin) on the Ark, *The Mysteries: The Nativity.*
© *Victoria and Albert Museum, London*

The Arbor

WRITTEN BY
Andrea Dunbar (1961–90)

DIRECTED BY
Max Stafford-Clark

DESIGNED BY
Peter Hartwell

- First performed in the full length version at the Royal Court Theatre, London, 24 June 1980.

① The Girl (Kathryn Pogson) and The Boy (Jeff Rawle).
© *Victoria and Albert Museum, London*

② David Bamber and Ron Cook. © *Victoria and Albert Museum, London*

SNAPSHOT

The Abor is an insider's view of life on the Buttershaw council estate in Bradford. The central character, The Girl, gets pregnant when she loses her virginity; coping with a drunken father and a school for unmarried mothers (they learn about 'trees and flowers'), she loses the baby. There is a bleak confrontation with the father, who won't believe it is his – 'and she never saw him no more'. In Act Two, she moves in with her Pakistani boyfriend, Yousaf; when she gets pregnant, Yousaf wants her to have an abortion. As he becomes violent, The Girl moves to a refuge with her friend Maureen; The Girl's practical mother refuses to be told the address of the refuge in case her husband beats it out of her. Yousaf threatens suicide, but doesn't go through with it. The Girl misses her family.

IMPACT

Andrea Dunbar was fifteen when she wrote the original first act; via a women's refuge and the actor/writer Liane Aukin, it found its way to the Royal Court and was staged at the Young Writers' Festival in the sixty-seat Theatre Upstairs. Its success prompted a transfer to the main space. This involved bringing Dunbar to London to write a second act, with director Max Stafford-Clark urging her on. His production was starkly simple. The set consisted of a few chairs, which served as everything from a sofa to the crashed stolen car in which a floundering pregnant Girl is abandoned by the panicky teenage driver. Actors spoke the stage directions to clarify Dunbar's sparse, unsentimental dialogue. The spare style suited Dunbar's immediacy and grim humour. Overall, it impressed the critics, although several felt she should have been

①

allowed to develop her craft at her own pace, not rushed into the larger theatre. However, Dunbar's was one of the few working-class female voices in this period; Shelagh Delaney called her 'a genius straight from the slums'. *The Arbor* vividly illustrated the consequences of the government's choice to let the north of England shift for itself as the country's manufacturing base declined. ('Do you spell arbour with an H?', asks a patronising teacher as if on safari to a distant country.)

AFTERLIFE

The play was performed in New York in 1983. Dunbar's second play *Rita, Sue and Bob Too* was staged at the Royal Court in 1982 and filmed by Alan Clarke in 1986. Dunbar continued to live on the Buttershaw Estate, where she died of a brain haemorrhage in 1990. In 2000, Stafford-Clark returned to Buttershaw to create a new play, *A State Affair*, documenting the changes since Dunbar's death; conditions had not greatly improved. In 2010, Clio Barnard made *The Arbor*, a film about Dunbar using archive film of her at the Royal Court, interviews with her family and neighbours and excerpts from the play performed on Buttershaw Green. While the recorded voices were authentic, they were lip-synched by actors; this slight distancing effect fitted the sometimes conflicting nature of the memories, creating a picture of a complex mind and life behind the plays. 'If she was alive today', says the voice of her daughter Lorraine, 'I'd have a lot to say to her'.

OTHER WORKS BY
Andrea Dunbar
Rita, Sue and Bob (1981)
Shirley (1986)

SEE ALSO
A Taste of Honey (1958)
by Shelagh Delaney
Road (1986)
by Jim Cartwright

1980–89

Translations

WRITTEN BY
Brian Friel (1929–)

DIRECTED BY
Art O'Briain

DESIGNED BY
Consolata Boyle

• First performed at the Guildhall, Derry, 23 September 1980.

OTHER WORKS BY
Brian Friel
The Freedom of the City (1973)
Faith Healer (1979)
Dancing at Lughnasa (1990)

SEE ALSO
The Plough and the Stars (1926)
by Sean O'Casey
The Romans in Britain (1980)
by Howard Brenton

SNAPSHOT

At first, *Translations* tricks the audience into assuming that it is a piece of naturalism. Set in a fictional village in Donegal in 1833, it shows the re-mapping of Ireland by British soldiers to mark the country's integration into the United Kingdom. The action takes place around the 'hedge school' of Hugh and his son Manus, whose livelihood is threatened by the new national schools where the learning of English will be compulsory. Hugh's other son, Owen, employed by the British Army to translate place names, arrives with two officers. By now, it has dawned on the audience that it cannot take the words that it hears for granted, but that it has to think hard about their meaning – for although the play is in English, the Irish characters are really speaking Gaelic (spiced with Latin and Greek). Owen, as interpreter, puts a glibly positive spin on the map-making: 'This survey demonstrates the government's interest in Ireland'. Maire, one of Hugh's pupils, and cartographer Yolland fall in love, but Yolland disappears (presumably attacked by Hugh's most belligerent pupils, the Donnelly twins). Soldiers drafted in to find Yolland threaten the locals with violent eviction. Owen discards his diplomatic translations for bald fact; the threat he was initially so keen to underplay he now proclaims unequivocally.

IMPACT

Translations premiered in Derry Guildhall, the focus of the civil rights march on Bloody Sunday in 1972 (and the site of the Saville Inquiry into that event set up in 1998). It was the first production of the Field Day company, established by Friel and Stephen Rea. Involving both Protestant and Catholic performers, Field Day aimed to give Derry a theatre of its own, a cultural space where a discourse of unity could be forged. Friel has repeatedly stated that *Translations* is not a political play, but a play about language. Critics drew comparisons with John Millington Synge and Sean O'Casey as they praised Friel's varied and ironic treatment of language: a young girl's struggle to acquire speech; exuberant Homeric recitals by Jimmy, a crusty drunk; and Owen's 'translations' taking on the sour taste of betrayal. However, labels like 'classic', used by *The Times*, ignore the resonance *Translations* inevitably accrued when speech itself became politicised in the mid-1980s. The government adopted a policy of denying the 'oxygen of publicity to terrorists', refusing supporters of the IRA in Sinn Fein access to the airwaves. Broadcasting corporations responded with a bizarre form of karaoke, whereby film of key players in the conflict, such as Gerry Adams, was shown with voices dubbed by actors – one of the most frequently used being Stephen Rea, the original Owen.

AFTERLIFE

The play was first performed in England in 1981 at the Hampstead Theatre Club, directed by Donald McWhinnie, where it garnered universally positive reviews and transferred to the National. It was revived there in 2005 and also staged in the USA and adapted for BBC radio. Field Day drew in other writers and critics, including poets Seamus Heaney and Tom Paulin, *Translations* was published widely, although its political influence has perhaps declined. Friel was named a Saoi ('wise one') of Aosdana, an association of people in Ireland distinguished in the arts, founded in 1981.

① Owen (Tony Doyle) and Hugh (Ian Bannen), Hampstead Theatre Club, 1981. © *Victoria and Albert Museum, London*

② Maire (Bernadette Short), Hugh (Ian Bannen) and Sarah (Máire ní Ghráinne), Hampstead Theatre Club, 1981. © *Victoria and Albert Museum, London*

②

The Romans in Britain

WRITTEN BY
Howard Brenton (1942–)

DIRECTED BY
Michael Bogdanov

DESIGNED BY
*Martin Johns (sets) and Stephanie
Howard (costumes)*

- First performed at the Olivier,
  National Theatre, London,
  16 October 1980.

① Romans (background), Second Soldier (Robert
Oates), Third Soldier (Peter Sproule) and First Soldier
(Robert Ralph) meet Celts (foreground) Viridio (Roger
Gartland), Marban (Greg Hicks) and Brac (Michael
Fenner). © *Victoria and Albert Museum, London*

② Caesar (Michael Bryant), Second Soldier (Robert
Oates), Marban (Greg Hicks) and First Soldier (Robert
Ralph). © *Victoria and Albert Museum, London*

③ Maitland (William Sleigh), Thomas Chichester
(Stephen Moore) and Corporal (Michael Beint).
© *Victoria and Albert Museum, London*

SNAPSHOT

The Romans in Britain makes bold leaps in time
and space to juxtapose Julius Caesar's invasion
of Britain, the Saxon invasion five centuries
later and the presence of British troops on
the border between Northern Ireland and the
Republic in the 1980s. There are no central
characters; like John Arden and Margaretta
D'Arcy's *The Island of the Mighty* (see p. 80),
it is as concerned with soldiers, servants and
slaves as with powerful men like Caesar, or
the well-born undercover intelligence officer
Chichester. The latter goes out of his mind
and is shot by the IRA as he struggles to
express his guilt. There are repeated collisions
between time frames. A slave uses a stone to
kill her Celtic captor and, with the sound of a
helicopter overhead, is killed in turn by British
squaddies. As soldiers recover Chichester's
body, a fat cook on the run from the Saxons
dreams of a democratic, peaceful king who
never was, known as 'any old name. Arthur?'

IMPACT

This colourful, broad-brush Brechtian epic
might have prompted debate about Anglo-
Irish relations, Brenton's accurate use of Latin
sources or the politics of imperialism, but
in the event the most prolonged discussion
concerned a few inches of flesh visible in
Scene Three: a penis or a thumb? A scene in
which Roman soldiers kill two young Celts and
set about the rape of a third, a Druid priest,
prompted a walkout by Sir Horace Cutler,
leader of the GLC and a board member of the
National Theatre (to which the GLC awarded
an annual grant). Though he complained that
his wife was so shocked she had to 'cover her
head', the grant was not withdrawn. Mary
Whitehouse of the National Viewers' and
Listeners' Association then looked into the
viability of a prosecution under the Theatres
Act of 1968, outlawing performances liable
to 'deprave and corrupt'. Advised against
this, she exploited a legal loophole to bring a
private prosecution against director Michael
Bogdanov, accusing him under the Sexual
Offences Act of 'procuring an act of gross
indecency by Peter Sproule [Third soldier] with
Greg Hicks [Druid]'. A potential jail sentence
for Bogdanov hung on surreal arguments in
court over the visibility (or otherwise) of
Sproule's penis from the back of the stalls. The
prosecution was eventually abandoned on the
advice of the Attorney General.

AFTERLIFE

There has been understandable unease on
the part of theatres about reviving the play.
However, in 2006, Samuel West mounted a
full-scale production at the Crucible Theatre,
Sheffield. The production was praised for its
clarity and vigour; so was Ralph Koltai's set of
twisted wood, with a deep pool from which
the young Celts emerged from bathing. The
production encouraged new questions. *The
Independent* likened the 'heartless flippancy'
of the rape scene to incidents involving the
mistreatment of inmates at Abu Ghraib prison
in Iraq, and Brenton compared the uneasy
alliances between Rome and complicit British
tribes to current Anglo-American relations. In
2005, BBC Radio 4 transmitted a play by Mark
Lawson, *The Third Soldier Holds His Thighs*, an
account of the Romans affair from rehearsal
to courtroom.

1980–89

Good

WRITTEN BY
C. P. Taylor (1929–81)

DIRECTED BY
Howard Davies

DESIGNED BY
Ultz

- First performed at the RSC Warehouse Theatre, London, 2 September 1981.

① Freddie (Pip Miller), Pianist (Nigel Hess) and Maurice (Joe Melia). © *Victoria and Albert Museum, London*

② Maurice (Joe Melia) and John Halder (Alan Howard). © *Victoria and Albert Museum, London*

SNAPSHOT

C.P. Taylor described *Good* as a 'musical-comedy'. It is also a Faustus story, about a scholar who effectively sells his soul. Goethe expert John Halder is not an anti-Semite – his best friend is a Jew. Most of his problems are ordinary: his mother has Alzheimer's, his wife is chronically needy and he is sleeping with one of his students. Halder's other problem is that, everywhere he goes, he is accompanied by imaginary bands. Sometimes they play works by Richard Wagner; sometimes selections from Sigmund Romberg's operetta *The Student Prince*; and sometimes even traditional Jewish songs. Is his subconscious dramatising his failure to grasp reality, he asks his friend and psychiatrist Maurice, or is that too glib? 'If you knew the unconscious like I do,' says Maurice, 'nothing's too glib for that bastard.' Halder never quite grasps this. Feted by the Nazis for his novel about euthanasia, he sees it as a compliment, not an attempt to recruit him. When they begin burning books, he tells himself it shows a 'less theoretical' approach to learning. While Maurice's situation as a Jew becomes ever more grave, Halder pontificates that there is no objective moral truth. By the end, Halder has a high-profile job at Auschwitz; the band that welcomes him there is real.

IMPACT

Taylor was an original and prolific writer, who at his death had written over seventy plays. Most of these were written and produced in the north, chiefly by the Traverse Theatre in Edinburgh and the Live Theatre Company in Newcastle upon Tyne. *Good* was one of his few works staged in the south. Although it has clear affinities with David Edgar's *Destiny* in its careful account of an ordinary citizen's drift to the far right, its lightness of touch was unique. Its daring lies in its simplicity: rather than spectacular iconic images of the Third Reich, it takes place in Halder's confused consciousness. Howard Davies's bare stage, on which all the cast were present throughout like judges, underlined the way in which the most private scenes of betrayal, such as Halder's flight from his incontinent mother, slid imperceptibly into political ones as he seamlessly engaged in planning 'reassuring' rooms for the extermination of the unfit. Alan Howard, after a run of heroic Shakespearean roles, was a revelation as Halder, universally praised for what the *Telegraph* described as 'humour and fine judgement'; his Halder was invariably blinking and sweet-natured as a teddy bear, leaving it to the audience to judge the man's corruption.

AFTERLIFE

The play transferred to the Aldwych and then to the Booth Theater in New York. Alan Howard won three awards for his performance. It has been revived numerous times: as part of a C.P. Taylor season at the Edinburgh Festival in 1992, by Michael Grandage at the Donmar in 1999, with Charles Dance as Halder, and by Polly Findlay at the Royal Exchange, Manchester, in 2011. In 2008, it was made into a film by Vicente Amorim with Viggo Mortensen as Halder. The published text is dedicated to Taylor's father: 'Max George Taylor, a refugee from anti-Semitism in Czarist Russia'.

①

OTHER WORKS BY
C.P. Taylor
Cleverness of Us (1971)
The Killingworth Play (1975)
And a Nightingale Sang (1979)

SEE ALSO
Rhinoceros (1960)
by Eugene Ionesco
Albert Speer (2000)
by David Edgar

Top Girls

WRITTEN BY
Caryl Churchill (1938–)

DIRECTED BY
Max Stafford-Clark

DESIGNED BY
Peter Hartwell

- First performed at the Royal Court Theatre, London, 28 August 1982.

① Angie (Carole Hayman) and Kit (Lou Wakefield).
© *Victoria and Albert Museum, London*

② Pope Joan (Selina Cadell) and Lady Nijo (Lindsay Duncan). © *Victoria and Albert Museum, London*

SNAPSHOT

Like most of Churchill's plays, *Top Girls* is radically original in form. The first act brings together famous women from history to celebrate the promotion of Marlene, managing director of the Top Girls Employment Agency. In a smart restaurant, six of them reflect on their triumphs and challenges: Marlene; Patient Griselda, the passive heroine of Geoffrey Chaucer's Clerk's Tale; Pope Joan; Nijo, a Japanese courtesan; Dull Gret, from Pieter Breughel's painting; and Isabella Bird, a Victorian explorer. The second act shows Marlene at work, busy with cut-throat office politics and interviewing women for jobs; she is visited by her rather slow niece, Angie. The third and final act takes place the previous year, as Marlene visits her sister Joyce and Angie; we learn that Angie is really Marlene's daughter, adopted by Joyce who makes her living cleaning for rich women. While Angie sleeps, the sisters squabble and make up, but then have a blazing political row as Marlene praises Margaret Thatcher to the passionate socialist Joyce. Angie comes downstairs, distressed by a nightmare, and utters the last word in the play, 'Frightening'.

IMPACT

Top Girls perplexed some reviewers. Some found it difficult to attune their ears to Churchill's innovative overlapping dialogue – although this rapidly became a standard technique for playwrights. *The Sunday Times* called the non-linear structure 'inchoate'; Harold Atkins's review for the *Telegraph* noted coyly that Churchill 'unobtrusively presents a feminist idea that the male sex is rather in the way'. Audiences were more responsive, enjoying the wit and the sophisticated use of doubling that linked Marlene's personal story to the first scene. For example, Carole Hayman played Gret, the peasant woman who storms into hell and beats up the devils, then Angie; both are inarticulate, but while Gret's situation allowed her scope for heroic resistance, Angie's prospects in the aggressively individualist 1980s are, as for all the vulnerable members of society, 'frightening'. This was the first play to produce a fully developed female protagonist who admired Thatcher – where other contemporary plays simply vilified her, *Top Girls* explores and challenges notions of what it meant to be a successful woman in the present and probes the limitations of role models from the past.

AFTERLIFE

Churchill won an Obie award for the play. Although not an instant box office success, the production went to Joseph Papp's Public Theatre in New York. Billed as a London triumph, it did excellent business and returned to the Royal Court. Now billed as a New York success, it attracted large audiences. In 2008, it made its Broadway debut at the Biltmore Theater. Notable British revivals have been staged by Thea Sharrock in 2002 and by Max Stafford-Clark with Out of Joint in 2011 at the Minerva Theatre, Chichester and subsequently at Trafalgar Studios in the West End. The cast included Suranne Jones, Stella Gonet and Lucy Briers. Named by Michael Billington as one of the ten best plays of the twentieth century, it is widely revived and studied all over the world.

①

1980–89

②

OTHER WORKS BY
Caryl Churchill
Cloud Nine (1979)
Fen (1983)
A Number (2002)

SEE ALSO
My Mother Said I Never Should (1987)
by Charlotte Keatley
Thatcher's Women (1987)
by Kay Adshead

WRITTEN BY
John Godber (1956–)

DIRECTED BY
Andrew Winters

- First performed by Yorkshire
  Actors Company, Rotherham Arts
  Centre, 25 March 1983.

Bouncers

The Company, 1984. *Photo by Steve Morgan © Steve Morgan, Photographer*

SNAPSHOT

A fast-moving four-hander, *Bouncers* does not so much tell a story as enact a ritual: Friday night at a club. The play is presented by the only people who see the 'midnight circus' from start to finish, bouncers Ralph, Judd, Les and Lucky Eric. From girls preening at the hairdresser's to stragglers vomiting in the small hours, the bouncers take on over thirty roles, including punks, rugger-bugger students and the stars of the Swedish porn movie they watch in their break – 'I'm unt der shower ... Oh, I've dropped the soapen,' breathes Lucky Eric huskily. The group's philosopher, Eric, delivers two monologues to the audience about his concern for the young girls at the club: 'Pure and dirty, innocent and vulgar; it all withers, washes away'.

IMPACT

Godber wrote the first version of the play when he was a twenty-one-year-old student at Bretton Hall college, for himself and a friend to perform at the Edinburgh Festival in 1977. Although the audience seldom outnumbered the cast, the actor Brian Glover provided encouragement. The four-handed version, although more complex, still reflects Godber's conviction that a theatre should be a bare space, not an imitation of life (he dislikes fancy sets, saying an audience should not have to 'clap wood'). As with Steven Berkoff's *East* (see p. 92), much of the pleasure lies in watching skilful and ingenious transformations: a burly man becomes a convincing young girl with only a handbag to denote the character; fingers splayed over the head create a punk with a Mohican haircut. Godber's background in teaching is evident in the care he takes to win over an audience unfamiliar with the medium of live theatre; the play assumes they have a sophisticated knowledge of movies and makes innovative use of filmic techniques such as freeze-frames and rewinds.

AFTERLIFE

Bouncers did not attract much critical attention until Godber began an association with the company of which he eventually became artistic director, Hull Truck, which performed the play at the Edinburgh Festival in 1984. The production transferred to the Donmar Warehouse in September. In the *Guardian*, Michael Billington noted the 'distinctive style which is that of lightning-cartoon caricature which still manages to say something about the tinny, tacky, curiously barren quality of disco culture', perhaps doing less than justice to the energy and fun of the play. However, *Bouncers* was to become, as critic Lyn Garder put it, '*The Mousetrap* of the Fringe' – the most performed play by the most frequently performed playwright in the world apart from Shakespeare or Alan Ayckbourn. In the original published version, or Godber's 1991 adaptation *Bouncers: 1990s Remix*, it is revived an average of eight times a year in the UK. In Hull alone, it has been seen seventeen times, including the performance given to mark Hull Truck's farewell to their original premises in 2009. Actors appearing in it have included John McArdle of *Brookside* and Michael Wattam, best known for his work in the anarchic TV comedy show *The Smell of Reeves and Mortimer*. *Bouncers* has been staged in twelve countries, and won seven Critics' Circle Awards in Los Angeles in 1986. Every version is different, with new lines, new jokes and new music. As Godber urges, 'Keep it alive for today'.

OTHER WORKS BY
John Godber
Up 'n' Under (1984)
Teechers (1987)
On the Piste (1990)

SEE ALSO
The Kitchen (1959)
by Arnold Wesker
Stags and Hens (1978)
by Willy Russell

Masterpieces

WRITTEN BY
Sarah Daniels (1957–)

DIRECTED BY
Jules Wright

DESIGNED BY
David Roger

- First performed at the Royal Exchange Theatre, Manchester, 1 May 1983.

① Rowena (Kathryn Pogson) and Trevor (Bernard Strother), Royal Court, 1983. © *Victoria and Albert Museum, London*

② Rowena (Kathryn Pogson) and Hilary (Patti Love), Royal Court, 1983. © *Victoria and Albert Museum, London*

SNAPSHOT

Masterpieces mixes naturalism and punchy monologues within a nightmare framework. At a dinner party an unoriginal misogynist joke sets off an argument about pornography, which the men dismiss as harmless. Rowena, a social worker, is inclined to agree. However, in a leap forward in time, we see Rowena on trial for pushing a man under a train, her marriage in shreds, and her attempts to defend or explain herself disregarded by court and psychiatrist alike. In a final scene with a young policewoman, Rowena describes her fury when shown a snuff movie at work, which prompted her to kill the stranger who casually leaned into her personal space. Rowena describes the film in harrowing detail.

IMPACT

Audiences at the first production tended to respond not by applauding but by sitting in silent shock and then talking among themselves long after the play was over, a response shared by the critic Michael Billington. In 1974, the noted radical-feminist writer Robin Morgan had famously asserted, 'Pornography is the theory, and rape the practice'. *Masterpieces* was the first radical-feminist play within the theatrical mainstream and the first to tackle the pornography issue head on. It remained a key text of the debate about the impact of pornography that ran through the 1980s. Some critics were fazed by the play. John Barber in the *Telegraph* noted Daniels's youth (she was twenty-four) and admired her 'blazing anger', but never fully grasped the level of violence in the material encountered by Rowena in the course of the play. (The film described is *Snuff*, a movie made in 1976 which grafted fake footage of the 'murder' of one of the cast onto an existing 'splatter' film and marketed itself as 'real', causing widespread outrage in the women's movement on both sides of the Atlantic.) Kathryn Pogson's impassioned Rowena was highly praised; there were even better reviews for Patti Love as Rowena's client Hilary, a young single mother. Her brilliantly bawdy monologue, refuting the oft-repeated allegation that the working class don't bother with contraception (and describing an extremely novel use for Coca-Cola) was the comic highlight of the play.

AFTERLIFE

The production transferred to the Royal Court Theatre on 7 October 1983 and Daniels was awarded the 1983 London Critics' Circle Theatre Award for Most Promising Playwright. The play has been revived in the UK, the USA and Australia, although the specific issues it raises have now been aired far more widely. Daniels went on to write extensively for the Royal Court and for television, where her sharp social observation and the vivacious and surreal nature of her comedy found a place in the series *Grange Hill*. She has also worked for Chicken Shed, a company for adults and children of all abilities, and for women and girls in the criminal justice system.

OTHER WORKS BY
Sarah Daniels
Byrthrite (1987)
Beside Herself (1990)
The Madness of Esme and Shaz (1994)

SEE ALSO
Progress (1984)
by Doug Lucie
Five Kinds of Silence (2000)
by Shelagh Stephenson

①

②

Glengarry Glen Ross

WRITTEN BY
David Mamet (1947–)

DIRECTED BY
Bill Bryden

DESIGNED BY
Hayden Griffin

- First performed at the Cottesloe, National Theatre, London, 15 September 1983.

SNAPSHOT

As one might expect from the nickname given to it by actors, 'Death of a Fucking Salesman', the play is about a group of foul-mouthed real estate vendors, who personify the state of the American dream in the 1980s as Arthur Miller's salesman did for the late 1940s. Their goal is the top spot on the sales graph known as the 'board'. The winner gets a Cadillac; the runner-up a set of steak knives; the bottom man gets the sack. Key to success are the 'leads', the names of promising clients. Ricky Roma, top of the board, has the right to the best leads. At the bottom is Shelly Levene, once called 'the Machine' for his killer sales pitch. The leads are stolen – we assume by two salesmen we have heard discussing the idea. As the police interview everyone, Roma battles to prevent a timid client having second thoughts. He and Levene brilliantly improvise a situation to reassure him, which office manager Williamson wrecks at the key moment. In a rage, Levene lets slip he was the thief. Roma consoles Levene by promising to work with him, but as Levene leaves, Roma asserts, 'My stuff is mine, whatever he gets, I'm taking half'.

IMPACT

Like Arthur Miller's *A View from the Bridge* (see p. 42), the play premiered in the UK, although not this time for political reasons. Mamet, uncertain about the script, showed it to Harold Pinter, who responded that it was ready for staging and sent it to the National Theatre. Director Bill Bryden, who staged the first European production of Mamet's *American Buffalo*, drew on a group of actors he had worked with closely, notably Jack Shepherd, Karl Johnson and Trevor Ray from *The Mysteries*. Their detailed ensemble work powerfully evoked the claustrophobic, sweaty world of the office. Reviewers found the language dazzling: Michael Billington praised 'the sharp contrast between the wheedling, ingratiating, fake-matey tone adopted towards a welching client and the big-mouth, four-letter abusiveness with which they bombard the head desk-wallah'. The play resonated in a Britain equally obsessed with market values and its linguistic vitality was entirely fresh. Language, in this play, is action; words make or break a career and have an almost sexual potency. 'Whoever told you you could work with *men*?' screams Levene to the manager who wrecks his sales pitch – the ultimate insult.

AFTERLIFE

The play won an Olivier for Best New Play in 1983 and the Pulitzer Prize for Drama in 1984. It was filmed by James Foley in 1992, with Jack Lemmon as Levene, Al Pacino as Roma and Kevin Spacey as Williamson; the budget was so small that most of the cast took significant pay cuts. It has had innumerable revivals – notably in the UK by James Macdonald at the Apollo in 2007. Jonathan Pryce played Levene and was compared by the *Telegraph* to a kicked dog still capable of turning nasty. Translated into many languages, it had particular success in Japan during the 1980s boom, where the word 'stress' had just entered the Japanese language. In the National Theatre's millennium poll, it was voted one of the 100 greatest plays of the century. Conor McPherson says it made him a playwright, 'The day I read [it] … I knew exactly what I was going to do'.

①

② 1980–89

① Richard Roma (Jack Shepherd) and Shelly Levene (Derek Newark). © *Victoria and Albert Museum, London*

② Richard Roma (Jack Shepherd), Dave Moss (Trevor Ray) and Shelly Levene (Derek Newark). © *Victoria and Albert Museum, London*

OTHER WORKS BY
David Mamet
American Buffalo (1975)
Speed-the-Plow (1988)
Oleanna (1992)

SEE ALSO
Death of a Salesman (1949)
by Arthur Miller
Dealing with Clair (1988)
by Martin Crimp

Loving Women

WRITTEN BY
Pam Gems (1925–2011)

DIRECTED BY
Philip Davis

DESIGNED BY
Jonathan Gems

- First performed at the Arts Theatre, London, 1 February 1984.

① Frank (David Beames) and Susannah (Marion Bailey).
© *Victoria and Albert Museum, London*

② Susannah (Marion Bailey). © *Victoria and Albert Museum, London*

SNAPSHOT

Pam Gems's comedy is elegantly symmetrical. In Act One, set in 1973, Susannah returns home from an educational project for deprived kids; her sick lover, wannabe writer Frank, is being nursed by a vibrant hairdresser, Crystal. Captivated by Crystal's cholesterol-packed cooking and sexy lingerie, Frank switches partners. By the end of the first act, he has married Crystal, has children and holds down a job. 'I feel real,' he announces. In Act Two, set in 1983, Susannah returns from Bolivia to find a peevish Frank, while a radiantly successful Crystal has a West End business and various lovers. Bemoaning the lack of a family, Susannah asks Frank to give her a child. Before he can answer, Crystal arrives. There is a flaming row. Frank sulkily prepares to leave; Crystal decides she will go; Susannah protests she ought to be the one. Crystal then suggests a large house for the three of them. Frank exits in a huff, but, as Crystal astutely remarks, 'He's left his books'.

IMPACT

Pam Gems was a founding member of the pioneering Women's Theatre Group established in order to develop better roles for women in the theatre and address issues of interest to them. In 1976, Verity Bargate invited the group to submit plays to the Soho Poly for lunchtime performance. Gems's play was *The Project*, effectively the first act of *Loving Women*. Gems liked to revisit and recycle work over a period of time, and by the time she revised it as a two-acter she had had a major success with *Dusa, Stas, Fish and Vi*. This is the tragedy of a brilliant young woman who cannot deal with the gap between revolutionary ideals and individual experience. *Loving Women* explores this dilemma from a comic perspective. However, while the first act gently satirises a world in which 'Bloody social democrat' is the worst insult one can hurl, and a man as inert as Frank can perceive himself as a 'lion' striving to satisfy two mates, the new second act has darker moments. It holds up a mirror to the changing spirit of the left in the 1980s, from optimistic infighting to beleaguered rage in a world obsessed with money. It is also one of the most poignant explorations of parenthood of the decade, depicting with equal force the longing of the childless Susannah and the glowing paternal joy of Frank, played by David Beame with wonder and tenderness. The play was described in the *Financial Times* as Gems's best, with Gwyneth Strong singled out for special praise as Crystal, 'like a carelessly exotic poodle on stilts', a downmarket version of Marlene in Caryl Churchill's *Top Girls*.

AFTERLIFE

The play has not been revived. However, other works by the prolific Gems, who wrote almost fifty plays, translations and adaptations, are still being performed, most notably her 1978 musical drama *Piaf*, an international success. She remains a key influence on the theatre, and one of the first playwrights to explore female experience that the playwrights in her own youth chose to leave unmentioned and undervalued.

OTHER WORKS BY
Pam Gems
Dusa, Fish, Stas and Vi (1975)
Piaf (1978)
Stanley (1996)

SEE ALSO
Entertaining Mr Sloane (1964)
by Joe Orton
Progress (1984)
by Doug Lucie

①

The Mysteries

WRITTEN BY
Tony Harrison (1937–)

DIRECTED BY
Bill Bryden

DESIGNED BY
William Dudley

MUSIC BY
John Tams

- First performed at the Cottesloe, National Theatre, London, 19 January 1985.

SNAPSHOT

The Mysteries trilogy is a new version of the festive whole-day cycle of plays with which the Middle Ages celebrated the story of God and Man. They begin with the fall of Lucifer, the Creation and the story of Adam and Eve. At the centre is the story of Jesus from his birth to his death and resurrection. The ending is set in the future – Doomsday, when the world ends and everyone goes to hell or heaven; the staging of the plays was an act of devotion by the Guilds, the trades unions of their day, who spared no effort or expense to make sure it was heaven.

IMPACT

Versions of the Mystery cycles have been regularly staged in the northern English towns, in which they originated, for years. Tony Harrison had greatly disliked a York production in the 1950s: 'God was terribly posh ... only the comic parts were allowed to be Yorkshire'. When the National Theatre invited him to translate them afresh, he saw it as a chance 'to reclaim Northern classics for the voice they were written for'. In his lively verse translation, Harrison preserved the Yorkshire voice for all the characters. Director Bill Bryden established that the plays were by and for the people: the first instalment of the three-part *Mysteries* cycle took place, like the original plays, outdoors, on the terrace; the actors – who welcomed the audience as they arrived – wore and used the symbols of modern trades. Homely items such as dartboards were transformed into stars in a heaven where God, played by a powerfully Yorkshire Brian Glover, stood on a forklift truck wearing a miner's helmet. The promenade-style production drew the audience in as much as possible. Children pelted Mak, the sheep stealer, with wet sponges. Their parents held torches around Mary as she gave birth in the stable, while the band sang the old Shaker hymn 'Lay Me Low'. Jesus still hung on the cross as the audience left after the second part of the play. The magic and beauty of the production were widely praised. Bryden had tapped into the same kind of need that produced the RSC *Nicholas Nickleby* in 1980 – the desire for a vibrant and celebratory theatre also engaged with the need for social justice. Some dissenting voices, however, felt the budget would be better spent on new plays.

AFTERLIFE

The plays went into the Cottesloe repertoire in 1985, then moved to the Lyceum, the first drama there since the 1940s. Bryden won three Best Director Awards. *The Mysteries* were revived by the National in 1999/2000 to celebrate the millennium. A new production was staged at the Globe in 2011, directed by Deborah Bruce. However, Harrison's trilogy was truncated into a single three-hour play; while the sweep of the original allowed for a stylistic and emotional range from the bawdy to the numinous, critics and audiences tended to be confused by the leaps in tone over such a short time.

OTHER WORKS BY
Tony Harrison
The Oresteia (1981)
The Trackers of Oxyrhyncus (1988)
The Common Chorus (1992)

SEE ALSO
Yiimimangaliso – a South African version of the Mysteries – (2000)
by Mark Dornford-May and Charles Hazlewood
We Are Three Sisters (2011)
by Blake Morrison

① The Crucifixion of Jesus (Karl Johnson), *The Passion.*
© *Victoria and Albert Museum, London*

② God (Brian Glover) creates the world, *The Nativity.*
© *Victoria and Albert Museum, London*

②

Pravda: A Fleet Street Comedy

WRITTEN BY
Howard Brenton and David Hare

DIRECTED BY
David Hare

DESIGNED BY
Hayden Griffin

- First performed at the Olivier, National Theatre, London, 26 April 1985.

① Ian Ape-Warden (Olivier Pierre), Lambert Le Roux (Anthony Hopkins) and Elliot Fruit-Norton (Basil Henson). © *Victoria and Albert Museum, London*

② Andrew May (Tim McInnery) and Lambert Le Roux (Anthony Hopkins). © *Victoria and Albert Museum, London*

SNAPSHOT

A Brechtian comedy of excess, the play is a satire on Fleet Street with a spectacular villain at its heart, South African tycoon Lambert Le Roux. The play tracks his takeover of the British newspaper industry: first he buys a provincial daily, then the tabloid *Daily Tide*, all 'dirty vicars and randy divorcees', and finally the upmarket broadsheet *Victory*. Parallel to the rise of Le Roux is the fall of an idealistic reporter, Andrew May. While May's colleagues fuss over layout and ignore content, or get drunk, or flaunt their classical education instead of addressing major issues, May makes a stand. He attempts to publish a leaked document proving that the Minister of Defence has lied about the risks involved in transporting plutonium. Le Roux decrees, 'We send back the document unread. And we publish the name of the person who gave it to us, so they can go to gaol'. Then he fires May. The editor of a rival paper who does publish the document is harassed by Special Branch. Desperate to write again at all costs, May becomes editor of the *Daily Tide*. He ends up screaming for better tits on page three, while Le Roux hurls a blizzard of insurance cards at sacked employees.

IMPACT

This was the first collaboration between Brenton and Hare since *Brassneck*, in 1973. While that was a broad-based satire, *Pravda* took on a specific aspect of the Conservative government's second term: the failure of the press to challenge Thatcherite ideology and apparent willingness to accept something approaching monopoly ownership. *Pravda*'s story of the leaked document had a parallel with events at the *Guardian*. Meanwhile, Rupert Murdoch controlled the *News of the World* and he had transformed the *Sun* into Britain's most popular tabloid, purveying jingoistic headlines such as its response to the sinking of the Argentine ship *General Belgrano* in the Falklands conflict – 'GOTCHA!' In 1981, he secured *The Times*. Murdoch was also about to break the power of the print unions in the UK. As Le Roux, Anthony Hopkins, shortly to move to Hollywood and the role of Hannibal Lecter, gave the finest stage performance of his career. He made no attempt to suggest Murdoch, but gave Le Roux a vivid physicality of his own, with a shrill South African accent, a forward lean like a rugby player in a high wind, and a serpentine viciousness that led critics to regret that a Richard III to rival Olivier's had been lost to the stage. Although dazzled by Hopkins, the press were understandably less keen on the account of newspaper life and ethics. 'An illiterate strip-cartoon,' thundered Bernard Levin.

AFTERLIFE

Pravda was a box-office success and won three Best Play awards. At its revival at Chichester Festival Theatre in 2006, it seemed prescient. As the Tories won their third term in 1992, the *Sun* headline had proclaimed 'IT'S THE SUN WOT WON IT'. Over the twenty years since the original production, Murdoch's News Corporation absorbed Twentieth Century Fox, the Wall Street Journal, HarperCollins, BSkyB and another 800 companies across fifty countries. By 2011, Brenton and Hare's satire seemed tentative. News Corp journalists were being accused of hacking into the phones of private citizens, bribery and corruption. The questions raised by the triumph of Le Roux still hang in the air.

OTHER WORKS BY
Howard Brenton and David Hare
Lay By (1971) with Brian Clark,
Trevor Griffiths, Stephen Poliakoff,
Hugh Stoddart and Snoo Wilson
England's Ireland (1972)
with Tony Bicât, Brian Clark, David
Edgar, Francis Fuchs and Snoo Wilson
Brassneck (1973)

SEE ALSO
Serious Money (1987)
by Caryl Churchill
Revengers' Comedies (1989)
by Alan Ayckbourn

The Castle

WRITTEN BY
Howard Barker (1946–)

DIRECTED BY
Nick Hamm

DESIGNED BY
Stewart Laing

- First performed at the Barbican Pit Theatre, London, 16 October 1985.

① Skinner (Harriet Walter). © *Victoria and Albert Museum, London*

② **Building the castle.** © *Victoria and Albert Museum, London*

③ Skinner (Harriet Walter) and Cant (Katharine Rogers). © *Victoria and Albert Museum, London*

SNAPSHOT

The Castle might be called a history play, although it does not take place in any recognisable time. Stucley, a knight, returns from the Crusades to find that his wife Ann and her lover, the witch Skinner, have transformed his land. They have torn down fences, closed the church, used the men too old for crusading as studs, and taken delight in their own bodies. Determined to recover his world, Stucley orders the captive Arab engineer, Krak, to build a vast fortress. Skinner is horrified, especially when Ann begins to feel desire for Krak. When spells don't work, Ann seduces and kills the chief builder, Holiday. Skinner is tortured and condemned to have Holiday's corpse tied to her until it falls to pieces. Trying to outdo all the castle-builders of the district, Stucley grows tyrannical. Women – including the pregnant Ann – kill themselves. When Stucley is finally killed, Skinner and Krak are left to decide what will happen; fighter jets are heard screaming over the medieval fields.

IMPACT

Ronald Reagan's presidency saw a furious escalation of nuclear weaponry, supported by the UK government. Prominent among the protesters were the women who encamped outside the base used by the US Air Force at Greenham Common in Berkshire. Barker's play could not have been more timely. However, *The Castle* offers no easy answers. Feminist idealism – 'the more they bore into the hill, the more we must talk love' – struggles with personal jealousy, rage and desire. Stucley is consumed by an architectural vision as well as a passion for power. The play is full of violent, striking images that do not yield to simple interpretation – Skinner tied to the corpse, and the bodies of women raining from the battlements as they kill themselves in a last protest against Stucley's regime – and the speech is dense, poetic and explicit. There was no consistent critical response; the reviews were full of contradictions, calling the play both

'miraculous' and 'monontous', 'powerful' and full of 'schoolboy silliness'. There was universal praise for Ian McDiarmid as Stucley, switching between tranced visionary and waspish spouse snapping, 'Christ knows what goes on here. You must explain it to me over the hot milk at bedtime'. Francis King of the *Sunday Telegraph* described him as 'carving a character out of living flesh with a razor'.

AFTERLIFE

Barker's commitment is to a Theatre of Catastrophe, which acts as an irritant, like grit to an oyster; he is less interested in clarity and accessibility than in sending the audience home 'disturbed or amazed'. His later work is less accessible than the vivid narrative of *The Castle*, but he is very much a writer's writer and a key influence on figures such as Sarah Kane. In 1988, actors from the RSC and the Royal Court formed the Wrestling School, a company focusing on Barker's plays and named for the necessity to 'wrestle' with them. For the company's twenty-first birthday on 21 October 2009, executive producer Sarah Goldingay devised 21 for 21, a series of Barker productions over four continents cascading across the globe as the earth turned. In Newcastle upon Tyne, a staged reading of *The Castle* involved a new generation of performers in the RSC, the company who originally performed it.

OTHER WORKS BY
Howard Barker
No One Was Saved (1970)
Victory (1983)
Gertrude – The Cry (2002)

SEE ALSO
The Sons of Light (1974)
by David Mercer
Light Shining in Buckinghamshire
(1976) by Caryl Churchill

Shirley Valentine

WRITTEN BY
Willy Russell (1947–)

DIRECTED BY
Glen Walford

DESIGNED BY
Claire Lyth

- First produced at the Liverpool Everyman, 13 March 1986.

OTHER WORKS BY
Willy Russell
Stags and Hens (1978)
Educating Rita (1979)
Blood Brothers (1981)

SEE ALSO
Woman in Mind (1985)
by Alan Ayckbourn
The Vagina Monologues (1996)
by Eve Ensler

SNAPSHOT

Shirley Valentine is a monologue about a woman's journey of self-discovery as she transforms from Mrs Joe Bradshaw back into fearless Shirley Valentine. In the kitchen of her Liverpool house, Shirley talks to the wall while cooking egg and chips for her husband Joe. Her children make her feel old and unadventurous, she and Joe have nothing in common and she feels as though life has left her behind. In the second act, she has escaped on a holiday to Greece, where she confides in a rock about her rekindled sexuality, her renewed courage and pleasure in her own company.

IMPACT

Since 1975, two Liverpool theatres, the Playhouse and the Everyman, have nourished innovative, politically radical productions, local writers such as Willy Russell, Alan Bleasdale and Chris Bond, and a generation of actors including Julie Walters, Bill Nighy, Jonathan Pryce and Pete Postlethwaite. Russell had enjoyed commercial success with his earlier works *Educating Rita* and *Blood Brothers*, both of which had transferred to the West End, so a new Russell play — especially one that employed just one actress while vividly evoking a host of other characters and Liverpool locations — was a brilliant prospect for the cash-strapped Everyman. (Russell memorably described it as 'a place where you could go and see an exciting new musical or a really good

Shakespeare while sitting on a bag of cement.') The emerging Scouse feminist who kicks against the way 'most of us die before we're dead' captured the imagination of audiences, and the play was a sell-out. As the Everyman could not afford an understudy for Noreen Kershaw, who played Shirley, Russell agreed to perform the role if needed. Kershaw was struck down with appendicitis and Russell found himself cooking chips and egg live on stage every night for three weeks. At the end of the year, Kershaw won the *Liverpool Echo* Best Actress Award and Russell was awarded Best Supporting Actress.

AFTERLIFE

The play arrived in the West End in 1988, two years after its Liverpool debut, with popular television actress Pauline Collins as Shirley. The production, directed by Simon Callow, was a success, winning the Olivier Awards for Best New Comedy and Best Actress. In 1989, it transferred to Broadway and Collins won a Tony. In the same year, Russell adapted the play into a film, also starring Collins, who was nominated for an Oscar. Although *Shirley Valentine* has been repeatedly revived its first major London revival was in 2010 at Menier Chocolate Factory with Meera Syal as Shirley. 'Shirley Valentine syndrome' has become a media catchphrase to describe older women who have sexual adventures on holiday, but there is more to Russell's heroine than that.

① Shirley Valentine (Pauline Collins), Vaudeville Theatre, 1988. © *Victoria and Albert Museum, London*

② Shirley Valentine (Pauline Collins), Vaudeville Theatre, 1988. © *Victoria and Albert Museum, London*

③ Shirley Valentine (Pauline Collins), Vaudeville Theatre, 1988. © *Victoria and Albert Museum, London*

③

Road

WRITTEN BY
Jim Cartwright (1958–)

DIRECTED BY
Simon Curtis

DESIGNED BY
Paul Brown

- First performed at the Royal Court Upstairs Theatre, London, 22 March 1986.

SNAPSHOT

Road is a collection of vignettes, glimpses of life in one street – it doesn't have a name because the sign is broken – in a dirt-poor town in Lancashire. We follow Scullery, who scratches a living stealing junk from derelict houses, as he weaves his way through the lives around him: an old lady painting her face, lost in dreams; a skinhead, who has turned to Buddha; the 'Professor', who collects stories; Valerie, who cannot help hating her unemployed husband and whose days are 'old damp sacks laid on top of one another'. Few of the thirty-odd characters have jobs, but some try to change their lives. A woman picks up a drunken soldier and makes a romance for herself as he slumps half conscious; a young couple decide to starve to death; four young people end up in a flat where there is a single record, Otis Redding's *Try a Little Tenderness*, and they drink to help each one let out their personal rage until they are all chanting, obsessively, 'Somehow a Somehow a Somehow – might escape!'

IMPACT

The play only got a reading through the tenacity of the Royal Court's assistant director, Antonia Bird. At the original promenade production, punk singer Ed Tudor-Pole as Scullery and six actors including Lesley Sharp and Neil Dudgeon moved among a packed audience that included the agent Peggy Ramsay. Its obvious impact prompted Max Stafford-Clark to engineer a transfer to the main house – as, perhaps, did several reviews remarking on the extreme discomfort of the space. For some critics, there seemed little difference between the misery of the characters' experience and the characters themselves. 'If this is all the young can do,' sniffed the *Guardian* about the explosive drinking scene, 'sex must be really ghastly.' For most audiences, however, the energy and wit informing the language suggested that, like Andrea Dunbar's *The Arbor* (see p. 108), the play offered a spirited challenge to the north–south divide and a timely reminder that of the country's three million unemployed, the majority lived in the north.

AFTERLIFE

The play won the George Devine Award and three others for Best Play. It returned to the Royal Court in 1987, with Ian Dury as Scullery and Jane Horrocks and Iain Glen among the cast. In 1987, the BBC released a film version directed by Alan Clarke with David Thewlis, Horrocks, Sharp and Dudgeon. The film cut Scullery's role and the theatrical frame it provided, but still offered a powerful picture of youth struggling to survive. In 1988, it was staged at the La MaMa theatre, New York. Looking at the set, theatre critic Frank Rich observed '*Road* could be *Cats* with a social conscience' and revivals have sometimes risked creating a kind of poverty theme park rather than exploring the real physical pain of unemployment conveyed by Cartwright's text. The large cast makes the play a favourite for drama schools but there have been many professional revivals in the UK too, as government attitudes to the unemployed harden. In 2008, Noreen Kershaw (the original Shirley Valentine) directed it in Jim Cartwright's native Lancashire, at the Bolton Octagon.

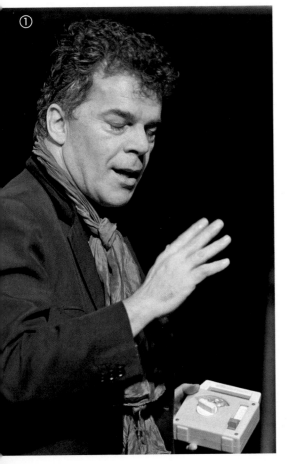

① Scullery (Ian Dury), Royal Court, 1987. © *Victoria and Albert Museum, London*

② Brink (Ewan Stewart), Carol (Mossie Smith), Louise (Jane Horrocks) and Eddie (Iain Glen), Royal Court, 1987. © *Victoria and Albert Museum, London*

③ Blowpipe (William Armstrong), Scullery (Edward Tudor-Pole) and Molly (Susan Brown). © *Victoria and Albert Museum, London*

1980-89

Serious Money

WRITTEN BY
Caryl Churchill (1938–)

DIRECTED BY
Max Stafford-Clark

DESIGNED BY
Peter Hartwell

- First performed at the Royal
  Court Theatre, London,
  21 March 1987.

OTHER WORKS BY
Caryl Churchill
Owners (1972)
Top Girls (1982)
Far Away (2000)

SEE ALSO
The Revengers' Comedies (1989)
by Alan Ayckbourn
Enron (2009)
by Lucy Prebble

SNAPSHOT

Serious Money is what the seventeenth century called a city comedy, a satirical play about money that dashes along in verse. Jake and his sister Scilla are born into the stockbroker class and the Tory shires, but in the wake of the deregulation of the London Stock Exchange, they have to deal with a world without rules. When Jake is found dead, Scilla plays detective, discovering his involvement in complicated and corrupt deals. She encounters figures of huge power: the corporate raider Corman, implicating himself in a sex scandal to mask his financial ones – 'Sexy greedy is the late eighties'; the Peruvian businesswoman Jacinta Condor, vamping a banker but never having the energy to consummate the affair because her Filofax is full. Scilla becomes less concerned with justice for Jake than with access to his accounts. The killer is never found and Scilla settles for a job with sinister American arbitrageur Marylou Baines. At the end, the whole greedy mob sings a hymn to Margaret Thatcher: 'send her victorious for five fucking morious, five more glorious years'.

IMPACT

Serious Money was developed using the Joint Stock Theatre Company's method of workshops and extensive research by the actors. However, its focus was unusual: plays such as Churchill's *Fen* explored the lives of the poor, but this time actors interviewed stockbrokers, or worked on the floor of the London International Financial Futures Exchange. It was clear that the government's decision to put London at the centre of world finance by permitting unfettered competition would have consequences, but few people outside the City grasped the implications. *Serious Money* set out to inform as well as entertain. It offered wonderful opportunities for actors. Gary Oldman as Corman was a whirlwind of corruption with a sinister moustache. Meera Syal, who played Jacinta Condor, embodied the cocaine-fuelled jet set that decides the fate of the Third World. Churchill's bouncy rhyming couplets captured the buccaneering zest of the traders as well as the corruption; they gave the play a fizzing life that made it the commercial success of Stafford-Clark's period at the Royal Court. However, it charmed the people it was satirising; the Royal Court seethed with pinstriped suits.

AFTERLIFE

The play was a major critical success, winning both an Olivier award and an Obie. The transfer to Wyndham's in the West End coincided with Thatcher's election victory, which was treated by some of the audience as worthy of celebration. Its success led the Court to build up an entrepreneurial team to profit from future opportunities, although Churchill was unhappy with its efforts to secure sponsorship deals during the Broadway run, eventually resigning from the English Stage Society Council in 1989. *Serious Money* coincided with Oliver Stone's movie *Wall Street* ('greed is good'), whose audiences also relished the entertainingly corrupt characters. However, as the recession began to bite and problems in the banking sector were traced back to the 1980s, the intent of the play became more visible. When revived at Birmingham Rep in 2009, it was described as 'prophetic'. Mathilde Lopez's production in Aberystwyth in 2011 had cast members address the audience directly and even sit next to them, underlining that we are all affected by the spectacular greed of the period.

① Jake (Julian Wadham) and Grimes (Gary Oldman).
© *Victoria and Albert Museum, London*

② Grimes (Gary Oldman) and Scilla (Lesley Manville).
© *Victoria and Albert Museum, London*

Mary Queen of Scots Got Her Head Chopped Off

WRITTEN BY
Liz Lochhead (1947–)

DIRECTED BY
Gerry Mulgrew

DESIGNED BY
Colin MacNeil

- First performed at the Lyceum Theatre Studio, Edinburgh, as part of the Festival Fringe, 10 August 1987.

SNAPSHOT

Mary Queen of Scots Got Her Head Chopped Off is a poetic and political cabaret. 'Twa queens. Wan green island,' announces La Corbie, the crow-narrator, marshalling the key players, Elizabeth I and Mary, Queen of Scots, like a circus ringmaster. Shot through with songs and dances, and using French and Lallans Scots as well as English, the play narrates a paradoxical story. Elizabeth, the Protestant 'Virgin Queen', is no such thing but cannot marry the man she wants because she will lose her power. Catholic Mary, at odds with the religious reformer John Knox who calls her 'the French whore', is a virgin when she marries the man she desires – and thereby rips Scotland apart before being beheaded with the complicity of Elizabeth. Instead of showing her execution, the final scene turns all the characters, including the queens, into modern slum kids playing a vicious game of 'proddies v. papes'.

IMPACT

Liz Lochhead offered an exuberant challenge to the assumptions that she felt pervaded writing and theatre of the time:

> 'The way it had to be said
> Was as if you were posh, grown-up,
> male, English and dead.'

She built the play around the skills of the original Communicado company, including dancer Frank McConnell, who played Mary's secretary Riccio, and Anne Wood, a fiddle player, whose music set up triumphal processions, a tender wedding night for Mary and a sound like an Orange Order marching band for John Knox. While its presentation of the grim options facing women – power within a damaging patriarchal structure, or more humane values

at the cost of social effectiveness – echoes Caryl Churchill's *Top Girls* (see p. 116), the play relates this dilemma to the still-festering sectarian divide in Scotland and the misogyny entwined with it. (Lochhead and Mulgrew, reared as Protestant and Catholic respectively, found that they had quite different perspectives on Mary's story; Lochhead remarked that the play is 'about us'.) A vivid device is used to embody not only the differences between the two queens and their circumstances, but also a wider class perspective: Mary and Elizabeth, who never met in real life, morph into each other's maids in scenes of private talk. Critics responded warmly to the variety and originality of Lochhead's handling of a familiar story, the *Guardian* commending the way she 'blasts Mary's myths not out of mindless radicalism, but because it has something more important to say about her and about us, about womanhood and the nation'.

AFTERLIFE

The play won a *Scotsman* Fringe First Award and transferred to the Donmar Warehouse in September 1987. Lochhead's most successful and popular play, it has become a Scottish classic and is frequently revived. It was staged at the Scottish National Theatre in 2009, at what the *Sunday Herald* considered a particularly resonant moment: 'As the torrid sectarian wound of our national history is reopened by the conclusion to another green-and-blue football season, the play speaks to Scotland's past and present with a welcome creative wit'. In 2011, two Scottish theatres, the Edinburgh Royal Lyceum and Dundee Rep mounted a new production to tour Scotland, directed by Tony Cownie. In 2011, Liz Lochhead became Scotland's 'makar' or national poet.

① John Knox (Gerry Mulgrew). *Photo by Sean Hudson* © *Communicado Theatre Company, through the good offices of the National Library of Scotland*

② Elizabeth I (Alison Peebles). *Photo by Sean Hudson* © *Communicado Theatre Company, through the good offices of the National Library of Scotland*

③ Mary (Anne Lacey) and Riccio (Frank McConnell). *Photo by Sean Hudson* © *Communicado Theatre Company, through the good offices of the National Library of Scotland*

1980-89

OTHER WORKS BY
Liz Lochhead
Dracula (1985)
Perfect Days (1998)
Miseryguts (2002)

SEE ALSO
Mary Stuart (1800)
by Friedrich Schiller
Vivat! Vivat Regina! (1970)
by Robert Bolt

Our Country's Good

WRITTEN BY
Timberlake Wertenbaker (1951–)

DIRECTED BY
Max Stafford-Clark

DESIGNED BY
Peter Hartwell

- First performed at the Royal
Court Theatre, London,
10 September 1988.

① Robert Sideway (Nick Dunning), Ralph Clark (David Haig), Mary Brenham (Lesley Sharp), Duckling Smith (Alphonsia Emmanuel) and Dabby Bryant (Mossie Smith). © *Victoria and Albert Museum, London*

② Dabby Bryant (Mossie Smith). © *Victoria and Albert Museum, London*

③ Ralph Clark (David Haig) and Capt Arthur Phillip (Ron Cook). © *Victoria and Albert Museum, London*

SNAPSHOT

Our Country's Good tells the true story of a group of convicts performing the first play in Australia in 1789 – George Farquhar's *The Recruiting Officer*. Marine Lieutenant Ralph Clark starts directing the play to please the Governor. Increasingly absorbed, he falls in love with convict Mary Brenham, who plays the heroine Silvia, and takes the role of her lover Captain Plume. The Governor and officers debate theatre and the penal code. Some find its harshness unbearable, including Harry Brewer, the Provost Marshall, haunted by the ghost of a man that he hanged. Though they rehearse in chains, the cast begin to discover their own worth: the monosyllabic, violent Liz Morden, sentenced to hang, finds a voice to defend her innocence; Wisehammer, the thief, composes a witty and subversive prologue; Ketch Freeman, the colony hangman, finds new dignity. The figure of an Aboriginal Australian comments throughout. At first he decides, 'This is a dream which has lost its way'. By the end of the play, he is dying of the plague brought by the colonists.

IMPACT

Impressed by Thomas Keneally's novel *The Playmaker*, Max Stafford-Clark commissioned Timberlake Wertenbaker to adapt it for the Royal Court as a companion to his production of *The Recruiting Officer*. Preliminary workshops included visits to Wormwood Scrubs prison – where a play by Howard Barker was being staged – and improvisations around the extreme brutality of the eighteenth-century penal code. As Farquhar's play went into performance, actors rehearsed drafts of the new script. Each actor played the convict who had his or her role in the 1789 *Recruiting Officer*, as well as one of the officers. Linda Bassett played both Lieutenant Will Dawes, indifferent to the theatre, and the brutalised Liz, transformed by her role as the vivacious Melinda. She had the moment of the play, as Liz turns to her judges and declares 'Your Excellency, I will endeavour to speak Mr Farquhar's lines with the elegance and clarity their own worth commands'. The production received standing ovations; Charles Spencer in the *Daily Telegraph* remarked there would be 'no justice' if it did not receive some awards. As subsidies continued to ebb from the

arts, such a powerful assertion of the value of professional theatre was welcome – but this was also the era of government rhetoric about a 'short sharp shock' for offenders, and the play was equally informed by a sense that drama had the same power for prisoners as it had in 1789.

AFTERLIFE

There were, as predicted, many awards: the Laurence Olivier Awards for Play of the Year, and for Actor of the Year in a New Play for David Haig's outstanding performance as Ralph. The play transferred to the Nederlander Theater, Broadway in 1991 and received the New York Drama Critics' Circle Award for Best Foreign Play. It has had countless revivals, perhaps the most interesting in Blundeston Prison; the prisoner playing Harry Brewer wrote to Wertenbaker, 'I got so much out of that one play. I was already on the Road but doing O.C.'s G. gave me the opportunity to take a short cut on my own Road to Reality'. Max Stafford-Clark wrote a short book, *Letters to George*, which was a series of letters to Farquhar about his experience with the twin productions.

OTHER WORKS BY
Timberlake Wertenbaker
The Grace of Mary Traverse (1985)
The Love of a Nightingale (1988)
After Darwin (1998)

SEE ALSO
The Island (1973)
by Athol Fugard, John Kani and
Winston Ntshona
A Chorus of Disapproval (1984)
by Alan Ayckbourn

The Revengers' Comedies

WRITTEN BY
Alan Ayckbourn (1939–)

DIRECTED BY
Alan Ayckbourn

DESIGNED BY
Roger Glossop

- First performed at the Stephen Joseph Theatre, Scarborough, 13 June 1989.

① Karen Knightly (Christine Kavanagh) and Tracey Willingforth (Claire Skinner). © *Scarborough Theatre Trust (The Stephen Joseph Theatre) and supplied by Alan Ayckbourn's official website www.alanayckbourn.net*

② Imogen Staxton-Billing (Elizabeth Bell) and Henry Bell (Jon Strickland). © *Scarborough Theatre Trust (The Stephen Joseph Theatre) and supplied by Alan Ayckbourn's official website www.alanayckbourn.net*

SNAPSHOT

The Revengers' Comedies, a two-parter, gleefully borrows the premise of Alfred Hitchcock's classic thriller *Strangers on a Train* – 'you avenge me, I'll avenge you'. Part One begins on Albert Bridge. Henry, intending to jump off, finds himself rescuing Karen Knightly, whose suicide has been thwarted by her belt catching on the ironwork. Mild-mannered, mildly depressed middle-aged Henry finds himself drawn into the psychotic Karen's plans. She proposes to destroy the man who replaced Henry at work, Bruce Tick, while Henry deals with Imogen, the wife of Karen's lover Anthony Staxton-Billing. Karen becomes a terrifyingly effective avenging angel, laying waste to Henry's former firm. Henry, however, falls in love with Imogen. Bumbling into a duel with the vile Staxton-Billing, he accidentally shoots him, and battles with his conscience about whether to marry Imogen or stick to his forced bargain with Karen.

IMPACT

Alan Ayckbourn wrote the plays to celebrate his fiftieth birthday. As usual, he chose a new form; although some of his best work, like *The Norman Conquests*, involved linked plays, this was a serial over two nights. It also placed his decent Everyman hero in a social context rather than hermetically sealed suburbia. Thanks to the deftness of designer Roger Glossop's widely praised use of trucked furniture, Scarborough's small in-the-round stage became the office of a big multinational, Karen's cavernous Gothic mansion, or the poky chicken shed where Henry and Imogen have their first kiss. While this let Ayckbourn create a whole spectrum of enjoyable caricatures from yuppies to thick aristocrats, it also brought a new political edge. This was recognisably the England of Caryl Churchill's *Serious Money* (see p. 136), where monetarist management-speak smoothly covered the violence done to ordinary lives. Henry bitterly describes his enforced redundancy as 'Redefining the job profile. Rationalising the department. Restructuring the management team'. In a world poisoned by economic ruthlessness, Karen can rise to the top by simply being her psychotic self. British reviews tended to see the play as minor Ayckbourn, although there was praise for the Scarborough cast. Christine Kavanagh's Karen was described by the *Daily Telegraph* as going from 'dowdy frumpishness through slatternly glamour to ice-cold chic ... a vicious lunatic on the loose'. US critics making the pilgrimage to Scarborough were more responsive to the state-of-the-nation aspect of the play. The *New York Times* thought Ayckbourn captured the 'national sport of hostile corporate takeovers, wholesale job "redundancies", and industrial destruction of the countryside'.

AFTERLIFE

Ayckbourn wanted the plays staged at the National Theatre, but Richard Eyre would only accept a condensed, one-night version. Eventually, in 1991, Michael Codron (who produced Harold Pinter's and Joe Orton's first plays) staged them at the Strand Theatre, a traditional proscenium-arch space that had problems with the fast-moving sets. The cast featured Griff Rhys-Jones as Henry, Joanna Lumley as Imogen and Lia Williams as Karen. Williams won the Critics' Circle newcomer's award for her performance. The play was filmed by Malcolm Mowbray in 1997, but had problems with distribution; it was shown on BBC2, and released on DVD in the USA as *Sweet Revenge*.

①

②

OTHER WORKS BY
Alan Ayckbourn
How the Other Half Loves (1969)
Season's Greetings (1980)
A Small Family Business (1987)

SEE ALSO
Serious Money (1987)
by Caryl Churchill
On the Ledge (1993)
by Alan Bleasdale

1990–99

British theatre limped into the 1990s bedevilled by cuts and outshone by blockbuster musicals. By the end of the decade, it was a central part of the 'Cool Britannia' brand thanks to daring works produced by a new generation of writers, and new works from established figures. Critic Aleks Sierz described it as 'in-yer-face' theatre: violent, sexually explicit and viscerally shocking. Phillip Ridley's *Fastest Clock in the Universe* and Mark Ravenhill's *Shopping and Fucking* showed a world of culturally and morally dislocated people struggling with the reality of a globalized, post-Communist world in which everything, including people, was a commodity. Sarah Kane's *Blasted* achieved notoriety for its scenes of rape, baby-eating and ultra-violence, and reconfirmed the Royal Court as the venue for radical drama heralding a renaissance in new writing.

Blasted also touched on another central preoccupation of 1990s theatre: the reshaping of Europe after the collapse of the Berlin Wall in 1989. The Yugoslavian wars, Kosovo, the reconfiguration of Czechoslovakia and the breakup of the Soviet Union and European Communism affected the whole world, and produced an extraordinary range of dramatic and cultural responses. In British theatre, this manifested itself in the work of new writers like Kane, Ravenhill and David Greig as well as in the work of established dramatists such as Caryl Churchill, David Hare and David Edgar.

▶ Guy (David Bamber), Daniel (John Sessions) and John (Anthony Calf), *My Night with Reg*, West End transfer, Criterion Theatre, 1994. © *Victoria and Albert Museum, London*

The Fastest Clock in the Universe

WRITTEN BY
Philip Ridley (1964–)

DIRECTED BY
Matthew Lloyd

DESIGNED BY
Moggie Douglas

- First performed at the Hampstead Theatre, London, 14 May 1992.

OTHER WORKS BY
Philip Ridley
The Pitchfork Disney (1991)
Vincent River (2000)
Mercury Fur (2005)

SEE ALSO
The Birthday Party (1958)
by Harold Pinter
Entertaining Mr Sloane (1964)
by Joe Orton

SNAPSHOT

In this darkly funny Gothic tale, set not in Transylvania but a disused fur factory in the East End of London, Cougar Glass is celebrating his nineteenth birthday – again. This ritual, organised by Cougar's besotted sidekick Captain Tock, involves the presence of a beautiful teenage boy for him to seduce (and, perhaps, to kill). This year's boy, Foxtrot Darling, arrives with a pregnant fiancée, Sherbet Gravel, who irritates Cougar; he attacks her, causing a miscarriage. A horrified Tock points a gun at Cougar, willing him to react. Cougar eats birthday cake, apparently unmoved. The standoff is interrupted by the ancient widow, Cheetah Bee, kept around by Cougar to contrast with his youth and beauty. She describes how mink are stripped of their fur while still alive: 'the cruelty of what I saw that day still chills me. But, oh ... [feels her fur coat] It is beautiful'.

IMPACT

The hints of Dracula and Dorian Gray reflect Ridley's work in movies about the supernatural, and the story of the title, about a selfish prince turned into a bird who can regain human form only by finding the fastest clock (love), is a reminder that he also writes fiction for children. But there is also a disconcerting realism: sometimes it feels as if Ridley had front seats at a row between Joe Orton and his lover and murderer, Kenneth Halliwell; and while Sherbet is sometimes as saccharinely sweet as her name, her obsession with all things 'traditional', from food to marriage, chimes with John Major's family-values campaign as he struggled to relaunch a government rocked by sex and money scandals. Ridley says his intent is to create a sensation in the audience. Prompted by controversy over his first play *The Pitchfork Disney*, which had done just that, artistic director Jenny Topper brought *The Fastest Clock in the Universe* to Hampstead Theatre, liking the way it countered the trend for 'tiny slices of life'. Critics were sharply divided, the *Sunday Times* seeing it as an 'exceptional aberration by the Hampstead Theatre' and Michael Billington as 'much the best new play Hampstead has discovered in a long while', with praise for Jude Law making his debut as Foxtrot Darling.

AFTERLIFE

Ridley won the *Evening Standard* Award for Most Promising Playwright and Most Promising Newcomer to British Film, the only person to win both awards. *Fastest Clock* was revived at the rebuilt Hampstead Theatre in 2009 as part of its fiftieth anniversary season and the production was more pertinent than ever to the culture's obsession with youth and the body. This time, however, the most significant figure to many of the critics was that of Sherbet Gravel. Jaime Winston received stellar notices for her debut in the role and was described by Charles Spencer as combining 'the cosiness of Barbara Windsor with the waspishness of Edna Everage'.

① Captain Tock (Jonathan Coy), Cheetah Bee (Elizabeth Bradley) and Cougar Glass (Con O'Neill). © *Victoria and Albert Museum, London*

② Foxtrot Darling (Jude Law), Sherbet Gravel (Emma Amos) and Cougar Glass (Con O'Neill). © *Victoria and Albert Museum, London*

②

Arcadia

WRITTEN BY
Tom Stoppard (1937–)

DIRECTED BY
Trevor Nunn

DESIGNED BY
Mark Thompson

- First performed at the Lyttleton Theatre, National Theatre, London, 13 April 1993.

① Bernard (Neil Pearson), Chloe (Lucy Griffiths), Valentine (Ed Stoppard), Thomasina (Jessica Cave), Septimus (Daniel Stevens) and Hannah (Samantha Bond), Duke of York's, 2009. © *Victoria and Albert Museum, London*

② Valentine Coverly (Samuel West) and Hannah Jarvis (Felicity Kendal). © *Victoria and Albert Museum, London*

SNAPSHOT

Arcadia is an intellectual comedy exploring the nature of free will, history, human attraction and the laws of the universe. It is set in one place, country manor Sidley Park, and two times, 1809–12 and 1993. The past shows events mistakenly reconstructed in the present by two researchers at Sidley. Hannah is a populist historian working on the story of Sidley's famous grounds. Bernard is a literature professor convinced Byron fought a duel at Sidley and killed a minor poet. Hannah finds evidence of a 'Sidley Hermit' who symbolises her arguments about Classical reason versus Romantic sentiment. Both are wrong: Septimus Hodge, friend of Byron, proves to be the hero of the hypotheses. He is tutor to the brilliant teenage daughter of the house, Thomasina, who takes on Fermat's last theorem and whose ideas anticipate the second law of thermodynamics, iterative algorithms and chaos theory. By the end, we have learned that Septimus took up residence in the hermitage after Thomasina's death on the eve of her seventeenth birthday, and went mad trying to solve the equation she scribbled in her notebook. Valentine, Sidley's twentieth-century mathematical genius, realises that Thomasina stumbled on the principles of chaos theory, but lacked a computer to work it out. Thomasina's work feeds into Valentine's, melding past and present. The timeframes merge in the final scene, as the modern characters don period dress for a ball while Thomasina flirts with Septimus. Honourably, he refuses to come to her room and, as the curtain falls, they waltz to celebrate the birthday she will never see.

IMPACT

Arcadia was a key point in Stoppard's career, his first major hit for ten years and showing – as all the critics remarked – a new tenderness. Like Howard Brenton's *The Genius* and Michael Frayn's *Copenhagen* (see p. 180), it tapped into a growing appetite for plays about science, but while they were primarily concerned with moral responsibility, *Arcadia* is about loss: the loss of heat for which Thomasina produces an equation that inadvertently describes entropy and the end of the universe, and the loss of characters we come to care about – this pert and clever girl and her stylish, flippant, kindly tutor. The stellar cast – Felicity Kendal as Hannah, Bill Nighy as Bernard, Samuel West as Valentine, Rufus Sewell as Septimus – had seminars on chaos theory and brought clarity to the way the characters live the theories outlined, in what *The Times* critic Benedict Nightingale called a 'marriage of ideas and high comedy'.

AFTERLIFE

The play ran for months at the National before transferring to the West End winning *Evening Standard* and Olivier awards for Best Play. During the run, Fermat's last theorem was proved by a British mathematician. *Arcadia* opened on Broadway in 1995. In 1996, Washington's Arena Stage mounted the first major regional production in the USA. Stoppard guested at the Mathematical Sciences Research Institute's 'Arcadia' event in 1999; its research director, Robert Osserman, described the opening – where Thomasina asks Septimus to define 'carnal embrace' while he sets her to work on Fermat – as 'the all-time greatest introduction to a mathematical theorem'. *Arcadia* was revived in the West End in 2009 with Stoppard's son Ed as Valentine and Daniel Stevens as Septimus.

OTHER WORKS BY
Tom Stoppard
The Real Thing (1982)
The Invention of Love (1997)
The Coast of Utopia (2002)

SEE ALSO
Give Me Your Answer, Do! (1997)
by Brian Friel
An Experiment with an Air Pump
(1998) by Shelagh Stephenson

Beautiful Thing

WRITTEN BY
Jonathan Harvey (1968–)

DIRECTED BY
Hettie MacDonald

DESIGNED BY
Robin Don

- First performed at the Bush
  Theatre, London, 28 July 1993.

SNAPSHOT

As befits its subtitle of 'urban fairytale', *Beautiful Thing* is a love story set on a London council estate. Fifteen-year-old Jamie lives with his mum, Sandra. His schoolmates live in the flats on either side: cheeky Leah, kicked out of school and obsessed with Mama Cass, and sporty Ste, who has a violent alcoholic father. One night when Ste's father has beaten him up, Sandra takes him in and he shares a bed with Jamie. Tentatively, they fall in love and experiment with a gay bar. Sandra, herself a bar manager, finds out and confronts Jamie, but she loves him far too much to make difficulties. As the story ends, Jamie and Ste, Leah and Sandra are dancing; a glitter ball transforms the dreary walkway of the flats.

IMPACT

Beautiful Thing was Harvey's seventh play, but he describes it as his first 'grown up' one, having previously written for youth groups and festivals. The story was timely: the idea of equalising the age of consent for all relationships was being widely discussed, though extended debates around Edwina Currie's proposal in the House of Commons in 1994 achieved only a compromise, lowering the age of consent for gay men to eighteen. Hettie MacDonald's production with Jonny Lee Miller as Ste sold out the tiny Bush Theatre. Audiences responded to the unpatronising and sunny characterisation that demolishes working-class stereotypes of truanting kids and single mothers. Sandra works hard and takes pride in her flat. Ste is striving for a job at the sports centre; his balcony is draped in clean washing and he does the domestic work for his family. Truanting Leah has an impressively inventive vocabulary of insults. Jamie and Ste's love scenes are tentative. Jamie rubs Ste's back bruised by his father. Not quite up to compliments, they bolster each other's confidence; Ste admires Jamie's glasses, Jamie manages a shy, 'I don't think you're ugly'. Some critics felt that Harvey ignored the tougher realities of growing up gay, but while there are elements of fantasy, the final dance is a vivid expression of spirited kindness in a small community.

AFTERLIFE

The play was revived with a new cast for a tour in 1994 and ended with a run at the Donmar Warehouse. Harvey won the George Devine Award and widespread acclaim for the play, the *Independent on Sunday* hailing it 'as the most heartening working class comedy since *A Taste of Honey*'. The West End success provoked an article by the veteran *Evening Standard* theatre critic, Milton Shulman, denouncing a 'plague of pink plays'. For most critics and audiences, however, plays challenging stereotypes of gay life – Kevin Elyot's *My Night with Reg* (see p. 154), Mark Ravenhill's *Shopping and Fucking* (see p. 162) – were no longer fringe events, but part of the theatrical mainstream. A new production opened in the West End in 1994 with Rhys Ifans as Tony. It was made into a film in 1996, directed by MacDonald. There have been over two dozen revivals in the UK, Australia and the USA, and in French, German and Dutch. The age of consent for both sexes in the UK was changed to sixteen in 2000.

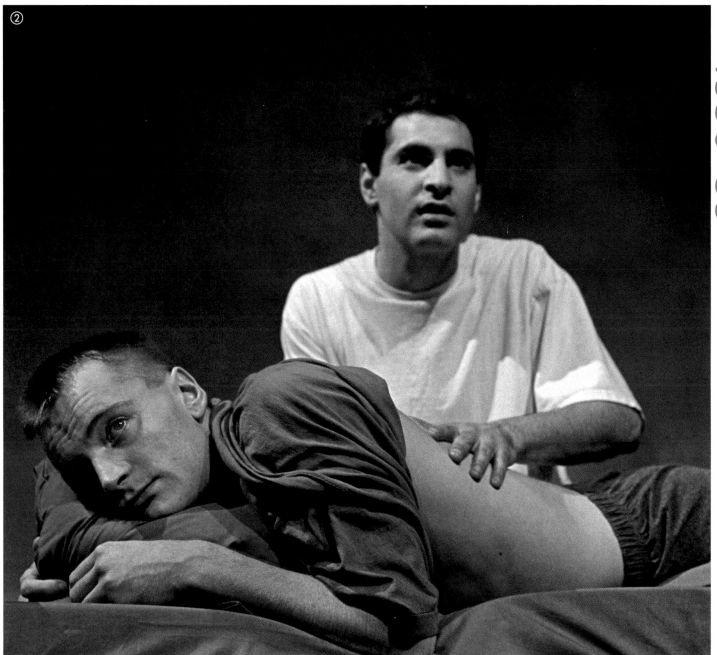

① Jamie (Mark Letheren) and Sandra (Patricia Kerrigan).
© *Victoria and Albert Museum, London*

② Ste (Richard Dormer) and Jamie (Zubin Varla),
Duke of York's Theatre, 1994. © *Victoria and Albert
Museum, London*

OTHER WORKS BY
Jonathan Harvey
Boom Bang-a-Bang (1995)
Guiding Star (1998)
Hushabye Mountain (1999)

SEE ALSO
Five Finger Exercise (1958)
by Peter Shaffer
Bent (1979)
by Martin Sherman

Angels in America (Parts 1 and 2)

WRITTEN BY
Tony Kushner (1956–)

DIRECTED BY
Declan Donnellan

DESIGNED BY
Nick Ormerod

- *Part 1, Millennium Approaches* and *Part 2, Perestroika,* performed together for the first time at the Mark Taper Forum, Los Angeles, directed by Oskar Eustis and Tony Taccone.

- First performed together in the UK at the Cottesloe, National Theatre, London, 20 November 1993.

OTHER WORKS BY
Tony Kushner
Homebody/Kabul
Caroline or Change

SEE ALSO
The Normal Heart (1985)
by Larry Kramer
Hushabye Mountain (1999)
by Jonathan Harvey

SNAPSHOT

Angels in America, 'A Gay Fantasia on National Themes', focuses on the public and private stories of a nation on the edge of the millennium. Prior, a gay man with AIDS, is visited by an Angel who hails him as a prophet. Louis, Prior's lover, can't cope with caring for him and falls for Joe, a Mormon Republican legal clerk. Joe anguishes about his sexuality; his wife Harper frets about the ozone layer, takes pills and imagines herself into a dream Antarctica. Joe takes a job with the corrupt McCarthyite lawyer, Roy Cohn, now dying of AIDS. In the 1950s, Roy secured a death sentence for the Rosenbergs, who passed atomic secrets to Moscow; now Ethel Rosenberg's ghost drops in with news of his disbarment. Prior's best friend, black drag queen and nurse Belize, needles the dying Roy into giving him his stash of AZT for Prior. In 1990, Prior celebrates his continuing survival with Louis, Belize, Joe's mother Hannah and the audience.

IMPACT

The mixture of history, myth and soap opera invites the question, 'what kind of world do we want?' The Angels want stasis. However, the humans who make it to 1990 with bodies and minds more or less whole know that their 'terminal, crazy and mean' America has to change, just as the Soviet Union had to change after the fall of the Berlin Wall. Joe's Reaganite values destroy him and others. AIDS ravages the gay community. During the gestation of the plays, treatments improved, as did attitudes to sufferers (slowly). Kushner draws on the epic techniques of Bertold Brecht (he has translated several Brecht plays) and Caryl Churchill's juxtaposition of historical and personal to create a Theatre of the Fabulous, which can be realised onstage in different ways. Declan Donnellan, best known for directing Shakespeare, gave the National production Shakespearean speed and simplicity, with the actors – including Daniel Craig as Joe, Jason Isaacs as Louis and Stephen Dillane as Prior – doubling as stagehands. The minimalist staging underlined the dazzling theatricality of key moments – Prior's wrestling match with his angel, or the scene that unites Louis and a ghostly Ethel Rosenberg to say Kaddish, the Jewish prayer for the dead, for Roy Cohn. The production drew a young audience to the National Theatre and they were visibly moved as Prior – whose life seemed so fragile at the end of the first half – proclaimed at the close 'We won't die secret deaths any more'.

AFTERLIFE

Angels won the Pulitzer prize and was named part of the Western Canon of major works of literature by Harold Bloom. It was filmed as a mini-series by HBO in 2003, with Al Pacino as Roy and Meryl Streep playing Ethel, an elderly rabbi, and Harper's mother. There have been many revivals, the most recent in the UK by Headlong in 2007. In 2004 it was made into an opera by Peter Eotvos for the Théâtre du Châtelet in Paris. Harrison David Rivers' play, *When Last We Flew*, described as a tribute to Kushner, was staged at the New York Fringe Festival in 2010 as *Angels* returned to New York and also opened in Harper's home town, Salt Lake City.

Angel (Nancy Crane) and Prior Walter (Stephen Dillane).
Photo by John Haynes, © John Haynes/Lebrecht Music & Arts

My Night with Reg

WRITTEN BY
Kevin Elyot (1951–)

DIRECTED BY
Roger Michell

DESIGNED BY
William Dudley

- First performed at the Royal Court Theatre Upstairs, London, 31 March 1994.

① John (Anthony Calf), Guy (David Bamber), Eric (Joe Duttine), Daniel (John Sessions), Bernie (Roger Frost) and Benny (Kenneth Macdonald), West End transfer, Criterion Theatre, 1994. © *Victoria and Albert Museum, London*

② Daniel (John Sessions), West End transfer, Criterion Theatre, 1994. © *Victoria and Albert Museum, London*

SNAPSHOT

Guy loves John. Dan, John's best friend, who loves Reg, encourages Guy to tell John – but then John confides to Guy that he loves Reg, and the moment passes. When Reg dies of AIDS, we discover he has slept around on an epic scale. Guy's decorator, Eric, encourages Guy to tell John he loves him – but the moment passes. Guy dies of AIDS, picked up in a drunken and brutal encounter on holiday. He leaves John everything.

IMPACT

As the *Guardian* delighted in pointing out, this is a 'small and perfectly-formed bourgeois comedy'. Despite the 'plague of pink plays' label Milton Shulman had slapped on Jonathan Harvey's *Beautiful Thing* (see p. 150) and other gay plays flourishing in London, most of the critics concurred. Its high-gloss elegance was relatively unusual fare for the Royal Court's Theatre Upstairs (it had originally been commissioned by Hampstead Theatre), but Elyot's craftsmanship constantly surprises, tipping the laughing audience abruptly into grief. For instance, the first scene ends with rain falling on Guy's roof at his flat warming;

when the second begins with the same sound, it seems minutes have passed. Then you realise Guy is hosting Reg's wake. The same device is even more shocking in the last act. A naked John appears in the flat and makes you believe, for one moment, that Guy has had his wish; then John is revealed as Guy's heir, not his lover. So far, most plays about AIDS had – like Tony Kushner's *Angels in America* (see p. 152) – been overtly political and extrovert. This was elegiac and English, its hero as restrained as Celia Johnson in David Lean's *Brief Encounter*. There was widespread praise for David Bamber as Guy. 'Every wry little grimace rings true,' noted John Gross in the *Sunday Telegraph*. Apparently doing nothing, Bamber managed to reveal Guy's whole heart as he repeatedly homed in on one memory – John at a student party, hinting he might fancy Guy, and the moment passing. His silent pain as he realises John's remark, 'You're the only one', means that Guy is the only one he can tell about Reg, not a declaration of love, is the high spot of the evening. John Sessions as camply self-dramatising Dan and Anthony Calf as John, 'the flying fuck of the first XV' now past his prime, were also praised for the delicacy of the comedy.

AFTERLIFE

Director Roger Michell said that he always assumed the play would be 'a huge commercial hit' and it transferred from the Royal Court to the Criterion Theatre in November 1994 and then to the Playhouse Theatre. It won not only a Writer's Guild Award for Best Fringe Play in 1994, but also *Evening Standard* and Olivier awards for Best Comedy and the Critics' Circle award for Most Promising Playwright. David Bamber also received an Olivier Award for Best Actor. *My Night with Reg* was made into a film in 1996, with the original cast. The play has been revived all over the world.

OTHER WORKS BY
Kevin Elyot
Coming Clean (1982)
The Day I Stood Still (1998)
Mouth to Mouth (2001)

SEE ALSO
Anti Body (1983)
by Louise Parker Kelly
Angels in America (Part One and Two)
(1993) by Tony Kushner

②

1990–99

Pentecost

WRITTEN BY
David Edgar (1948–)

DIRECTED BY
Michael Attenborough

DESIGNED BY
Robert Jones

- First performed at the Other Place, Stratford-upon-Avon, 12 October 1994.

① Oliver (Charles Kay) and Gabriella (Jan Ravens), Young Vic, 1995. © *Victoria and Albert Museum, London*

② Gabriella (Jan Ravens) and Oliver (Charles Kay), Young Vic, 1995. © *Victoria and Albert Museum, London*

SNAPSHOT

Pentecost examines the breakup of Eastern Europe and its effect on local, national and international relations. In an unspecified Balkan country in the 1990s, a newly discovered fresco – which may be the first ever use of perspective, turning received art history on its head – could place the country on the map. Gabriella, the local museum curator, hopes so, but she and Oliver, a British art historian, are plunged into a diplomatic and cultural nightmare. While churchmen, nationalists and the pragmatic American art expert, Leo Katz, are arguing over the building – which has been a church, a mosque, a stable, a warehouse and a 'Museum of Atheism and Progressive People's Culture' – a group of international refugees take them (and the fresco) hostage, demanding asylum in countries of their choice. As communication gradually develops, Oliver posits a new attribution for the painting – an Arab colourist encountering European tradition. Suddenly soldiers overpower the hostage-takers; they shoot a number of the refugees, as well as Oliver, who had traded clothes with one of them.

IMPACT

Pentecost was workshopped by Edgar and the RSC during the breakup of Yugoslavia and the conflict raging between its ethnic groups. For Edgar, the heart of the play was language; in fragmenting Eastern Europe, language defines you – your own or the one your enemy imposes. Each character in *Pentecost* speaks in their own language; the audience gathers the gist from the reactions of others, or from translations into English that are sometimes halting, or self-serving, or deliberately misleading. For the church, Pentecost signifies the moment the Holy Spirit imparted a miraculous ability to speak and understand a multitude of languages, a symbol of unity. Here there is a constant struggle between unity and self-expression, individual beliefs and national ones. Sometimes this is comic; Jan Ravens, best known as an impressionist, gently satirised Oliver (Charles Kay) for his Eurocentricity ('East Europe ... where they botch up socialism and make even bigger botch of market system too') while quite clearly beginning to fancy him.

Sometimes the issues are sharper: Leo points out that efforts to recover the fresco have wiped away the names written on the walls by victims of Nazi torture. During the struggle to understand words, bits of the painting are emerging, demanding to be interpreted, and asking us whether art is more important than human lives. *Pentecost* brought the large cast, big issue play back to subsidised theatre, and was generally welcomed, although some critics complained of the length and density of the arguments.

AFTERLIFE

The play moved to the Young Vic and won the 1995 *Evening Standard* Award for Best Play. It was revived in the USA at Yale, Oregon, Berkeley and San Diego, though it did not reach New York until 2005 with a production by the Barrow Group. The fragmentation of Eastern Europe found its way into many new plays in the 1990s, including Sarah Kane's *Blasted* (see p. 160), David Greig's *Europe* (see p. 158) and Pinter's *One for the Road*. *Pentecost* is the central part of a trilogy about negotiation within Eastern Europe; *The Shape of the Table* was staged in 1990 shortly after the collapse of the Soviet Union, and *The Prisoner's Dilemma* just before 11 September 2001.

①

OTHER WORKS BY
David Edgar
The Shape of the Table (1990)
Continental Divide (2003)
Testing the Echo (2008)

SEE ALSO
Professional Foul (1977)
by Tom Stoppard
One for the Road (1984)
by Harold Pinter

Europe

WRITTEN BY
David Greig (1969–)

DIRECTED BY
Philip Howard

DESIGNED BY
Kenny MacLellan

- First performed at the Traverse Theatre, Edinburgh, 21 October 1994.

① Morroco (Chris Ryman), Horse (Cameron Mowat) and Billy (Graeme Rooney), Barbican, 2007. © *Douglas McBride, Photographer*

② Adele (Samantha Young), Katia (Michelle Bonnard), and Sava (Hannes Flaschberger), Barbican, 2007. © *Douglas McBride, Photographer*

③ Kaita (Michelle Bonnard), Fret (Robert Paterson) and Sava (Hannes Flaschberger), Barbican, 2007. © *Douglas McBride, Photographer*

SNAPSHOT

Europe explores the effects of the fall of Communism and globalisation on 'a small town on the border, at various times on this side, and, at various times, on the other', somewhere in Europe. The town's significance has always been tied to this border status; the railway station was a hub for travellers and for those inspecting passports and permits. Now the opening up of Europe's borders means trains no longer stop, leaving the town economically and socially isolated. The factory is shut; the station is closed. 'Economic migrants,' Sava and his daughter Katia, are stranded. Stationmaster Fret, and his daughter, Adele, lose their jobs and their sense of identity. Fret and Sava bond over their love of the railway and unite in opposition to the station's closure, while Adele dreams of leaving with Katia. Local entrepreneur Morocco accepts and exploits the change. He tells his friends from the former factory, Billy, Horse and Berlin, that a border is 'A magic money line. See. You pass something across it and it's suddenly worth more. Pass it across again and now it's cheaper'. However, unable to accept change, they join a racist group, beat up Sava, and set fire to the station, destroying the town's last link with the outside world. Their actions briefly give the town an identity once more. 'They know,' Berlin remarks, 'that in our own way, we're also Europe.'

IMPACT

Shortly before the start of Scottish devolution, David Greig founded his own company, Suspect Culture, and worked on a number of plays with them before writing *Europe*. When it drew the interest of both the Royal Court Theatre Upstairs and the Traverse, he chose the larger space. As a result, little of his work has appeared in London, but he became an important part of the flowering of Scottish writing that has taken place from the work of Liz Lochhead in the 1980s to Gregory Burke in 2007. *Europe* led *The Scotsman* to identify Greig as 'the most important playwright to have emerged north of the border in years'. Its appeal to the imagination was a double one. It commented, like Sarah Kane's *Blasted* (see p. 160) and David Edgar's *Pentecost* (see p. 156), on the fragmentation of Europe and the homelessness and aggression towards migrants resulting from it; but, as Greig remarked, 'That border town could just as easily be Motherwell' in its poverty and interracial strife. Any small town in England, for that matter, could make sense of the world shown, where opportunity goes thundering by like a high speed train and gives the impression of plenty and progress, but leaves communities fractured.

AFTERLIFE

It was revived at Dundee Rep in 2007; Douglas Rintoul's production then came to the Barbican Pit later that year, one of the first of Greig's plays to appear in London. In the same year, he had three plays running at the Edinburgh Festival. *Europe* has been played in six European languages.

OTHER WORKS BY
David Greig
The Cosmonaut's Last Message to the Woman He Once Loved in the Former Soviet Union (1999)
Outlying Islands (2002)
The American Pilot (2005)

SEE ALSO
Mad Forest (1990)
by Caryl Churchill
Pentecost (1994)
by David Edgar

②

③

Blasted

SNAPSHOT

Like all Sarah Kane's work, *Blasted* is innovative in form. At first, it looks like a naturalistic two-hander. In a bland expensive hotel, journalist Ian and the vulnerable Cate swing between tenderness and abuse. He pleads for sex and sympathy but sees her as a mentally ill prick-tease. She is affectionate, uneasy and violent, and prone to blackouts. When morning comes, he has raped her and she has escaped through the bathroom window. A soldier enters. The room is blasted by a mortar bomb. The soldier demands that Ian tell his stories of atrocity and loss; Ian refuses – 'this isn't a story anyone wants to hear'. The soldier rapes Ian, sucks out his eyes and then commits suicide. Cate returns with a dead baby. She comforts Ian, stops him killing himself, and buries the dead baby before going to look for food. Ian masturbates, tries to strangle himself, hugs the dead soldier, eats the dead baby and 'dies with relief' until revived by rain. Cate returns and feeds him.

IMPACT

The reviews used every word in the 'Disgruntled Critics' Phrasebook': 'farrago', 'gratuitous welter of carnage', 'adolescent', and, most famously, in the *Daily Mail*, 'disgusting feast of filth'. The play became news, prompting reporters to pursue Kane. Meanwhile, Harold Pinter sent her an encouraging letter. Caryl Churchill, Martin Crimp and Edward Bond spoke up on her behalf, and Michael Billington, regretting his dismissive review, urged a reassessment. The row did not surprise the Royal Court; at a first reading, some staff expressed reluctance to work on the play. The actors who did take part – Pip Donaghy, Kate Ashfield and Dermot Kerrigan – had a blazing conviction that even the critics admired. The extreme violence was Kane's response to viewing the siege of Srebrenica on television. War blows the set apart; it breaks the bodies of the characters; it fragments the language into monosyllables; it fractures time, so the last scenes are briefly lit moments. But it all links back to the initial, ordinary cruelties – as Kane said, 'one is the seed and the other is the tree'. Ian hurts Cate more casually than the soldier – who saw his girlfriend hacked to pieces – maims and kills. The play is shot through with tenderness, touch and nourishment; every scene ends with the sound of rain, hinting at the possibility of healing and redemption.

AFTERLIFE

By the time of her death in 1999, Kane was perceived as a major theatre voice. James MacDonald revived *Blasted* at the Royal Court in 2001, with Kelly Reilly and Neil Dudgeon. Thomas Ostermeier brought a German language production to the Barbican in 2006 and Sean Holmes revived it at the Lyric Hammersmith in 2010. Meanwhile, Kane's reputation in Europe grew. *Blasted* was staged six times in Germany, and in France, Belgium, Italy, Serbia and Australia. Her first director, James Macdonald, commented on her importance in redefining the shape of political drama: 'she gave the lie to a laziness in thinking which insists on the superiority of a certain kind of play ... kitted out with signposts indicating meaning, and generally featuring a hefty state-of-the-nation speech ... More than anyone, she knew that this template is no use to us now'.

OTHER WORKS BY
Sarah Kane
Phaedra's Love (1996)
Cleansed (1998)
Crave (1998)
4.48 Psychosis (2000)

SEE ALSO
Saved (1965)
by Edward Bond
The Romans in Britain (1980)
by Howard Brenton

WRITTEN BY
Sarah Kane (1971–99)

DIRECTED BY
James Macdonald

DESIGNED BY
Franziska Wilcken

- First performed at the Royal Court Theatre Upstairs, London, 12 January 1995.

① Ian (Pip Donaghy) and Cate (Kate Ashfield). © *Ivan Kyncl, Photographer*
② Ian (Pip Donaghy). © *Ivan Kyncl, Photographer*

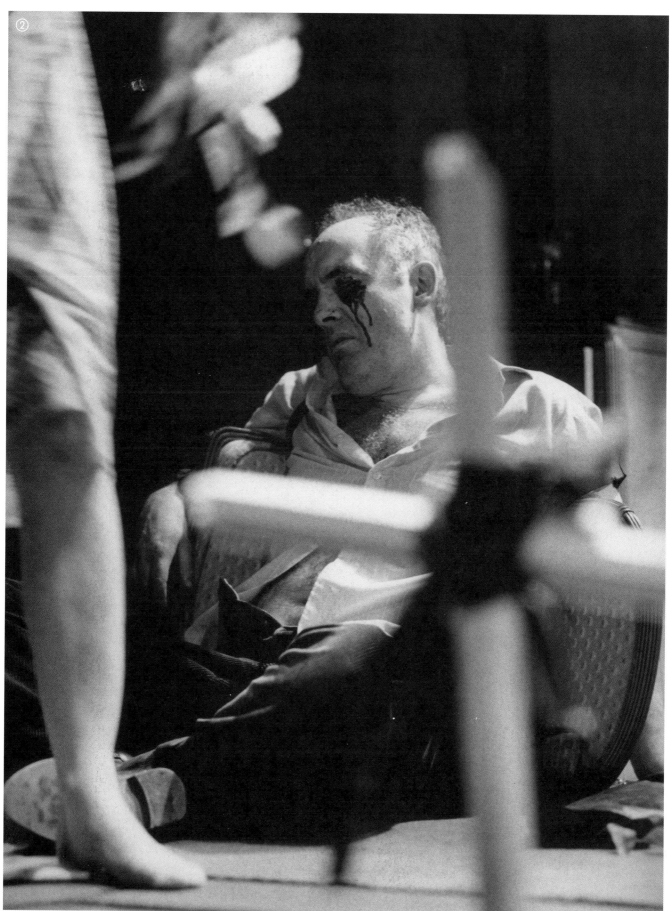

Shopping and Fucking

WRITTEN BY
Mark Ravenhill (1966–)

DIRECTED BY
Max Stafford-Clark

DESIGNED BY
Julian McGowan

- First performed at the Royal
Court Theatre Upstairs at the
Ambassadors Theatre, London,
26 September 1996.

① Brian (Robin Soans) interviews Lulu (Kate Ashfield).
© *Victoria and Albert Museum, London*

② Robbie (Andrew Clover). © *Victoria and Albert
Museum, London*

SNAPSHOT

Robbie, Lulu and Mark live in a dingy flat,
subsisting on convenience food and casual
jobs. Mark leaves for an addiction centre. Lulu
has a job interview with creepy businessman
Brian, who weeps over *The Lion King*, but makes
her 'act' Chekhov in her bra before giving her
a job selling Ecstasy. She passes the pills to
Robbie. High on E and desire, he gives them
all away. Robbie and Lulu resort to phone
sex to repay Brian. Mark brings home Gary, a
fourteen-year-old sex worker. Robbie offers
to act out (for cash) Gary's fantasy of being
dominated by a father figure. He and Mark
abuse Gary, but hesitate when he demands to
be penetrated with a knife. Gary says, 'When
someone's paying, someone wants something
and they're paying, then you do it'. Mark
agrees. Lulu and Robbie leave and Gary says,
'I want it over. And there's only one ending'.
In the next scene, there is no sign of Gary.
Brian arrives, forces them to chant 'Money is
civilisation' and waives the debt because 'you
have learnt'. They share convenience food as
the play ends.

IMPACT

Shopping and Fucking was part of the Royal
Court's drive to encourage younger audiences.
It was, perhaps, the play that most clearly
merited the 'in-yer-face' label coined to
describe the new drama – not just for its
explicitness but also for the ruthless social
indifference experienced by the young. There is
no protection for Gary from the Welfare State;
parents are represented by Brian and Gary's
abusive father; education by the fragments
of Shakespeare and the Bible Lulu and Robbie

quote to brighten up their phone sex. Young
audiences responded, attracted by the subject
matter, the funky temporary space at the
Ambassadors, the pounding techno soundtrack
and the neon backdrop. Inevitably, the title,
of the play, provoked controversy. Producing
company Out of Joint were warned that to
show it in full on any printed material would
breach the 1889 Indecent Advertisements Act;
even now, posters and covers are spangled
with asterisks. David Blunkett, then Education
Secretary, described the play as 'a waste
of public money' without ever seeing it.
However, most audiences and reviewers – and
the Culture Secretary, Chris Smith – were
quick to defend it as a profoundly moral
play about people whose ability to act or
believe collectively has been fractured by a
consumerism that treats them commodities.

AFTERLIFE

The play transferred to the West End, first to
the Gielgud and then to the Queen's Theatre
(with a new cast in 1998), and formed part
of a British Council Euro Theatre 98 festival
in Brussels. It has also been produced off-
Broadway (with Philip Seymour Hoffman
as Mark) and in a notable production at
the Baracke Theater by Thomas Ostermeier.
One speech has also gained currency as
a crystallisation of the 1990s: Robbie's
observation: 'I think we all need stories, we
make up stories so that we can get by. And I
think a long time ago there were big stories.
Stories so powerful you could live your whole
life in them ... But they all died or the world
grew up or grew senile or forgot them so now
we're all making up our own stories'.

OTHER WORKS BY
Mark Ravenhill
Some Explicit Polaroids (1999)
Mother Clap's Molly House (2001)
Pool (No Water) (2006)

SEE ALSO
Trainspotting (1997)
by Harry Gibson
Disco Pigs (1996)
by Enda Walsh

②

East is East

WRITTEN BY
Ayub Khan-Din (1961–)

DIRECTED BY
Kristine Landon-Smith

DESIGNED BY
Sue Mayes

- First performed at the Birmingham Repertory Theatre, 8 October 1996.

① Abdul (Paul Bazely), Ella (Linda Bassett), George (Nadim Sawalha), Annie (Lesley Nicol), Mr Shah (Kris Dosanjh), Munir (Emil Marwa) and Tariq (Jimi Mistry), Royal Court Theatre Upstairs (Ambassadors Theatre), 1996. © *Victoria and Albert Museum, London*

② Ella (Linda Bassett) and George (Nadim Sawalha), Royal Court Theatre Upstairs (Ambassadors Theatre), 1996. © *Victoria and Albert Museum, London*

SNAPSHOT

East is East is an autobiographical play with political undertones, but it also has much in common with old-fashioned north-country family comedy. George Khan ('Genghis') runs a fish and chip shop in Salford. He has been married for twenty-five years to Ella, the English woman he took as his second wife, leaving a family in Pakistan. He wants to raise his seven children as Pakistani Muslims; but one has left home to be a hairdresser, his daughter prefers football to wearing a sari, Saleem is studying art instead of engineering and twelve-year-old Sajit is so conflicted about his identity that he refuses to take off his parka. George plots to marry two sons to the daughters of posh Mr Shah; when things don't go to plan, Ella supports the rights of her children and George strikes her. Ella is forgiving, but as the play ends, we do not know whether George can ever accept his family as it is (although Sajit has thrown away his parka).

IMPACT

The play was developed collaboratively between the Royal Court and Tamasha Theatre Company. Tamasha (the name means 'commotion') had been launched in 1989 to bring contemporary Asia-focused drama to the British stage. Its first major success, Kristine Landon-Smith's production drew a multiracial audience and was rapidly recognised as a modern classic. It showed British Asian life in a new way, balancing broad comedy (it opens with Sajit being forcibly inspected by his Auntie Annie to confirm he hasn't been circumcised) with a sharp awareness of what it was like to live in a time when Enoch Powell's inflammatory 'rivers of blood' speech drew out the very worst of British racism. 'Enoch Powell was always being thrown in my face as a child,' Khan-Din remarks. The role of George was one of the strongest roles for a mature Asian actor written in English. Nadim Sawalha's performance never concealed George's narrowness and rage, but, as reviews were quick to recognise, also showed a clearly decent man under pressure, helplessly watching the TV news as war between India and East Pakistan threatened to obliterate his national identity. Linda Bassett as Ella was praised for the dignity she brought to the role, a tribute to Khan-Din's mother.

AFTERLIFE

After two London runs and a national tour, the play transferred to the West End (Royal Court Downstairs at the Duke of York's). Ayub Khan-Din won the John Whiting and Writers' Guild Awards. The play was made into a film in 1999. Although some aspects of the plot were simplified and Om Puri took over the role of George, Linda Bassett played the role she originally created and won a Best Actress award at the Valladolid International Film Festival. *East is East* also won Best Picture at Valladolid that year. Jimi Mistry, as older son Tariq, went on to have a very successful film career. The film won sixteen national and international awards. A sequel, *West Is West*, followed in 2010, which took the Khan family to Pakistan and showed a more relaxed Sajit discovering a new world and aspects of himself. Khan-Din has suggested that the Khan story is not yet complete and that it may become a trilogy.

①

1990–99

OTHER WORKS BY
Ayub Khan-Din
Last Dance at Dum Dum (1999)
Rafta Rafta (2007)

SEE ALSO
As Times Goes By (1971)
by Mustapha Matura
Hobson's Choice (2003)
by Tanika Gupta

Art

WRITTEN BY
Yasmina Reza (1959–)

TRANSLATED BY
Christopher Hampton

DIRECTED BY
Matthew Warchus

DESIGNED BY
Mark Thompson

- First performed at Wyndham's Theatre, London, 15 October 1996.

① Yvan (Ken Stott), Serge (Tom Courtenay) and Marc (Albert Finney). © *Victoria and Albert Museum, London*

② Marc (Albert Finney). © *Victoria and Albert Museum, London*

③ Yvan (Ken Stott), Serge (Tom Courtenay) and Marc (Albert Finney). © *Victoria and Albert Museum, London*

SNAPSHOT

Middle-aged, twice-divorced dermatologist Serge splurges 200,000 francs on an all-white painting. Marc, his bombastic friend who prefers the classics, is wounded by Serge's trendy choice. Yvan, pathetically eager to please, and preoccupied with his forthcoming marriage, tries desperately to act as peacemaker and of course ends up as the focus of everyone's anger. Serge proves that 'he cared more about him than he did about the painting' by inviting Marc to draw on it with a felt tip pen. However, he knows the ink isn't indelible.

IMPACT

Like David Edgar's *Pentecost* (see p. 156), the play is about the value of art, but in Reza's comedy the stakes are money and friendship rather than human lives. The white painting allows her to satirise controversies about contemporary art; the media was currently full of debate about the Young British Artists, and the value and meaning of works such as Tracey Emin's bed or Damien Hirst's dead animals. A headline in the *Guardian* accused Reza of producing a 'Nazi piece of work' that 'seeks to smother all intelligent cultural debate in the name of a mindless populism'. Translator Christopher Hampton responded by pointing out that Marc's traditionalist perspective was not necessarily that of the author; all three characters address the audience and offer different points of view. The dramatic value of the painting, however, is that it provides, literally, a blank canvas onto which each character projects their own insecurities. The way Marc eventually describes the picture – 'it represents a man who moves across a space and disappears' – is also a perfect definition of male mid-life anxiety about loss and change; Marc has always seen himself in the role of mentor, and doesn't find it easy to watch his protégé making his own choices. While there are countless plays about sexual, familial and professional relationships, there are not so many about friendship. This may explain the positive response of actors to the play. It was originally produced in France; Micheline Roquebrune, Sean Connery's wife, saw it and bought the English language rights. The relish of the first cast – Albert Finney as Marc, Tom Courtney as Serge and Ken Stott as Yvan – was apparent. Michael Billington suggested a 'Hydra-headed' triple award for Best Actor. But while Finney's bullish Marc and Courtenay's little flashes of cruelty as the cultured Serge gave life to the central conflict, most critics awarded the honours to Ken Stott's bewildered peacemaker, whose fit of weeping drew an 'aaahh' from the audience.

①

AFTERLIFE

Reza's first reaction to the laughter was to ask her translator Christopher Hampton, 'What have you done?' In France, the play had been seen as a play of debate. However, in the UK, Hampton's light comedy translation helped win the first ever Olivier Best comedy Award for a non-Anglophone work. *Art* became a West End phenomenon, with a constantly changing trio of famous actors enjoying the chance of intimate ensemble work and audiences making a point of revisiting each cast change. It ran for eight years, the last cast being *League of Gentlemen* stars Steve Pemberton, Mark Gatiss and Reece Shearsmith. *Art* has been performed in fifty theatres across Europe, translated into more than thirty languages and has grossed almost £200 million worldwide.

OTHER WORKS BY
Yasmina Reza
Conversations After a Burial (1987)
The Unexpected Man (1995)
God of Carnage (2006)

SEE ALSO
Leonardo's Last Supper (1969)
by Peter Barnes
Three Birds Alighting on A Field (1991)
by Timberlake Wertenbaker

Attempts on Her Life

WRITTEN BY
Martin Crimp (1956–)

DIRECTED BY
Tim Albery

DESIGNED BY
Gideon Davey

- First performed at the Royal Court Theatre Upstairs at the Ambassadors Theatre, London, 7 March 1997.

① Kacey Ainsworth, Danny Cerqueira, David Fielder, Ashley Jensen, Hakeem Kae-Kazim, Etela Pardo, Sandra Voe, and Howard Ward. © *Victoria and Albert Museum, London*

② Danny Cerqueira and Howard Ward. © *Victoria and Albert Museum, London*

SNAPSHOT

Attempts on Her Life is a postmodern melange of styles in an episodic structure. The 'her' of the title is Anne, or Anya, Annie, Anny or Anushka, and we never see her. Instead, people talk (or even sing) about her. Anne may be a teenager, or about forty. She may be a student, a film star, a terrorist, a porn actress, a mother, a suicide, an artist, a victim of war. She may even be a make of car: 'The Anny comes with electric windows as standard'. Some scenes are in a mix of languages, and we have no idea of Anne's nationality. The seventeen disparate 'scenarios' do not assign the dialogue to particular characters; it is for the director and company to shape the play.

IMPACT

This was Crimp's eleventh play, or as he describes it, 'anti-play', in which he deliberately challenged what he perceived as the conservatism of most Royal Court productions. There was universal praise for the way the production looked; Gideon Davey's evocative sets constantly surprised the audience, evoking everything from a TV studio to an airport runway, and the cast of eight briskly transformed into a series of roles from pretentious art critics to torture victims. The play itself, however, sharply divided the critics. Crimp was adamant that it was not in any sense an 'in-yer-face' play; despite the violence it sometimes narrates, the tone is coolly austere. Some found it heartless or pretentious; others found its originality exhilarating. While the text was fragmented, it was driven relentlessly forwards by a clear sense of rage against a consumerist culture that classified people purely in terms of their use – whether as porn actors or purchasers of the latest car that has 'no room for gypsies, Arabs, Jews, Turks, Kurds, Blacks or any of that human scum'. Michael Billington drew an analogy between Anne and Eva Smith, the dead girl in J.B. Priestley's *An Inspector Calls* (see p. 12) – not a 'character' but the catalyst for an anti-materialist understanding of the world.

①

1990–99

AFTERLIFE

The earliest revivals were in Europe, where the play's radical originality was embraced at once; it has been translated into twenty languages. It is now widely studied and frequently produced in Anglophone universities too. Most recently it was revived by Katie Mitchell at the National Theatre in 2007. This high-tech production filled the stage with lights, cameras and video screens that were operated by the cast; screens above the stage showed the action using a huge variety of film techniques; Anne was, literally, constructed afresh every night for the audience. Mitchell's cast were given the freedom to develop their work as they chose, and she ensured that they were billed with her as directing the production. Crimp's experiment with unattributed dialogue had a wide influence. Sarah Kane was greatly moved by it and her last two plays, *Crave* and *4.48 Psychosis*, shifted away from character and narrative, with the latter an 'open text' like Crimp's. Simon Stephens also developed *Pornography* (see p. 210) as fragmented scenes without a narrative order.

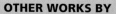

OTHER WORKS BY
Martin Crimp
The Treatment (1993)
The Country (2000)
The City (2008)

SEE ALSO
An Inspector Calls (1945)
by J.B. Priestley
Pornography (2007)
by Simon Stephens

The Censor

WRITTEN BY
Anthony Neilson (1967–)

DIRECTED BY
Anthony Neilson

DESIGNED BY
Julian McGowan

- First performed at the Finborough Theatre, London, 1 April 1997.

① Miss Fontaine (Jan Pearson) and the Censor (Alastair Galbraith), Royal Court at the Duke of York's, 1997.
© *Victoria and Albert Museum, London*

② Miss Fontaine (Jan Pearson) and the Censor (Alastair Galbraith), Royal Court at the Duke of York's, 1997.
© *Victoria and Albert Museum, London*

③ The Wife (Alison Newman) and the Censor (Alastair Galbraith), Royal Court at the Duke of York's, 1997.
© *Victoria and Albert Museum, London*

SNAPSHOT

The Censor examines attitudes to sex, pornography and censorship through a series of encounters between the Censor and Fontaine, writer/director of a pornographic film he is assessing, interspersed with scenes of his home life. The opening echoes a porn film, with Fontaine standing in her bra in the Censor's office. But instead of interminable sex scenes with lame dialogue, the audience is confronted with passionate discussion about the nature of art and sex. When Fontaine touches the Censor sexually, she makes Sherlock Holmes-style deductions about his marriage and his insecurities; she claims his belief that sex and love are necessarily linked is too narrow, and that sexuality is 'the most sophisticated level of interaction attainable'. She exposes the reason for his impotence, his belief that his sexual fantasies are disgusting, and fulfils them therapeutically. Later, he reads of her murder, and weeps.

IMPACT

Like Liz Lochhead, Neilson grew up when theatre group 7.84 was making a major impact on Scottish theatre and the intimate spaces of fringe theatre are the natural home of his work. *The Censor* was his fourth play at the Finborough Theatre, an important centre for new writing throughout the decade. Identified as part of the 'in-yer-face' movement for his graphic images, Neilson believes theatre should have a 'very direct, very basic force'. *The Censor* bears witness to this, confronting the audience with explicit images (including masturbation and defecation). However, it has a rare optimism about the possibility of change in attitudes to sex and power, and the education of an authority figure by someone he initially sees as inferior is handled with the gentle comedy of Willy Russell's *Educating Rita*. The Censor struggles to see the 'subtext' behind Fontaine's film are both satirical, puncturing critical pretension and censorship bureaucracy, and a tenderly comic indication of his growing desire for Fontaine. *The Censor* also has some witty and reasonable arguments. 'Without censorship there'd be no allegory, no metaphor, no restraint – I mean – *Brief Encounter* is a story about two lovers, but you don't have to see Trevor Howard's penis thrusting in and out of Celia Johnson, do you?' The majority of critics found the Finborough Theatre production touching and humane, with praise for Alastair Galbraith as the Censor and Jan Pearson as Fontaine. When it transferred to the Royal Court, which was still based in the West End at this time. It went to the Duke of York's theatre in June, and then the Ambassadors theatre later, in September. The Ambassadors' reviews were mixed and there were some audience walkouts. However, even conservative newspapers continued to admire it, the *Daily Mail* describing it as 'a healing and finally tragic love story'.

AFTERLIFE

The play won the Writers' Guild Award for Best Fringe Play and a Time Out Live Award. It was revived on the London fringe in 2004 and at the Chapter Arts Centre in Cardiff in 2009, in response to an act of censorship. Neilson has continued to challenge audiences and theatrical forms with plays that combine naturalism with fantasy and that push the boundaries of acceptability. He directed the controversial RSC fiftieth anniversary season production of *Marat/Sade* (see p. 60).

OTHER WORKS BY
Anthony Neilson
Normal (1991)
The Wonderful World of Dissocia
(2004)
Realism (2006)

SEE ALSO
Collaborators (2011)
by John Hodge
Wastwater (2011)
by Simon Stephens

Closer

WRITTEN BY
Patrick Marber (1964–)

DIRECTED BY
Patrick Marber

DESIGNED BY
Vicki Mortimer

- First performed at the Cottesloe, National Theatre, London, 22 May 1997.

OTHER WORKS BY
Patrick Marber
Dealer's Choice (1995)
Howard Katz (2001)
After Miss Julie (staged 2003)

SEE ALSO
Betrayal (1978)
by Harold Pinter
Sexual Perversity in Chicago (1976)
by David Mamet

SNAPSHOT

Closer is an acid comedy of desire between four people. In its dance-like structure, we see the first and last meetings of every possible pairing. Larry and Dan compete over sophisticated Anna and exploit self-styled 'waif' Alice as a diversion or a consolation prize. At the end, Alice is dead, killed by a car in New York. The surviving three visit Postman's Park, the site of a memorial to ordinary people who died saving others; they discover that Alice took her name from one of the figures named there. They reflect that they hardly knew her; by now, they barely seem to know one another and each person leaves alone.

IMPACT

Patrick Marber worked as a stand-up comedian and also adapted *Miss Julie* by Strindberg for BBC2; both these aspects of his work are evident in *Closer*. He said his intention was 'to create something that has a formal beauty into which you can shove all this anger and fury'. The settings for the fast, fragmented and colloquial encounters are different in every scene; from a hospital to a strip club, they were realised on Vicki Mortimer's evocative set where discarded props from each scene piled up as carelessly as the characters discarded one another. The most striking innovation was Marber's use of the Internet. In a dark echo of Shakespeare's cross-dressing heroines, Dan, at home, pretends to be Anna and seduces Larry in a chat room called 'London Fuck'. While

Larry sits in his surgery in a doctor's white coat – occasionally breaking off the sexual chat to diagnose skin complaints – Dan-as-Anna brings herself to orgasm online with a 'oooooooooooooooooooooooooooo+)*^%$£*) £$%%%^^^%&&*&&*&((&*((£££'. A darker note to this practical joke is the way Dan steals some of Alice's phraseology to characterise his 'Anna'. Critics and audiences were instantly impressed with the sexy wit and Marber's snappy lines were widely quoted, especially Anna's speech about male attitudes to psychological baggage: 'They deny all knowledge of it … "They're in love" … they have none. Then … just as you're relaxing … a Great Big Juggernaut arrives … with their baggage. It Got Held Up'. As the play shifted into the bigger space of the Lyttleton, some critics expressed reservations. Despite its sharp observation of sex and power, the play did not bring new insights, like Sarah Kane or Martin Crimp, or open up new areas as Jonathan Harvey and Kevin Elyot had done. The high gloss insulated the characters from the rest of the world, and even Liza Walker's touching performance could not hide the lack of social context for Alice. However, as Dominic Dromgoole pointed out, the one-liners are as irresistible as the sweeties thrown from the stage at a pantomime: 'Nobody does it better than Marber'.

AFTERLIFE

Closer won four Best New Play awards and the New York Drama Critics' Circle award for best foreign play, and transferred to the West End and then Broadway. Audiences continued to respond to both the comedy and the savagery (there is an urban legend about a couple having sex in a theatre box). In 2004, it was made into a film starring Jude Law, Clive Owen – Marber's original Dan, now playing Larry – Natalie Portman and Julia Roberts. It has been staged in thirty countries and was revived at the National Theatre in 1999.

① Anna (Sally Dexter) and Dan (Clive Owen). © *Victoria and Albert Museum, London*

② Alice (Liza Walker) and Dan (Clive Owen). © *Victoria and Albert Museum, London*

The Weir

WRITTEN BY
Conor McPherson (1971–)

DIRECTED BY
Ian Rickson

DESIGNED BY
Rae Smith

- First performed at the Royal
Court Theatre Upstairs at the
Ambassadors, London,
4 July 1997.

SNAPSHOT

The Weir is an Irish ghost story with no ghosts. In Brendan's pub in Sligo, middle-aged mechanic Jack, his assistant Jim and businessman Finbar tell ghost stories to entertain a stranger – Valerie from Dublin, renting a property from Finbar and causing a stir in the small community. The stories initially come from local folklore, before going into the realm of more direct experience. Then Valerie tells her own story – not to compete, but because their willingness to raise the subjects of death and loss empowers her to talk about her young daughter who drowned while swimming. Valerie may, or may not, have heard her dead child's voice on the phone, but it is clear that she is painfully stuck in grief, and her sense that her daughter 'still needs me' is making her marriage difficult and her life lonely. As Brendan closes up for the night, Jack tells a different kind of story, about a stranger's simple act of kindness when he was at a low ebb.

IMPACT

This was a fertile period for new writing at the Royal Court and one of the elements in it was a strain of Irish drama, including plays by Martin McDonagh, Sebastian Barry and later, from the north, Gary Mitchell. McPherson's play eased a difficult transitional period for the Court; Ian Rickson re-directed it more than a dozen times. Its phenomenal success took everyone by surprise, and the *Daily Express* described it as 'a modern masterpiece'. It tapped into a market for ghost plays created by Stephen Mallatratt's adaptation of Susan Hill's novel, *The Woman in Black* (as of 2012, in its twenty-third year in the West End). *The Weir*, however, is rooted more solidly in contemporary reality. As the stories unfold, we see a community haunted by an awareness of child abuse, where lives are hard and lonely and the population is ebbing away to the city. The very thought of Valerie brings out in the men a mix of chauvinism and awe, born of a long-term lack of female

1990–99

company. They are freed by her into a more gentle and truthful mode, while she is liberated from the loneliness of her grief. At Stephen Daldry's suggestion, the pub setting became the environment for the audience too, and, like the performers, they sat on stage, in a carefully replicated Irish bar. They often responded emotionally, both to the well told (if not necessarily truthful) tales of the men and the stark experience of Valerie.

AFTERLIFE

The Weir transferred from the Theatre Upstairs at the Ambassadors to the 600-seat Duke of York's under the Court's aegis; a commercial production at the same theatre followed, and it toured the UK before opening on Broadway. It won four awards, including an Olivier for Best New Play, and was voted one of the 100 most significant plays of the twentieth century in the National Theatre millennium poll.

① Jim (Kieran Ahern), Finbar (Des McAleer), Brendan (Brendan Coyle), Jack (Jim Norton) and Valerie (Julia Ford), Royal Court at the Duke of York's, 1998. © *Victoria and Albert Museum, London*

② Jack (Jim Norton). © *Victoria and Albert Museum, London*

③ Valerie (Julia Ford), Jack (Jim Norton) and Brendan (Brendan Coyle). © *Victoria and Albert Museum, London*

OTHER WORKS BY
Conor McPherson
This Lime Tree Bower (1995)
Shining City (2004)
The Seafarer (2006)

SEE ALSO
The Woman in Black (1993)
by Susan Hill and Stephen Mallatrat
By the Bog of Cats (1998)
by Marina Carr

The Lonesome West

WRITTEN BY
Martin McDonagh (1970–)

DIRECTED BY
Garry Hynes

DESIGNED BY
Francis O'Connor

- First performed as part of the Leenane Trilogy at the Town Hall Theatre, Galway, Ireland, 10 June 1997.
- First performed in the UK as part of the Leenane Trilogy at the Royal Court Theatre Downstairs at the Duke of York's Theatre, London, 19 July 1997.

① Valene (Brian F. O'Byrne), Girleen (Dawn Bradfield) and Coleman (Maelíosa Stafford), Royal Court at the Duke of York's, 1997. © *Victoria and Albert Museum, London*

② Valene (Brian F. O'Byrne, lying down), Coleman (Maelíosa Stafford) and Girleen (Dawn Bradfield), Royal Court at the Duke of York's, 1997. © *Victoria and Albert Museum, London*

SNAPSHOT

The Lonesome West is a black comedy of sibling rivalry set in Leenane, a small village in Galway. As the play begins, brothers Coleman and Valene, foul in thought, word and deed, return from their father's funeral. They are accompanied by the kindly, whiskey-sodden priest, Father Welsh, and visited by Girleen, a teenager they fancy but who loves Father Welsh. Eventually, Coleman declares outright to Welsh that he shot his father and the avaricious Valene agreed to pretend it was accidental in return for Coleman's share of the inheritance. Their callousness drives Welsh to suicide; his last note pleads with them to confess their crimes to each other. Enjoying this idea, they commence a passive/aggressive duel of apologies culminating, inevitably, in violence.

IMPACT

The play concludes McDonagh's Leenane Trilogy – major hit *The Beauty Queen of Leenane*, *A Skull in Connemara* and *The Lonesome West* – a triple success for the Royal Court. Fast on the heels of Conor McPherson's contemplative, melancholy *The Weir* (see p. 174), MacDonagh presented a very different Ireland: a dysfunctional community of murderous, delusional, lonely drunks, sketched in broad, garish cartoon strokes. Critics enjoyed spotting the literary pastiche: McDonagh

exuberantly rips off Sam Shepard's sibling-rivalry play, *True West*, the Bible story of Cain and Abel, and (not for the first time in the trilogy) the most famous Irish play of all, J.M. Synge's tale of a lad who boasts of killing his father, *The Playboy of the Western World*. The mix works because, like Joe Orton, MacDonagh constructs a world through language. The rhythms and turns of phrase are those of Galway, but, although the environment initially seems timeless, the characters' talk is shot through with allusions to the children's game Ker-Plunk, *Take-a-Break* magazine, soap operas and half-digested world news. When Coleman vengefully crushes Valene's bargain bag of crisps 'to skitter', he whines, 'There's Bosnians'd be happy to have them Taytos'. However, comedy is challenged by the death of Father Welsh, knowing his parishioners' true violence but recognising that 'betting on the horses and impure thoughts is all them bastards ever confess'. In David Ganly's performance, he was young and handsome, a credible love object for Girleen. This subtext of longing gave force to his suicide 'note', a monologue diagnosing the siblings' hatred as the product of 'a sad and lonesome existence'.

AFTERLIFE

The play is often compared unfavourably with *The Beauty Queen of Leenane*; McDonagh's style staled with familiarity. However, in opening up the theme of the church in decline, hinted at throughout the trilogy, McDonagh touched on some gentler human values. Watching the trilogy in a single day, Charles Spencer of the *Telegraph* regretted that McDonagh sacrificed these to a comic ending, and wished 'he had a heart as big as his talent'. The play won an Alfred Radok Award for Best Play and Brian F. O'Byrne got a Tony nomination for his toxic Valene. It transferred to Broadway in 1999. McDonagh continues to juxtapose the perception of rural Ireland as a bucolic backwater with outlandish tales of violence that provide a sugar rush of vicious amusement.

OTHER WORKS BY
Martin MacDonagh
The Beauty Queen of Leenane (1996)
The Lieutenant of Inishmore (2000)
The Pillowman (2003)

SEE ALSO
The Playboy of the Western World
(1907) by J.M. Synge
Flint (1970)
by David Mercer

Yard Gal

WRITTEN BY
Rebecca Prichard (1971–)

DIRECTED BY
Gemma Bodinetz

DESIGNED BY
Es Devlin

- First performed at the Royal Court Theatre, London, 7 May 1998.

OTHER WORKS BY
Rebecca Prichard
Essex Girls (1994)
Fair Game (1997)
Futures (2006)

SEE ALSO
Ashes and Sand (1994)
by Judy Upton
Gone Too Far! (2007)
by Bola Agbaje

SNAPSHOT

Yard Gal is a tragi-comic story of a girl gang in Hackney. Marie and Boo describe how they met, the members of their 'posse', and their criminal activities. The tales begin with a cocky account of how they got the better of the police, but gradually the tone gets darker, with the tragic death of their friend Deanne who falls from a tower block high on glue. Marie is stabbed in a fight, the gang disperses and Boo turns to prostitution and drugs. When they are reunited, Marie, who is pregnant, glasses a rival in a nightclub. Boo covers for her and ends up in prison. As they reach the end of their story, it is clear that their long-standing ('from time') friendship has not weathered the separation.

IMPACT

Rebecca Prichard wrote the play for Clean Break, a theatre company working with women in the criminal justice system (for whom Sarah Daniels has also done noteworthy work). While teaching creative writing at Bullwood Hall prison, she interviewed women about their lives and helped them devise their own pieces. She discovered that they 'created their own culture with both black and white elements in it' and used their Cockney-Caribbean language in *Yard Gal*. The extensive input of the women is reflected in the way the story-telling process constantly challenges the theatrical frame. Rather than giving 'case histories' that show them as passive victims of society, the girls present themselves as morally aware individuals with a complex relationship to their narrative. Telling it is both an obligation and a catharsis. They act the roles of their friends and their enemies with a wit and conviction that shows real understanding of their world, before ending in a display of childlike bravado as they try to outstare the audience, demanding 'Can we go?' Prichard had been profoundly affected by the reception of Sarah Kane's *Blasted* (see p. 160) and considered that 'plays should be about character and story to really land; that if an audience can switch off to the horror and "spectate" then you can't make your ideas land'. In *Yard Gal*, the ideas did land and the same critics who derided *Blasted* for indulging in 'an adolescent desire to shock' praised Prichard's 'unsentimental compassion'. There was universal praise for Sharon Duncan-Brewster as Boo and Amelia Lowdell as Marie.

AFTERLIFE

Prichard won the Critics' Circle Award for Most Promising Playwright. *Yard Gal* toured the country and was performed in prisons using Augusto Boal's technique of forum theatre, which allows the audience to suggest alternative courses of action for the characters and see the actors improvise accordingly. It went on to America, where the New York Times praised the cast for the 'biting, proprietary zest' with which they owned the distinctive language. It was revived at the Oval House in 2008 by the twenty-one-year-old Stef O'Driscoll, a production described by the *Evening Standard* as 'astonishing', and at the Albany in 2012. An experimental rather than prolific writer, Prichard has since written three plays. The most recent, *Dream Pill* – about two trafficked children – was presented in 2010 at the Soho Theatre as part of a project by Clean Break.

① Marie (Amelia Lowdell) and Boo (Sharon Duncan-Brewster). © *Victoria and Albert Museum, London*

② Boo (Sharon Duncan-Brewster, facing left) and Marie (Amelia Lowdell). © *Victoria and Albert Museum, London*

Copenhagen

WRITTEN BY
Michael Frayn (1933–)

DIRECTED BY
Michael Blakemore

DESIGNED BY
Peter J. Davison

- First performed at the Cottesloe, National Theatre, London, 21 May 1998.

SNAPSHOT

Copenhagen explores the nature of history, memory and ethics; after their deaths, Werner Heisenberg and his former mentor Niels Bohr re-create versions of their famous meeting of 1941 in Nazi-occupied Copenhagen, when Heisenberg was in charge of the German atomic energy research programme. Frayn's structure replicates the process of nuclear fission – each newly remembered event triggers a different reaction and therefore a different interpretation of the event and the motives behind it. In each re-enactment, Heisenberg's motives vary. He is working on atomic weapons for his country; or just building a reactor. He wants solutions to the problems his team encounter; he is trying to avoid those solutions in order to fail and prevent the development of a German bomb. He is seeking discussion on the ethics of the 'practical exploitation' of Bohr's groundbreaking work – or is it absolution? As the scientists debate and re-debate, Bohr's wife Margarethe acts as a human reference point and referee.

IMPACT

Frayn expresses the characters using a version of their own celebrated 'Copenhagen interpretation of quantum mechanics' – that is, particles behave differently when observed. Heisenberg's most famous contribution to this theory is the uncertainty principle, and this is the chief characteristic of his behaviour. In contrast, Bohr's theory of complementarity states how things can be, at one and the same time, the opposite of each other. This epitomises his character in the play, notably the way that, despite the fact that he contributed to the development of the bombs dropped on Hiroshima and Nagasaki, he manages to maintain the moral high ground. Each 'draft' of the meeting also includes an account of the drowning of Bohr's son Christian; each time with a glimmer of hope, but each time the ending is the same. Nothing can be un-done. The audience is the judge in this spiritual courtroom. At the National the audience sat around a bare circular stage furnished only with three chairs. Critical responses varied: some enjoyed the intellectual excitement (this was the most lucid explanation of the science since Ewan MacColl's *Uranium 235* (see p.. 14)); others admired the way that Frayn expressed the conflict in human terms; others had reservations about the fictionalisation of a controversial event.

AFTERLIFE

Copenhagen won five Best Play awards and transferred to the Duchess Theatre where it ran for two years. It opened on Broadway in 2000 and has had several revivals. In 2002, it was adapted as a television film, with Daniel Craig as Heisenberg and Stephen Rea as Bohr. Copenhagen re-established Frayn as a major British dramatist and was at the forefront of a new trend for 'faction' plays about real events, such as Lucy Prebble's *Enron* (see p. 218), over the next decade. The play marked a new departure for Frayn, best known in the theatre for his farce *Noises Off*. He subsequently wrote *Democracy*, about the German chancellor Willy Brandt, and *Afterlife*, about the impresario Max Reinhardt.

① Bohr (David Burke), Margrethe (Sara Kestelman) and Heisenberg (Matthew Marsh). © *Victoria and Albert Museum, London*

② Bohr (David Burke), Margrethe (Sara Kestelman) and Heisenberg (Matthew Marsh). © *Victoria and Albert Museum, London*

③ Bohr (David Burke) and Heisenberg (Matthew Marsh). © *Victoria and Albert Museum, London*

OTHER WORKS BY
Michael Frayn
Noises Off (1982)
Benefactors (1984)
Democracy (2003)

SEE ALSO
Uranium 235 (1946)
by Ewan MacColl
The Genius (1983)
by Howard Brenton

The Colour of Justice, the Stephen Lawrence Inquiry

SNAPSHOT

The Colour of Justice was the fourth of Tricycle Theatre's pioneering 'tribunal plays' – verbatim reconstructions of public inquiries. On 22 April 1993, Stephen Lawrence, an eighteen-year-old black student, was stabbed to death. Although it was clearly a racist murder, the police failed to bring successful charges against the prime suspects. Two were initially charged but the Crown Prosecution Service refused to continue the case for lack of evidence. The Lawrence family launched a private prosecution against three of the suspects, but the judge ruled vital evidence 'unreliable'. In the face of continued complaints about the conduct of the investigation, the Home Secretary called a public inquiry chaired by Sir William Macpherson. It lasted sixty-nine days and its report uncovered dubious police practice, racism, incompetence and corruption.

IMPACT

The Tricycle had established its reputation for groundbreaking verbatim work with *Half the Picture*, a dramatisation of the Scott Arms to Iraq Inquiry written by Norton-Taylor and John McGrath. *The Colour of Justice*, a distillation of over 11,000 pages of material, had a seismic impact. The *Financial Times* noted that it 'may change your view of the world'. Nicolas Kent's simple and uncluttered production preserved the witnesses' hesitations and awkwardness with the microphone recorded in the transcript. What emerged was the almost imperceptible way in which racism and corruption operate: not only the vile language of the suspects fantasising about mutilating black footballers but also the Police Inspector's assumption that the victim had been fighting; and the blank-faced DI writing off his dismissal of a vital witness with 'I was up to my eyeballs in other things'. One of the most moving performances came from Tim Woodward as a witness, Conor Taaffe, who admitted that his first response had been suspicion, not compassion, but went on to describe how his wife cradled Stephen's head and how he had later washed Stephen's blood from his own hands and poured the water onto a rose tree in his garden. This was not a traditional courtroom play; it could not have the dramatic conclusion of a verdict, but ended with a minute's silence in memory of Stephen Lawrence. The discussions that followed the play reflected how troubled the public were by the way in which law enforcement had failed him.

AFTERLIFE

The play transferred to the Theatre Royal Stratford East and then the West End; it toured extensively and appeared at the National Theatre before being shown on BBC2. In 2011, advances in forensic science and changes in the law made it possible to try two of the original suspects, Gary Dobson and David Norris, for murder. They were found guilty and sentenced respectively to a minimum of fifteen and fourteen years, terms that reflected their youth at the time of the killing. The judge made it clear that police should not regard the case as closed.

The Tricycle continued to produce tribunal plays and received a Liberty Human Rights Award in 2010. In 2011, Kent left after government cuts slashed more than forty per cent of the Tricycle's budget.

1990–99

WRITTEN BY
Richard Norton-Taylor (1944–)

DIRECTED BY
Nicolas Kent with Surian Fletcher-Jones

DESIGNED BY
Bunny Christie

- First performed at the Tricycle Theatre, London, 6 January 1999.

① Facing: Sir William Macpherson (Michael Culver) and Asst. Commissioner Ian Johnston (Tim Woodward). © *Victoria and Albert Museum, London*

② Sir William Macpherson (Michael Culver) and Jamie Acourt (Christopher Fox). © *Victoria and Albert Museum, London*

③ Jamie Acourt (Christopher Fox). © *Victoria and Albert Museum, London*

OTHER WORKS BY
Richard Norton-Taylor
Half the Picture (1994)
with John McGrath
Nuremberg (1996)
Justifying War (2003)

SEE ALSO
Sus (1979)
by Barrie Keeffe
Fallout (2003)
by Roy Williams

Mnemonic

WRITTEN BY
Complicité

DIRECTED BY
Simon McBurney

DESIGNED BY
Michael Levine

• First performed at the Lawrence Batley Theatre, Huddersfield, 24 June 1999.

① Katrin Cartlidge and Simon McBurney, Riverside Studios, 1999. © *Victoria and Albert Museum, London*

② Katrin Cartlidge and Catherine Schaub Abkarian, Riverside Studios. © *Victoria and Albert Museum, London*

③ Simon McBurney (lying on table) and the Company, Riverside Studios, 1999. © *Victoria and Albert Museum, London*

SNAPSHOT

Mnemonic explores our experience of dislocation, from our ancestors and from our sense of a future generation. Combining physical theatre, documentary, lecture and psychotherapy, it interweaves stories from different points in time and space: that of Virgil's love affair with Alice, who leaves him and crosses Europe to learn about her father (who may, or may not, be a Lithuanian Jew who played piano), and that of the Neolithic man found in a glacier on the Austro-Italian border in 1991. Everyone Alice meets, from taxi drivers to Jewish tourists seeking their past in Auschwitz, feels cut off from 'home'. Connectedness must be achieved through will: Alice phones Virgil to say she has failed to find the truth and can't come home; he tells her, 'Imagine'.

IMPACT

Complicité (originally Théâtre de Complicité) named themselves in honour of their original teachers in Paris, mime artists Jacques Lecoq and Philippe Gaulier. While they are based in Britain and their style uses European traditions in a unique, playful and popular way, they have toured the world as their reputation has grown. *Mnemonic* represents the input of at least fifty named individuals to this constantly evolving show. It begins with the smashing of boundaries. The director, Simon McBurney, playing himself, asks the audience to hold a leaf, put on a blindfold and explore how memory works on objects to re-create a personal past; then to visualise all the ancestors to whom they are connected. Surreptitiously, this combination of lecture and stand-up comedy transforms itself. While the blindfolds are on, the 'director' is replaced with his own recorded voice, to which McBurney listens in his new role, Virgil. The high-tech trickery is matched by an imaginative use of purely physical skill: McBurney lies naked on a table, playing both Virgil and the corpse; around him, Alice makes love to a man she meets in Europe – or is Virgil imagining it? Scenes of the scientific examination of the Neolithic Ice Man and the fragments of wood, ash and grass offering clues to his life touch, like Tom Stoppard's *Arcadia* (see p. 148), on chaos theory and the

interconnectedness of all things. Here the idea is physicalised as the cast collectively create and operate a puppet version of the Ice Man. Eventually, each of them in turn adopts the position of his naked body in its museum case, because, ultimately, they, and we, are all linked to him by blood. Continuously rolling into the place of the Ice Man in an acrobatic chain, they reiterate that the body itself, the one thing all humans share, constitutes our real home.

AFTERLIFE

Mnemonic has won ten international awards. It has also been performed on Radio 3. There have been two major revivals, in 2001 and 2002–3. Its 2003 appearance at the Riverside Theatre, marking the company's twentieth anniversary, drew a tribute from Charles Spencer in the *Telegraph*: 'I cannot think of a more imaginative, enthralling or moving devised show than this. Only the work of Robert Lepage runs it close'. Their work has informed that of other companies but remains unique. As Peter Brook says, Complicité 'have created their own tradition, and this is why they are so special'.

OTHER WORKS BY
Complicité
Street of Crocodiles (1992)
The Elephant Vanishes (2003)
A Disappearing Number (2007)

SEE ALSO
Far Side of the Moon (2000)
by Robert Lepage
Faster (2003)
by Filter and Stephen Brown

2000–10

The noughties were a riotous decade. Theatre proliferated in every direction, in form and location. The newly established National Theatres of Scotland and Wales decided they could do without buildings and staged shows in drill halls, nightclubs, army training camps and city centres. In the tunnels under the Old Vic as well as in its auditorium, outside the National Theatre, in abandoned factories, warehouses, forests and railway arches, audiences watched physical theatre, documentary drama, plays with songs and plays with puppets. The decade began well, with a £25 million injection of cash into the theatre economy in recognition of years of under-funding, and ended badly, with the Arts Council being forced into more cuts.

In the face of this turbulent future, British theatre continued to show its ability to respond to world events and also provide an escape from them. The wars in Iraq and Afghanistan provided the impetus for Gregory Burke's *Black Watch* and many other plays, while the effects of the 'war on terror' in the UK were discussed in Simon Stephens' *Pornography*, set on 7/7, and Richard Bean's *England People Very Nice*. Elsewhere, the same themes recurred. Corporate greed, previously explored in Howard Brenton and David Hare's *Pravda*, Caryl Churchill's *Serious Money* and Alan Ayckbourn's *The Revengers' Comedies*, was analysed in Lucy Prebble's *Enron*. Racism, starkly illustrated in Barrie Keeffe's *Sus*, David Edgar's *Destiny* and Richard Norton-Taylor's *The Colour of Justice*, was still an issue in Roy Williams' *Fallout*. More than 30 years after the abolition of the Lord Chamberlain's powers to control the content of plays, censorship was seen to be alive and well as public outcry closed Gurpreet Kaur Bhatti's *Behzti* and the National Theatre experienced its first stage invasion in protest against *England People Very Nice*.

The decade also saw an explosion of documentary and fact-based drama, which many saw as a response to a loss of faith in Britain's traditional sources of information and authority. The media, government and police had lost credibility in the wake of allegations of corruption and the spread of misinformation. Theatre held to account those in authority through its own investigations and reports on micro and macro-levels: David Hare and Out-of-Joint dramatised the history of corporate neglect that led to a spate of rail crashes in *The Permanent Way*, while *Black Watch* drew on the experiences of soldiers in Iraq, and Alecky Blythe interviewed prostitutes in Bournemouth to offer a glimpse into their lives.

It was a decade that not only saw the continuing success of established playwrights such as Alan Bennett and David Hare, but also witnessed younger playwrights lobbying for space on large-scale national stages. The Monsterist manifesto, written by a group including Richard Bean, Roy Williams and David Eldridge, demanded access to large spaces (rather than being consigned to small studios), large casts and equality with dead writers in terms of visibility and allocation of resources. Visibility and allocation of resources were also on the agenda at the Eclipse Theatre Conference, where leading black and Asian practitioners gathered to establish a launch pad for their work. The efforts of both groups are evident in the plays selected here, but there is still a long way to go before our theatre achieves equality.

▶ Kenzie (Scott Fletcher) and Fraz (Jamie Quinn), *Black Watch*.
© *Manuel Harlan, Photographer*

Blue/Orange

WRITTEN BY
Joe Penhall (1967–)

DIRECTED BY
Roger Michell

DESIGNED BY
William Dudley

- First performed at the Cottesloe, National Theatre, London, 7 April 2000.

① Bruce (Andrew Lincoln), Christopher (Chiwetel Ejiofor) and Robert (Bill Nighy). © *Victoria and Albert Museum, London*

② Bruce (Andrew Lincoln), Christopher (Chiwetel Ejiofor) and Robert (Bill Nighy). © *Victoria and Albert Museum, London*

③ Robert (Bill Nighy) and Christopher (Chiwetel Ejiofor). © *Victoria and Albert Museum, London*

SNAPSHOT

This darkly comic play about the treatment of mental health follows a struggle between two doctors over Chris, a young black man who has been sectioned and diagnosed with Borderline Personality Disorder. Chris is due for release, but Bruce wants to extend his stay, believing him to be schizophrenic. He asks consultant Robert for a second opinion. Robert confirms the BPD diagnosis and says that Chris should be discharged. He justifies this with a persuasive mix of pragmatism and selfishness, claiming that it is 'fair and right and just and textbook medically beneficial. And apart from anything else we don't have the beds'. But he also wants evidence for his work on race and mental illness. Bruce nudges Chris into displaying the delusional tendencies that back up his schizophrenia diagnosis, including his conviction that oranges are blue and that Idi Amin is his father. Robert promptly suggests that Bruce's diagnosis is racist. Chris becomes a pawn in a power struggle between the medics. He is released into a 'community' and 'support' system we know to be non-existent.

IMPACT

The first production in the Cottesloe set the action in a boxing ring to fit the combative nature of the debate. Dudley's design emerged from a visit that he made with Roger Michell to Guy's Hospital: Chris is anatomised before the audience like a cadaver before students in the old lecture theatre. Andrew Lincoln and Bill Nighy as the psychiatrists were widely praised for their handling of plausible, contradictory arguments and for the comically competitive vulnerability beneath. The production launched the career of Chiwetel Ejiofor as Chris, who seemed to justify every diagnosis in turn yet remain an enigma. The exploration of Chris's background is a frightening gloss on the mental-health cliché of the period, 'care in the community'. It suggests a fractured society, people cut off from their families, the inability of state services to cope, police harassment, racist assaults and, for Chris, medication that 'will paralyse him from the skull downwards'. Penhall had already written several plays about mental health but this fusing of psychiatric issues, racial tension and political correctness, not to mention the raw fringe energy *Blue/Orange* brought to the National, caught the public imagination.

AFTERLIFE

The play won *Evening Standard*, Olivier and Critics' Circle awards; Chiwetel Ejiofor won an *Evening Standard* Award for Outstanding Newcomer and went on to success in Hollywood. The original cast transferred with the show to the Duchess Theatre in the West End in 2001 for the first three months of its seven-and-a-half month run. It was made into a film in 2005 with Brian Cox, John Simm and Shaun Parkes, and revived by Kathy Burke at the Sheffield Crucible, also in 2005. It has been revived many times since, including an all-female version at the Arcola Theatre, Hackney.

①

2000–10

Far Side of the Moon

WRITTEN BY
Robert Lepage (1957–)

DIRECTED BY
Robert Lepage

DESIGNED BY
Robert Lepage with Ex Machina Theatre Company

- First performed at Le Théâtre du Trident, Québec City, 29 February 2000.
- First performed in the UK at the Lyttleton, National Theatre, London, 9 July 2001.

SNAPSHOT

Far Side of the Moon is a one-man show with the idea of travel at its heart. Two brothers – Philippe, a tubby loser about to get his PhD thesis on narcissism and space exploration failed for the third time, and his brother, gay, successful and apparently carefree TV presenter Andre – face a spiritual void after the death of their mother. Philippe tries to enlist support for his thesis from Alexey Leonov, the first man to walk in space, but waits in vain for him to keep their appointment in a bar. Then he makes a video for a competition organised by SETI (Search for Extra Terrestrial Intelligence), filming the minutiae of his life to explain it to another world. He gets an opportunity to fly to Moscow and deliver a paper but, receiving the news that his terminally ill mother took her own life, he is distraught and arrives only when the hall has emptied. On the phone, he and Andre reach an awkward peace over the death of their mother's goldfish and Philippe learns he has won the SETI competition. As the play ends, he flies in space.

IMPACT

Like Complicité's *Mnemonic* (see p. 184), *Far Side of the Moon* explores relationships between technology and loneliness, travel and interconnectedness. Lepage's association with the National began when he became the first North American to direct Shakespeare there with *A Midsummer Night's Dream* in 1992. This marked the beginning of a rich period at the National when Richard Eyre brought in a succession of innovative companies, like Kneehigh and Complicité, who explored all the elements of theatre – music, technology, movement and media. The set of *Far Side of the Moon* uses a series of sliding panels, constantly transforming the environment to let Lepage in his multiple roles evoke reality, or memory, or dream: a washing machine door becomes a space capsule and also the birth canal through which Andre, a puppet in a tiny spacesuit, is born. A few lights suggest the achingly empty bar where Philippe tells an invisible barman his question for Leonov, 'How do you manage to reconcile the infinitely banal with the infinitely essential?' The answer,

it seems, lies in the way theatre creates magic from the everyday. As the actor moves on the ground, an arrangement of mirrors allows us to see Philippe floating weightless in space like an astronaut, to the haunting music written for the play by Laurie Anderson. Lepage once said that he felt pessimistic about the art of film but very optimistic about the art of theatre. *Far Side of the Moon* combines the resources of film with the simplicity of a barebones theatre that depends for its effects on pure performance skill. Audiences responded with excitement to the imaginative links Lepage created between the majesty of space exploration and a simple human story. As Lyn Gardner put it in the *Guardian*, it's 'like discovering that the party conjuror is actually a real magician'.

AFTERLIFE

In 2001, the play won the *Evening Standard* Theatre Award for Best Play and the London Critics' Circle Theatre Award for Best Director. It was made into a film in 2003. It has continued to tour the world, with the actor Yves Jacques.

① Phillipe (Robert Lepage). © *Sophie Grenier, Photographer*

② Mom (Robert Lepage). © *Sophie Grenier, Photographer*

③ Phillipe (Robert Lepage. © *Sophie Grenier, Photographer*

OTHER WORKS BY
Robert Lepage
The Seven Streams of the River Ota (1994)
The Dragons' Trilogy (2003)
The Andersen Project (2005)

SEE ALSO
Krapp's Last Tape (1958)
by Samuel Beckett
Misterman (2011)
by Enda Walsh

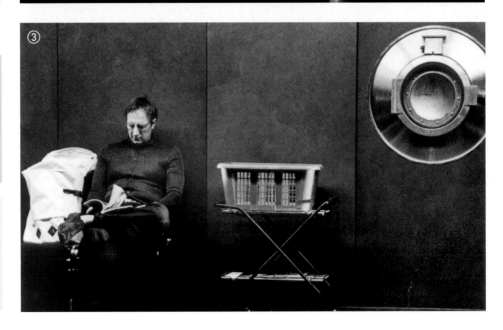

Elmina's Kitchen

WRITTEN BY
Kwame Kwei-Armah (1967–)

DIRECTED BY
Angus Jackson

DESIGNED BY
Bunny Christie

- First performed at the Cottesloe, National Theatre, London, 29 May 2003

SNAPSHOT

Deli is trying to make a living as an honest man running a West Indian takeaway on Hackney's murder mile, but Hackney won't let him. His nineteen-year-old son, Ashley, is desperate to follow in the footsteps of Deli's childhood friend, Digger, a gangster who conducts his business from the restaurant. For Deli, every day is a struggle in the battle to remain on the straight and narrow and keep Ashley there with him. The strong, sexy Anastasia comes to work in the restaurant and introduces a more positive atmosphere, making no secret of her disapproval of Digger and her attraction to Deli. Deli's brother is killed on his release from prison and Clifton, Deli's absentee father, returns for the funeral. Deli asks Digger not to talk about his business in the restaurant. Insulted, Digger takes Ashley into his gang and eventually demands protection money from Deli. Deli refuses to pay, leading to a standoff at gunpoint. Questioned by the police, Deli informs on Digger to save Ashley. Digger orders Ashley to shoot Deli and, as Ashley is about to do so, Digger shoots Ashley instead. Deli covers the body of his dead son and leaves the restaurant.

IMPACT

One of first new plays to be produced under Nicholas Hytner's tenure at the National, *Elmina's Kitchen* reflected another side of the nation. Kwei-Armah, a household name from long-running British TV series *Casualty*, thrust the issue of British black male identity and gang culture into a predominantly white, middle-class stronghold. As he stated in the programme note, 'I'm concerned about the rites of passage of black youths. Among a certain section of society, the badge of blackness is earned through the façade of criminality'. The critics were united in their praise for the play's clear-eyed dissection of the issues and its steady refusal to offer simplistic solutions; they also appreciated the vivid humour, the *Guardian* praising Kwei-Armah's language as 'peppery, poetic and full of wit', while Paterson Joseph received excellent notices as Deli.

AFTERLIFE

Kwei-Armah won the *Evening Standard*'s Most Promising Playwright Award. In 2005, he took over the role of Deli when the production transferred to the West End; he was only the second black British playwright to have a play staged there. He also adapted the play for television. First broadcast on BBC4 in 2005, it continued to be shown until 2008, earning Kwei-Armah a BAFTA nomination for his adaptation of the script.

① Deli (Kwame Kwei-Armah) and Clifton (Don Warrington), Garrick Theatre, 2005. © *Victoria and Albert Museum, London*

② Anastasia (Dona Croll) and Deli (Paterson Joseph). © *Victoria and Albert Museum, London*

③ Baygee (Oscar James) and Clifton (George Harris). © *Victoria and Albert Museum, London*

②

OTHER WORKS BY
Kwei-Armah
Fix Up (2004)
Let There Be Love (2008)
Seize the Day (2009)

SEE ALSO
Random (2008)
by debbie tucker green
Off the Endz (2010)
by Bola Agbaje

③

Fallout

WRITTEN BY
Roy Williams (1968–)

DIRECTED BY
Ian Rickson

DESIGNED BY
Ultz

- First performed at the Royal Court Theatre Downstairs, London, 12 June 2003.

① Emile (Marcel McCalla), Joe (Lennie James), Perry (O.T. Fagbenle), Dwayne (Michael Obiora) and Shanice(Ony Uhiara). © *Victoria and Albert Museum, London*

② Joe (Lennie James) and Emile (Marcel McCalla). © *Victoria and Albert Museum, London*

SNAPSHOT

Fallout explores racism and crime on the streets of south London. It begins with a gang of black teenagers kicking a schoolboy, Kwame, to death. The murderers are his ex-classmates, who despise him as an African and upwardly mobile; expelled from school, they hang around the estate occasionally committing crimes. The policemen investigating the murder have their own issues: Joe, a black officer from the estate, hates the glorification of gang culture, and Matt, white, is heavily influenced by the Macpherson Report on the death of Stephen Lawrence. While in Kwame Kwei-Armah's *Elmina's Kitchen* (see p. 192) women are powerfully resistant to the violence, here teenage Shanice is at its centre, a source of tension between her boyfriend Emile and gang leader Dwayne. Her claim that Kwame was 'sexing' her, a ploy to get Emile's attention ('Yu stop noticin me … yu made me lose faith, not juss in yu, but in me, man'), precipitated the murder, which now haunts Emile. With a mixture of motives, Ronnie, her clingy and jealous friend, tells the police she witnessed the murder. Desperate for a conviction, Joe coaches Ronnie but she collapses under questioning. The gang breaks up; Kwame's murder goes unpunished and Joe's career is in tatters.

IMPACT

The play was a response to the death of Nigerian schoolboy Damilola Taylor at the hands of twelve- and thirteen-year-old members of a predominantly black British gang in Peckham. Williams noted, 'I remember following the Damilola Taylor case, and the feelings that I had. Anger with the killers, anger with whoever had let those kids down. I felt it was important as well as necessary to write a piece that allowed all my feelings, and the feelings of those kids and police to be expressed'. Williams' teenagers are volatile; their preoccupation with sex and status provides some comic moments, but also horrifying ones. When Shanice refuses Dwayne's advances, he responds, 'I hope they rape yu up bad'. Williams' handling of the characters challenges the audience to re-think their perceptions. The girls mug the teacher who expelled them, but does her refusal to tolerate disruptive pupils mean she is responsible for what happens to them? The audience's role as arbiter of such questions was enhanced by Ultz's arena-like set. Rather than confining the action safely behind the proscenium arch, he created an oval surrounded by a wire fence, separating actors and audience by a cage. The stage represented the confinement of the estate, future confinement in prison and a space of judgement like that of Michael Frayn's *Copenhagen* (see p. 180); the sense of detachment was counterpointed by the extreme youth of the actors – Michael Obiora as Dwayne was only 16 – which stressed their vulnerability. The *Telegraph* considered it 'the most important play to emerge from [the Royal Court] since Sarah Kane's *Blasted* (see p. 160) and Mark Ravenhill's *Shopping and Fucking*' (see p. 162). However, some black critics saw it as confirming stereotypes. *Fallout* provided a focus for media debate on the allure of crime for young black men, alongside *Elmina's Kitchen* at the National.

AFTERLIFE

In 2008, Williams rewrote *Fallout* for *Disarming Britain*, a Channel 4 series on gun and knife crime, and in 2009 Nicholas Kent commissioned Williams, Kwei-Armah and Bola Agbaje to revisit the subject for the *Not Black and White Season* at the Tricycle.

①

2000–10

The Permanent Way

WRITTEN BY
David Hare (1947–)

DIRECTED BY
Max Stafford-Clark

DESIGNED BY
William Dudley

- First performed at the York Theatre Royal, 13 November 2003.

OTHER WORKS BY
David Hare
The Absence of War Trilogy: Racing Demon, Murmuring Judges, The Absence of War (1989–1993)
Skylight (1995)
Stuff Happens (2004)

SEE ALSO
The Laramie Project (2000)
by Moisés Kaufman
The Riots (2011)
by Gillian Slovo

SNAPSHOT

The Permanent Way is a documentary drama about four major railway crashes that occurred in the wake of post-privatisation restructuring of British Rail: at Southall, where the driver had not been trained to use the warning system; at Ladbroke Grove, where the signal was known to be unclear; at Hatfield, when a rail broke; and at Potter's Bar, where the nuts holding the points came loose. The play begins on an almost comic note with a series of customer complaints. It continues with the Civil Service and the Treasury, painfully aware that they are creating a potentially chaotic new system 'like beads thrown on a table', and goes on to introduce railway workers and policemen. Finally, it becomes a study in grief, showing survivors and the bereaved negotiating a fragile relationship; the Potter's Bar crash is described by two survivors, Nina, whose husband was killed, and the man who helped her.

IMPACT

The play has much in common with 'tribunal plays' such as Richard Norton-Taylor's *The Colour of Justice* (see p. 182). It also reflects the working practices of theatre company Joint Stock founded by Hare, David Aukin and Max Stafford-Clark in 1974, whose actors would do extensive research and conduct interviews before a play such as Caryl Churchill's *Serious Money* (see p. 136) was created. Stafford-Clark commissioned Hare to compose *The Permanent Way* for his touring company Out of Joint after reading Ian Jack's *The Crash That Stopped Britain*. The script was grounded in interviews conducted by the actors. These are sometimes used verbatim, including a statement from a bereaved mother of which Hare said 'D.H.

Lawrence couldn't write that'. Hare's main concern was to efface any sense of authorship from the script – 'The illusion is that I'm not present'. Over the previous decade, he had composed a trilogy of state-of-the-nation plays for the National, and more intimate pieces such as *Amy's View*; *The Permanent Way* returns to the documentary style of his first Joint Stock piece about the Chinese Revolution, *Fanshen*, in 1975. *The Permanent Way* is about honour – of the survivors and the bereaved who would not accept easy excuses – and dishonour – of the companies putting profit before safety and of both the Major and Blair governments for letting them do so. Reviewers and post-show discussions warmed to the theme, with Nicolas de Jongh describing his response in the *Evening Standard* as 'pure fury ... I intend a compliment'. The most shocking line in the play is spoken by a Senior Operating Executive from GNER, a concerned individual still dealing with the flak from an earlier incident. Told that the Hatfield crash has been caused by a broken rail, his response is 'Thank Christ it's not us'.

AFTERLIFE

Out of Joint's policy was to seek out audiences who might not usually go to a theatre. York was chosen as the opening venue because of its long association with railways, and the play toured to a variety of venues all over the country, including working men's clubs. It played the National Theatre in 2004 (at the Cottesloe and then the Lyttleton), Hare's twelfth play to be staged there. It was also adapted for radio and broadcast on BBC Radio 3. The production won the Theatre Management Association Award for Best Touring Production in 2004.

Ian Redford, and Souad Faress. *Photo by John Haynes,*
© John Haynes/Lebrecht Music & Arts

The History Boys

WRITTEN BY
Alan Bennett (1934–)

DIRECTED BY
Nicholas Hytner

DESIGNED BY
Bob Crowley

- First performed at the Lyttleton, National Theatre, London, 18 May 2004.

OTHER WORKS BY
Alan Bennett
Forty Years On (1968)
Talking Heads (1992)
The Habit of Art (2009)

SEE ALSO
Class Enemy (1978)
by Nigel Williams
Punk Rock (2009)
by Simon Stephens

SNAPSHOT

The History Boys is a comedy about a group of sixth formers and the battle between their charismatic teachers over the purpose of education – should it produce rounded individuals or get exam results? Eccentric Hector – whose tendency to grope the boys is taken for granted – takes the former view: his classes freewheel from French improvisations (the Headmaster interrupts a brothel scene where desire must be expressed in the subjunctive) to poems learnt for spiritual solace in later life. Irwin, the supply teacher brought in to improve the boys' chances of going to Oxbridge, demands snappy essays arguing a minority view for effect; there's a blazing row when as a result one boy downplays the Holocaust. Meanwhile, the boys navigate their way through A-Levels and a burgeoning desire for sex.

IMPACT

Bennett's long and productive working relationship with Nicholas Hytner had already resulted in several stage and movie successes, including *The Madness of George III*. Bennett called *The History Boys* 'an expiation' for his own slick approach to exams in the 1950s, but its subject resonated with audiences. While plays such as Roy Williams' *Fallout* (see p. 194) examined the failure of education for the underclass and the consequent poverty and crime, Bennett's – although a light-hearted piece set in the 1980s – concentrated on the psychic cost of the current government panacea, a target-based education policy. At the end, which is set in the present, none of the boys has really fulfilled his promise. It proved Bennett's most successful play ever, with extremely positive reviews and full houses. Some dissenting voices felt that Bennett had dismissed the question of abuse with a few brisk assurances that Hector's fumblings are 'more appreciative than investigatory', and that he idealised both the intellectual standards of the sixth form and their capacity for sexual tolerance. Hector's most enthusiastic adherent, Posner, for example, laments 'I'm a Jew. I'm small. I'm homosexual. And I live in Sheffield. I'm fucked', but experiences no intolerance, merely unrequited love for fellow pupil Dakin. If there is an element of fantasy about Bennett's sixth form, however, it offered an attractive image of education as intellectual adventure. There was universal praise for the sparky and intelligent young cast, for whom the experience created a kind of university environment. Most of them went on to major success, including James Corden, Russell Tovey and Dominic Cooper.

AFTERLIFE

The play won six Best Play awards. It toured extensively for four years and went to Broadway. It continues to be extensively revived in the UK, America and Australia. In 2006 it was made into a film, directed by Nicholas Hytner, featuring the original stage cast.

① Posner (Sam Barnett), Dakin (Dominic Cooper), Rudge (Russell Tovey), Lockwood (Andrew Knott) and Akthar (Sacha Dhawan). © *Victoria and Albert Museum, London*

② Hector (Richard Griffiths), Mrs Lintott (Frances de la Tour) and Irwin (Stephen Campbell Moore). © *Victoria and Albert Museum, London*

③ Posner (Sam Barnett), Lockwood (Andrew Knott, back row), Dakin (Dominic Cooper), Crowther (Samuel Anderson, back row) and Timms (James Corden). © *Victoria and Albert Museum, London*

Behzti (Dishonour)

WRITTEN BY
Gurpreet Kaur Bhatti

DIRECTED BY
Janet Steel

DESIGNED BY
Matthew Wright

- First performed at the Birmingham Repertory Theatre, 9 December 2004.

OTHER WORKS BY
Bhatti
Behud (2010)

SEE ALSO
Jerry Springer the Opera (2003)
by Richard Thomas and Stewart Lee
England People Very Nice (2009)
by Richard Bean

SNAPSHOT

Behzti, a dark family comedy, centres on ailing widow Balbir and her thirty-year-old daughter Min. Min has a tentative relationship with Balbir's black care assistant Elvis, but Balbir worries that her daughter is losing her bloom. At the gurdwara – the temple – she arranges for Min to meet Mr Sandhu, chairman of the Gurdwara Renovation Committee and local wheeler-dealer, so he can find her a husband. Sandhu reveals to Min that he had a homosexual relationship with her father, who killed himself. Overcome by Min's resemblance to the man he loved, he rapes her. She staggers onstage bleeding. Sandhu offers to marry her. Balbir is briefly gratified by this prestigious match; her friends only then reveal that Sandhu is an habitual rapist, who also abused them. Enraged at the conspiracy of silence, Balbir kills Sandhu with a kirpan, a sacred sword. The lights go down on mother, daughter and carer, a shattered family.

① Balbir (Shelley King), Polly (Pooja Kumar), Min (Yasmin Wilde), Teetee (Harvey Virdi), Background; Mr Sandhu (Madhav Sharma). © *Robert Day, Photographer*

② Polly (Pooja Kumar), Balbir (Shelley King). © *Robert Day, Photographer*

IMPACT

At a private preview, local leaders objected to the setting in the gurdwara and the use of sacred objects; they asked if the action of the play could be shifted to a community centre. Bhatti refused on the grounds that Sandhu is the chief builder of the temple and his office there is the centre of his power. On 18 December, 400 people stormed the theatre; a weekend of violence erupted, causing thousands of pounds' worth of damage. The theatre was forced to cancel and the playwright fled into hiding following death threats. The resulting debate was bitter and prolonged. This was by no means the only clash between religious traditionalism and theatre during the decade (Richard Thomas and Stewart Lee's *Jerry Springer: the Opera* was barracked by Christian groups, for instance) but, as Asian playwright Ash Kotak pointed out in the *Guardian*, the 'swirl of prejudice' encountered by all Asians, regardless of religion, since 9/11 had generated understandable sensitivity. A letter supporting Bhatti's right to free speech was signed by 700 figures in the arts, including Ayub Khan-Din, Willy Russell and Prunella Scales. The furore involved far more people than had seen the play and tended to eclipse critical response to it. The Social Affairs Unit published a long web article by Christie Davies – based on the script, not the performance – alluding to Bhatti's work on *EastEnders* and describing the play's conclusion as 'truly batty'. Helen Cross in the *Birmingham Post*, however, considered it 'terrific ... offensive, and furious and bloodthirsty and angry in all the right places'.

AFTERLIFE

Short-listed before its brief run began, *Behzti* won the 2005 Susan Smith Blackburn prize and was staged abroad. However, it was not until 2010 that Bhatti's next play, *Behud*, was performed, at the Belgrade Theatre, Coventry and at the Soho Theatre, which also staged the first English revival of *Behzti* with many of the original cast. It was a low-key event, which passed quietly. In *Behud*, a writer struggles to accommodate community leaders, councillors and an excitable director. Her characters mutiny and sack her, but she picks up her pen and continues writing. Bhatti expressed relief that *Behzti* had found some sort of outlet; she hoped it might eventually achieve a full production and the debate might carry (amicably) on.

①

Nights At The Circus

ADAPTED BY
Tom Morris and Emma Rice from the novel by Angela Carter

DIRECTED BY
Emma Rice

DESIGNED BY
Bill Mitchell and Vicki Mortimer

• First performed at the Lyric Hammersmith, London, 20 January 2006.

SNAPSHOT

Nights at the Circus adapts Angela Carter's magic realist novel through Kneehigh's trademark physical theatre. It is the end of the nineteenth century and a new age is dawning. Journalist Jack Walser is investigating the celebrity of the day, Fevvers, a beautiful trapeze artiste with real wings. Mesmerised by Fevvers and her story about her upbringing in a brothel, Walser joins the circus to be near her. Fevver's dresser and adoptive mother Lizzie doesn't trust him. The chief clown turns him into a comedy chicken. He rescues the clown's brutalised mistress, Mignon, from a tiger, only to get beaten up by the clown and her lover the Strong Man. Then he is slapped down by a jealous Fevvers and made to dance with a female tiger. The circus heads for disaster as the tiger goes wild, the Strong Man shoots the clown, and Lizzie defends Fevvers from a scalpel-wielding wing-collector with the bomb she keeps in her handbag. But they pick themselves up and Fevvers announces she will make Jack 'a fitting mate for the new woman, and we'll march onward hand in hand through the New Century'.

IMPACT

Emma Rice's manifesto for Kneehigh states, 'I want the world to transform in front of the audience's eyes and demand that they join in with the game' and the production used all the skills of physical theatre: music, on brass, accordion and washboard; puppetry, as Lizzie tenderly manipulates a puppet Fevvers in her first flying lesson; and, above all, trapeze, in a wildly fearless aerial display as Fevvers and Jack express their love. Gísli Örn Gardarsson, the circus-trained international gymnast whose charming accent made Carter's American newshound into an Icelander, and Natalia Tena, whose Fevvers was described by Carter's friend Susannah Clapp as 'radiant', both received high praise; reviews responded not only to the show's visual beauty but also to its lively and sophisticated treatment of gender. Right from the outset when the actors make themselves up in the foyer, in tatty old-fashioned underwear with fake genitals roughly stitched to the outside, the message of the New Century is clear: you can be whatever you want to be. An elegant male impersonator in a tuxedo sings 'Die, old century die', and in the new world whores run seminars on feminism and battered women turn into beauties.

AFTERLIFE

Like a real circus, the play went on an extended tour, to consistently excellent reviews. It marked a watershed in the life of the company. Based in Cornwall and working closely as a group, they had long been known for their dark and surreal treatment of old stories. Carter's novel was the first modern text to receive their unique treatment. Its success led to explorations of other works that had rooted themselves in the popular imagination, such as Noël Coward's *Brief Encounter* and Michael Powell and Emeric Pressburger's film *A Matter of Life and Death* at the National Theatre.

① Fevvers (Natalia Tena). *Victoria and Albert Museum, London*

② Ma Nelson (Amanda Lawrence), Fevvers (Natalia Tena) and A Creature of the Theatre (Andy Williams). © *Victoria and Albert Museum, London*

③ Ma Nelson (Amanda Lawrence), Fevvers (Natalia Tena), A Creature of the Theatre (Andy Williams) and Walser (Gisli Örn Gardarsson). © *Victoria and Albert Museum, London*

OTHER WORKS BY
Kneehigh
The Red Shoes (2000)
Tristan and Yseult (2005)
Brief Encounter (2008)

SEE ALSO
New Anatomies (1981)
by Timberlake Wertenbaker
Playhouse Creatures (1993)
by April de Angelis

Black Watch

WRITTEN BY
Gregory Burke (1968–)

DIRECTED BY
John Tiffany

DESIGNED BY
Laura Hopkins (set) and Jessica Brettle (costumes)

- First performed at the Edinburgh University Drill Hall as part of the Edinburgh Festival, 5 August 2006.

① Macca (Cameron Barnes). © *Manuel Harlan, Photographer*

② On the right Fraz (Jamie Quinn). © *Manuel Harlan, Photographer*

①

SNAPSHOT

This is the story, told by themselves, of soldiers from the Black Watch regiment sent to support the Americans in Iraq's 'triangle of death'. It is also the story of the regiment, threatened as part of a military economy drive. It opens with a flourish of bagpipe and drum before the narrator, Cammy, saunters on in civvies, explaining, 'I didnay want tay day this'. He and others from the regiment describe their experience to a naive writer in a pub. Flashbacks arise spectacularly out of the set, the pool table splitting as Fraz and Kenzie emerge from it in combat dress. In one scene, 'Fashion', Cammy narrates the history of the regiment while the squad dress him in a variety of period uniforms, an elaborate military manoeuvre rather like assembling a gun carriage. The men express scepticism and rage about their situation, Stewarty threatening to break the arm of the writer who bleats 'what was it like?' Early on, Alex Salmond, leader of the Scottish National Party, is heard on the radio responding to a suicide attack that killed three members of the regiment and their interpreter. Towards the end, Fraz, Kenzie, the Sergeant and their interpreter die that way; three bodies fly in agonizingly slow motion towards Cammy and the others. The final scene is a parade to bagpipes, the men drilling until they fall, but always helping one other to rise and carry on.

IMPACT

The original performance was described by the *Observer* as 'a high point not just of the festival but of the theatrical year'. The high-octane theatricality and the contrast between the wild violence and the disciplined drills made an instant impact on the audience. Critics were divided over the lack of analysis from the Iraqi point of view – 'I thought it was about our story?' says Stewarty when this is raised – but most found it refreshing to see a play about soldiers that treated them as intelligent, capable of making moral choices and aware of history. However, there were no illusions about the legal status of the war and a clear anger at what Alex Salmond called the political 'chicanery' that led to their deployment in order to free up US troops for an attack on Falluja in time for the presidential election.

AFTERLIFE

On 6 June 2007, Alex Salmond, now First Minister, asked Vicky Featherstone, artistic director of the National Theatre of Scotland, to stage the play to mark the opening of the Scottish Parliament on 30 June. Three performances were given: one for veterans, one for the public and one for MSPs. The event shows the status the play had acquired, not just as spectacular drama but also as a symbol of Scotland. *Black Watch* continues to be a calling card for the National Theatre of Scotland and has been on perpetual tour of three continents since it opened in 2006. It has won numerous awards, including four out of the ten Critics' Awards for Theatre in Scotland (CATS) and the Award for Best Foreign Play from the New York Drama Critics' Circle, the NTS's first ever US award.

OTHER WORKS BY
Gregory Burke
Gagarin Way (2001)
The Straits (2003)
On Tour (2005)

SEE ALSO
The Long and the Short and the Tall (1959) by Willis Hall
Motortown (2006) by Simon Stephens

Generations

WRITTEN BY
debbie tucker green

DIRECTED BY
Sacha Wares

DESIGNED BY
Miriam Buether

- First performed at the Young Vic,
  Maria Studio, London,
  22 February 2007.

① Grandad (Louis Mahoney), Mother (Michele Austin)
and Grandma (Nomhle Nkonyeni). © *Victoria and Albert
Museum, London*

② Grandma (Nomhle Nkonyeni) and Junior Sister
(Davinia Anderson). © *Victoria and Albert Museum, London*

SNAPSHOT

Generations explores the impact of AIDS on a
South African family simply by replaying the
same scene with a diminishing number of
characters. As the play begins, a black South
African choir ranged around the space lament
a long list of the dead: 'another leaves us,
another has gone'. The action then switches
to the family kitchen where three generations
– grandparents, parents and children – are
discussing how each couple met, 'he asked her
if she could cook', and how the skill of cooking
was passed on. At the end of each scene, the
choir call a character to join them, signifying
their death. By the end, only the grandparents
remain. AIDS is never mentioned, but in the
last two repetitions of the scene, Grandmother
fleetingly mentions 'this big dying thing'.

IMPACT

'This runs for fewer than thirty minutes, but
will last you a lifetime,' noted Lyn Gardner
in the *Guardian*. The simple structure, like a
child's game where people are eliminated one
by one, affected all those who saw it. As the
same words were repeated each time, their
meaning shifted. The cheerful family comedy,
full of flirtation and teasing, was replaced with
ever-increasing poignancy as the younger
characters were called away, a violation of
the natural order that the food and affection
had created. Moments of what tucker green
calls 'active silence' between the characters
indicated that they were at a loss to speak
of what was happening; even the most lively
words of the old people began to suggest that
they were repeating them as a kind of talisman
to ward off another death. The choir's 'wordless
dirge' created an emotional atmosphere that
generated a sense of the whole play as a
funeral rite: by the third scene, the audience
was all too aware that the whole family would
be taken, one by one. AIDS plays in the West,
such as Tony Kushner's *Angels in America* (see p.
152) and Kevin Elyot's *My Night with Reg* (see
p. 154), had so far dealt with the experiences
of gay men. tucker green placed the plight of
Africa squarely in the public domain.

①

AFTERLIFE

The play was first produced as a Platform performance (actors and choir but no set) at the National Theatre as part of its G8 series in 2005. In 2007, it was given a full performance at the Young Vic on a set designed by Miriam Buether. She filled the space with red sand, created a square kitchen in the middle of it and sat the audience around the square on upturned plastic buckets. The space was light and bright with cheerful colours and family pictures; a stew bubbled on a real working stove, filling the auditorium with its scent. The choir entertained the audience and inspired them to clap along, before they shifted to the periphery and began to chant the names of the lost, like a heavenly choir; at the close, they sang the classic assertion of African life and resistance, 'Nkosi Sikelel' iAfrika'.

OTHER WORKS BY
debbie tucker green
Dirty Butterfly (2003)
Trade (2005)
Random (2008)

SEE ALSO
My Night with Reg (1994)
by Kevin Elyot
Stoning Mary (2005)
by debbie tucker green

War Horse

WRITTEN BY
Nick Stafford from the novel by Michael Morpurgo

DIRECTED BY
Marianne Elliot and Tom Morris

DESIGNED BY
Rae Smith

PUPPETS BY
Basil Jones and Adrian Kohler for Handspring Theatre Company

- First performed at the Olivier, National Theatre, London, 9 October 2007.

SNAPSHOT

War Horse, based on the 1982 children's novel by Michael Morpurgo, follows the bond developed between farm boy, Albert Narracott, and his horse, Joey, and their experiences during the First World War. They are parted when war is declared and Joey is sold to the cavalry. Albert vows that they will meet again, and eventually enlists giving a false age. Joey serves in the British cavalry, and is then taken and serves in the German ambulance corps and artillery. Through an extraordinary series of events, Albert and Joey are reunited at a casualty clearing station.

IMPACT

The play was conceived as an epic piece of theatre for family audiences. Director Tom Morris, who had worked with theatre company Kneehigh on Tom Morris and Emma Rice's *Nights at the Circus* (see p. 202), saw it as an opportunity to bring the innovative South African puppet company, Handspring, to Britain. The horses are represented by full-size bamboo puppets; they have an uncanny range of movement, but their human handlers are always clearly visible. Audience members can simultaneously see that they are not real but respond emotionally as if they are. The mix of serious subject matter and innovative theatrical techniques was an instant success and reviews were generally stellar. Morpurgo has attributed the play's success to the determination and vision of Morris and Elliot to realise large set pieces, such as the battle of the Somme, while remaining focused on the human, an effect underlined by the folk-flavoured songs of John Tams, who had provided the music for *The Mysteries*. Morpurgo has also suggested that as Britain once again accustoms itself to seeing young soldiers return home dead or maimed, the suffering of the characters in *War Horse* gives us 'an excuse to cry'. While the focus on an animal predictably drew some accusations of sentimentality – 'It had them from the word "horse"', complained Matt Wolf in the *Guardian* – the beautiful sympathy between puppeteer and puppet stressed Joey's real function: a way for his various riders to engage in a relationship in the midst of the horror and hang on to their own humanity. The play brought the suffering of the First World War alive for a younger generation.

AFTERLIFE

War Horse has been seen by more than a million people since 2007. It transferred from the National to the New London Theatre in 2009 after two sold-out seasons at the National and was still playing in 2012. The creative team has won an array of awards for its design and choreography, and its phenomenal success at the box office has allowed the National Theatre to take a cut in government funding while expanding its operations. Steven Spielberg's film *War Horse* for Dreamworks opened in 2011, making $35 million in its first week ($15 million in its first weekend; total US gross $78 million; worldwide $126 million. The budget was $105 million). Nicholas Hytner, however, noted that, 'I'll stick my neck out and predict the play will be more profitable to us than the movie will be to Dreamworks'.

① Joey Head (Craig Leo), Albert (Luke Treadaway). © *Simon Annand, Photographer*

② Joey Head (David Grewcock), Albert (Matthew Aubrey), New London Theatre, 2010. © *Simon Annand, Photographer*

③ Members of the Company, New London Theatre, 2010. © *Simon Annand, Photographer*

OTHER WORKS BY
Nick Stafford
Back of the Bus (1991)
Love Me Tonight (2004)
Luminosity (2001)

SEE ALSO
Oh What a Lovely War (1963)
Theatre Workshop
The Accrington Pals (1981)
by Peter Whelan

Pornography

WRITTEN BY
Simon Stephens (1971–)

DIRECTED BY
Sean Holmes

DESIGNED BY
Paul Wills

- First performed at the Schauspielhaus, Hanover, 15 June 2007.
- First performed in the UK at the Edinburgh Traverse, 28 July 2008.

① Billy Seymour, Sam Spruell, Sheila Reid, Amanda Hale, Frances Ashman, Sacha Dhawan, Jeff Rawle and Loo Brealey. © *Robert Day, Photographer*

② Sam Spruell and Amanda Hale. © *Robert Day, Photographer*

③ Billy Seymour, Amanda Hale, Sam Spruell and Frances Ashman. © *Robert Day, Photographer*

SNAPSHOT

On 7 July 2005 – the week of London's successful Olympic bid and the Live 8 concert – a series of co-ordinated suicide attacks took place on London's public transport system during the morning rush hour, killing fifty-two people. *Pornography* was written in response to the event. It has seven scenes, one of which is a recital of brief obituaries for the victims. All other characters are fictional, including a suicide bomber.

IMPACT

The bombings took place while Stephens was in London working on his play *Motortown* for the Royal Court. *Pornography*, however, premiered in Germany, and had been staged there four times before Edinburgh Traverse staged a co-production with Birmingham Rep. The formal structure of the play is one perhaps more appreciated in Europe than in the UK: like Martin Crimp's *Attempts on Her Life* (see p. 168), it consists of a series of scenarios that do not attribute dialogue to specific speakers and can be played in any order. Stephens notes that they reflect the 'Seven Ages of Man' speech in Shakespeare's *As You Like It*. Although the audience doesn't need to be aware of this to make sense of the action, the Shakespeare connection underlines that this is a play about Englishness, an England that shapes the handful of lives shown here, including that of the bomber. The lives are not 'typically' English – there is no such thing; they are odd, troubled and very much themselves. A young mother adores her baby and gets back at her boss; a vicious – and victimised – schoolboy stalks his teacher; a scholar makes a pass at a student; siblings have sex. None of these characters are directly linked to the bombing. However, the fictional bomber has much in common with them. He is a commuter, a father, an office worker, with the destructive anarchy of the schoolboy – 'Wipe it all off the skin of the world. Scratch it away'. He does not have our sympathy, but he does have a context. We know what his act will mean, because one of the characters is an elderly widow who shares his loathing of society; she talks of her pleasure in watching footage of the Iraq war. But, walking home like everyone else after the bombing, she asks some people having a barbecue to give her a piece of chicken; and they do. Despite a headline in the *Telegraph*, 'The most shocking play of the Edinburgh Festival', there was praise for the play and for the performances, especially for Sheila Reid as the widow.

AFTERLIFE

The play eventually opened in London at the Tricycle in 2009. Reviewers tended to divide over Stephens's structure. Some, like Benedict Nightingale of the *Times*, felt that it offered a moving account of the fragmented and complex nature of England on a fateful day. Others – notably the *New English Review* – complained that the bomber never spoke about jihad, or described his motives, but focused, like everyone else, on the specifics of his day. The play continues to be widely discussed.

①

2000–10

OTHER WORKS BY
Simon Stephens
On the Shore of the Wide World (2005)
Motortown (2006)
Harper Regan (2008)

SEE ALSO
Terrorism (2000)
by Oleg and Vladimir Presnyakov
(The Brothers Presnyakov)
Taking Care of Baby (2007)
by Dennis Kelly

The Girlfriend Experience

WRITTEN BY
Alecky Blythe

DIRECTED BY
Joe Hill-Gibbins

DESIGNED BY
Lizzie Clachan

- First performed at the Royal Court Theatre Upstairs, London, 18 September 2008.

① Poppy (Lu Corfield), Tessa (Debbie Chazen) and Suzie (Beatie Edney). © *Alastair Muir, Photographer*

② Man (Alex Lowe) and Suzie (Beatie Edney). © *Alastair Muir, Photographer*

③ Tessa (Debbie Chazen). © *Alastair Muir, Photographer*

SNAPSHOT

The Girlfriend Experience carried verbatim theatre to a new level. It follows a group of prostitutes working in a Bournemouth brothel over a twelve-month period. The play uses Blythe's interviews with the women, and conversations among them and their clients, recorded during the project, in a style unique to Blythe's company, Recorded Delivery. Performers are fed their lines via earpieces, so they retain the exact cadences and rhythms of the person they are playing on stage. The story begins with Suzie and Tessa setting up on their own and moving into a new flat, which Tessa has rented. We hear about Suzie's elderly father, Tessa's teenage daughter, the difficulty of maintaining a relationship and her plans for the future. By the end of the play, Suzie's father is dead and Tessa's daughter has just achieved a string of GCSE results leading Tessa to proclaim: 'So hookers can do it, you see? We can have – a good family life, an' bring up children – in the right way'.

IMPACT

Blythe set out to challenge popular perceptions about prostitutes and the way they are portrayed in the media and in fiction: 'either high-class escorts, drug-addicted street walkers or pimped victims of human trafficking'. The women in the play are in control of their environment, safe and mutually supportive; they offer 'the Girlfriend Experience' – a service that goes beyond sex and leads them to feel affection for some of their clients. They seem, for the most part, to enjoy their work. But 'the Girlfriend Experience' carries risks, blurring the boundaries between work and life for the women when they date clients – and getting older is as hazardous as it is for any other self-employed person, as cheery fifty-odd Tessa is aware. The play has some uncomfortable moments, for example when Poppy, the youngest hooker, with a history of self-harm and alcohol abuse, is nearly pressured into unprotected anal sex. It is also very funny in its frequent collisions between the domestic and professional, such as the women's very detailed discussion of a client's extremely specialised requirements while they assemble some flat-pack furniture. Reviews were overwhelmingly positive, with high praise for Debbie Chazen's upbeat Tessa and for Alex Lowe who played all nine of the punters, from the socially inept to the sinister.

AFTERLIFE

The Girlfriend Experience moved Blythe's work and technique into the mainstream and the play transferred from the Royal Court to the Young Vic for an extended run. It continued to receive good notices, the *Telegraph* recommending it as a good alternative to the sold-out production of Tennessee Williams's *A Streetcar Named Desire* at the Donmar. Blythe went on to write *London Road* for the National Theatre. This explored a year in the life of the community in Ipswich where a group of prostitutes was murdered. It used the verbatim techniques of Recorded Delivery, but the words were set to music by Adam Cork.

①

OTHER WORKS BY
Alecky Blythe
Come Out Eli (2003)
Cruising (2006)
London Road (2011)

SEE ALSO
Everything in the Garden (1962)
by Giles Cooper
Unprotected (2006)
by Esther Wilson

England People Very Nice

WRITTEN BY
Richard Bean (1956–)

DIRECTED BY
Nicholas Hytner

DESIGNED BY
Mark Thompson

- First performed at the Olivier, National Theatre, London, 4 February 2009.

① Ensemble. *Photo by Johan Persson,* © *Johan Persson/ ArenaPAL*

② Phillipa (Olivia Coleman). *Photo by Johan Persson,* © *Johan Persson/ArenaPAL*

③ Mushi (Sacha Dhawan). *Photo by Johan Persson,* © *Johan Persson/ArenaPAL*

SNAPSHOT

England People Very Nice is a play about 'immigration, integration, terrorism, housing, racism, religion, power, hatred and love – in fact, all the staples for a comedy with songs' according to Richard Bean. In Pocklington Immigration Centre, a group of refugees is awaiting the results of their applications and rehearsing a play about immigration in Britain. Set in and around Bethnal Green in East London, the play shows four separate waves of immigrants arrive, assimilate and greet the next wave with indignation and violence. In each wave, a cross-cultural love story is snuffed out before it can develop, and the landlord, barmaid and philosopher in the local pub go through the same process of hostility followed by acceptance, stressing the timelessness of the process. The final wave of immigrants, the Bangladeshis, assimilate, but their children, born in England, become radicalised and hostile, leaving the end open to interpretation: is assimilation on its way or finished? At the close of the rehearsal, the refugees get the results of their applications to remain in the UK – a test of whether England people really are 'very nice'.

IMPACT

Bean is part of the Monsterist group of writers whose mission is to write big plays for big stages with 'action that shows rather than tells' the issues. Hytner was keen for him to write a big play for the National and *England People Very Nice* was the result. The characters are deliberately crude stereotypes: kneejerk racists of every colour and creed; East End criminals with hearts of gold who love their mums; Jewish anarchists; Muslim terrorists. Chunks of history were imparted on stage through bold graphics and animations by Pete Bishop that owed a lot to Terry Gilliam's work on Monty Python's Flying Circus. The play caused enormous controversy; it was the subject of the first stage invasion in the National's history, when a teacher and a playwright walked on stage with placards during Bean's Platform talk, lobbying Hytner for a public debate on the subject. This did nothing to harm the box office, as audiences rushed to see what the fuss was about. Critics were divided sharply: some, like the *Sunday Times*, found the bouncy stereotypes provocative but allowing for 'humane, edgy comedy'; others, like the *Evening Standard*, considered the play merely 'cruel'.

①

AFTERLIFE

Some days into the run, the journalist Yasmin Alibhai-Brown recorded that, while the talent of the multi-racial cast, especially Rudi Dharmalingam and Sacha Dhawan (one of the original *History Boys*), proved there was no racist intent, she experienced very mixed feelings at the play. She had laughed, but later wished she had not. The context, she suggested, was the problem; the present wave of anti-immigration hostility needed analysis, not jokes, and the National should have been more sensitive: 'England people very naïve.' A meeting was arranged between Hytner and a delegation of East End writers and community activists. The play finished its run, but whether, like Howard Brenton's *The Romans in Britain* (see p. 112), it gets another production will depend on some very complex shifts in social attitudes.

OTHER WORKS BY	SEE ALSO
Richard Bean	*Our Country's Good* (1989)
Toast (1999)	by Timberlake Wertenbaker
Harvest (2005)	*Testing the Echo* (2008)
One Man Two Guvnors (2011)	by David Edgar

Jerusalem

WRITTEN BY
Jez Butterworth (1969–)

DIRECTED BY
Ian Rickson

DESIGNED BY
Ultz

- First performed at the Royal
Court Theatre Downstairs,
London, 10 July 2009.

SNAPSHOT

It's St George's Day in Flintock, a small Wiltshire village, and the annual fair is about to begin. From a battered caravan in the woods, John Rooster Byron dispenses drugs, booze, advice and tall tales to a gang of teenagers and local misfits, and fights off an eviction order from the council. Flintock Fair celebrates the beginning of spring and the birth of new life, but Byron's future looks shaky. The residents of the nearby estate want him gone, a local thug believes he's sheltering his under-age stepdaughter, and he's finally been banned from every pub in the village. None of this perturbs him; he asserts that Byron boys don't rot, but just lie in their graves like stones waiting to be called back to life. By the end of the day, he's been beaten and branded but is still unbowed. He lays a curse on anyone who disturbs the wood, douses his caravan in petrol and summons his ancestors and the giants of English folklore to do battle against the South Wiltshire police. As he drums – on the earring of a giant he says he once met – the branches of the wood shake.

IMPACT

Butterworth wrote the part of Byron for Mark Rylance, one of England's greatest Shakespearean actors, and a large part of the huge box-office success sprang from his performance, widely regarded as one of the finest of the decade. Critics responded to the epic flawed hero, a Pied Piper who encourages the young to misbehave but also protects ancient rites and rituals and provides a sanctuary for the abused and damaged, and praised both the charisma with which Rylance delivered tales of magic and the sudden flashes of vulnerability in his relationship with his estranged wife and son. The play begins with a young girl singing William Blake's 'Jerusalem' and it is as much a state-of-the-nation play as David Hare's *The Permanent Way* (see p. 196). It is not just Byron but England that is under siege, not from the ravers whose music eclipses the hymn, but from the forces of law and order who seek to regulate them. The play poses questions about the rights of the individual and about the countryside and its ownership that resonated with British audiences who witnessed debates about ancient woodland, traveller's encampments and hunting throughout the play's first three runs.

AFTERLIFE

The play won a string of awards, including the *Evening Standard* Best Play, and Olivier and Tony Awards for Rylance. The play transferred from the Royal Court to the West End then on to Broadway, where it was a sell-out despite its peculiarly English nature and gained a Tony nomination for Mackenzie Crook's much-praised performance as Byron's creepy sidekick Ginger. It returned to the West End for a sold-out run in 2011. Rylance has hinted that he may return to the part in the future. Butterworth told a journalist, 'I don't see how anyone else could do it as well as he does'.

① Rooster Byron (Mark Rylance). © *Victoria and Albert Museum, London*

② Rooster Byron (Mark Rylance) and Ginger (Mackenzie Crook). © *Victoria and Albert Museum, London*

③ Ginger (Mackenzie Crook), Tanya (Charlotte Mills), Wesley (Gerard Horan), Rooster Byron (Mark Rylance), Lee (Tom Brooke), Davey (Danny Kirrane) and Pea (Jessica Barden). © *Victoria and Albert Museum, London*

OTHER WORKS BY
Jez Butterworth
Mojo (1995)
The Winterling (2006)
Parlour Song (2008)

SEE ALSO
Sport of My Mad Mother (1958)
by Ann Jellicoe
Fair (2005)
by Joy Wilkinson

Enron

WRITTEN BY
Lucy Prebble (1981–)

DIRECTED BY
Rupert Goold

DESIGNED BY
Anthony Ward

• First performed at the Minerva Theatre, Chichester, 11 July 2009.

OTHER WORKS BY
Lucy Prebble
The Sugar Syndrome (2002)

SEE ALSO
Serious Money (1987)
by Caryl Churchill
The Power of Yes (2009)
by David Hare

SNAPSHOT

Enron is an all-singing, all-dancing account of the implosion of the 'World's Most Innovative Company'. It tracks the rise and fall of Jeffrey Skilling, who received the longest sentence for corporate crime in history after Enron went bankrupt to the tune of $38 billion. Skilling is appointed president over the head of his rival Claudia Roe – a fictional character who is the conscience of the play. He has a 'vision' for the company as a 'powerhouse for ideas' rather than as a supplier of concrete resources. His sidekick, nerdy financial officer Andy Fastow, creates phantom companies where Enron's mounting debts can be disguised – until the inevitable crash. At the end, Skilling quietly changes into prison garb, while a chorus of Enron employees relates the maths: bonuses of $55 million for the executives; 20,000 people out of work. Skilling, still bewitched by the world that has crashed round his ears, sees himself as an Everyman: 'They'll realise they were banishing something of themselves along with me. I believe that'.

IMPACT

Lucy Prebble's first play, *The Sugar Syndrome*, which won the George Devine Award in 2004, was relatively intimate and naturalistic. Rupert Goold was best known as a director of Shakespeare when he worked on *Enron* and the result of their collaboration was an exuberant stylistic mix. At times the play uses simple, clear illustration to convey complex financial processes in the style of Ewan MacColl's *Uranium 235* (see p. 14). Fastow's scheme of phantom companies is explained with homely containers – the room, a desk, a shoebox, a matchbox – until he reaches a tiny, red, glowing box that represents the only real money. This is juxtaposed with extravagant effects like those of the musicals currently burgeoning in the West End: stock analysts sing in close harmony; a traders' corps de ballet wields light sabres to celebrate the deregulation of electricity. Reviewers responded to the theatrical dazzle – the *Sunday Telegraph* drew parallels with *Lear*, Goold's most recent success – and to the clarity. 'Even financial innocents can follow this,' commented Michael Billington. Above all, they praised Samuel West's very human Skilling, an overweight ugly duckling transformed by success into the best-dressed, slimmest man on the block.

AFTERLIFE

Enron transferred to the Royal Court Theatre in September 2009 and the Noël Coward Theatre in January 2010, before touring the country. It continued to receive excellent reviews and there were awards for both Goold and Prebble. It went to the Broadhurst Theater on Broadway in 2010. However, the play was less well received in the USA. *The New York Times* gave it the kind of review that inevitably meant closure. Richard D. North, author of *Rich Is Beautiful*, complained that Prebble glossed over Skilling's transition into actual illegality, suggesting he'd missed the play's point about the smoke-and-mirrors culture that allowed the transition at all. However, the play has acquired new layers of relevance in the face of world recession; it is hard to imagine that it will not be around for a long time to offer an insight into something affecting millions.

① Trader (Tom Godwin). © *Victoria and Albert Museum, London*

② News Reporter (Eleanor Matsuura), Trader (Tom Godwin) and the ensemble. © *Victoria and Albert Museum, London*

③ Ramsay (Ashley Rolfe), Hewitt (Eleanor Matsuura), Fastow (Tom Goodman-Hill), Senator (Orion Lee) and Lay (Tim Pigott-Smith). © *Victoria and Albert Museum, London*

Posh

WRITTEN BY
Laura Wade (1977–)

DIRECTED BY
Lyndsey Turner

DESIGNED BY
Anthony Ward

- First performed at the Royal Court Theatre Downstairs, London, 9 April 2010.

① Hugo Fraser-Tyrwhitt (David Dawson) and Miles Richards (James Norton). *Photo by Johan Persson, © Johan Persson/ArenaPAL*

② Hugo Fraser-Tyrwhitt (David Dawson). *Photo by Johan Persson, © Johan Persson/ArenaPAL*

③ Alistair Ryle (Leo Bill) and Hugo Fraser-Tyrwhitt (David Dawson). *Photo by Johan Persson, © Johan Persson/ArenaPAL*

SNAPSHOT

Posh examines privilege, tribalism and cronyism as demonstrated by 'The Riot Club', an elite Oxford dining society whose members are recruited for their wealth, breeding and future status. An attempt to return the club to its glory days – when a good dinner finished with the restaurant trashed and diners waking up in another country – ends with the landlord of the pub hosting the dinner beaten almost to death. The club decides that for the sake of their futures one member must take the blame. They nominate the unlikeable but clever Alistair Ryle. Aloof from the undignified scrabble for supremacy, Alistair is well connected. Not only does the aristocratic network save him from jail, but they are also so impressed with his ruthless understanding of power that they promise him a glittering future.

IMPACT

Posh was timed to open just before the 2010 General Election (Press Night coincided with the three party leaders' live TV debate). Newly elected Conservative Prime Minister David Cameron and Chancellor George Osborne were former members of Oxford's Bullingdon club, very similar to the Riot, their efforts to distance themselves being undermined by the *Daily Mirror*'s front-page photograph of Cameron in his fancy Bullingdon tailcoat. Wade spent three years researching the play by interviewing members of dining clubs, their friends and families. She was adamant that the play was not about Cameron and his cronies, but about the sense of entitlement in those circles: 'The idea that I can go somewhere and do as much damage as I like because I can afford to pay for it afterwards seemed completely alien to me as a person, and to the class I come from'. A number of reviews complained that characters were two-dimensional. However, most also relished Wade's sharp ear for tribal language and the wit of Lyndsey Turner's staging as the cast sang, danced, rapped and froze into tableaux suggesting tradition and modernity, mixing current chart music with portrait poses. There was more division over the ideas; conservative critics, such as Charles Spencer, complained of the 'paranoid conspiracy' element of the ending. However, the horrible Ryle's escape from justice provides a vivid counter-image to the ending of Roy Williams' *Fallout* (see p. 194), staged in the same space seven years previously. Both plays show the failure of justice and a brutal killing from remarkably similar motives of dislike and distrust. The Riot boys are baffled and resentful of a world where people 'beneath' them feel entitled to social mobility and respect. Their latent violence emerges only when Chris, the landlord, refuses to accept the trashing of his pub and calls the police instead of taking money like a proper inferior. Though the outcome is not lethal, his fate startlingly mirrors the death of Kwame in *Fallout*.

AFTERLIFE

When Dominic Cooke became artistic director of the Royal Court in 2006, he announced a shift of focus away from 'naturalist plays set in the north of England that involved unspeakable sexual acts'. *Posh* was the latest in a long line of Royal Court plays that did this, following the success of Lucy Prebble's *Enron* and Jez Butterworth's *Jerusalem*. Its relevance to contemporary English politics assured lively press coverage beyond the theatre pages, and is set to continue during its 2012 West End transfer.

2000–10

Index of Plays

Index of Playwrights

Methuen Drama in association with V&A Publishing, London.

10 9 8 7 6 5 4 3 2 1

First published in Great Britain in 2013 by Methuen Drama in association
with V&A Publishing, London.

Methuen Drama, an imprint of Bloomsbury Publishing Plc

Methuen Drama
Bloomsbury Publishing Plc
50 Bedford Square
London WC1B 3DP
www.methuendrama.com

ISBN 978 1 408 16480 8

Available in the USA from Bloomsbury Academic & Professional,
175 Fifth Avenue /3rd Floor,
New York,
NY 10010.

A CIP catalogue record for this book is available from the British Library

Printed and bound in India by Replika Press Pvt. Ltd.